Gothic Plays and American Society, 1794–1830

Gothic Plays and American Society, 1794–1830

M. Susan Anthony

McFarland & Company, Inc., Publishers
Jefferson, North Carolina, and London

Portions of Chapters 1, 3, 4 and 5 were published in "'Draw Close the Cord of Virtue': Instructive Plays and American Society" in the *Journal of American Culture* 27 (March 2004): 43–53. Used by permission of Blackwell Publishing.

Chapter 2 was partially drawn from "This Sort of Thing: Productions of Gothic Plays in America" in the *Journal of American Drama and Theater* 8 (Fall 1996). Used by permission of the Martin E. Segal Theatre Centre.

Chapter 9 was drawn from "Made in America: Adaptations of British Gothic Plays for the American Stage," published in the *Journal of American Drama and Theater* 6 (Spring/Fall 1994). Used by permission of the Martin E. Segal Theatre Centre.

LIBRARY OF CONGRESS CATALOGUING-IN-PUBLICATION DATA

Anthony, M. Susan, 1958–
    Gothic plays and American society, 1794–1830 / M. Susan Anthony.
        p.   cm.
    Includes bibliographical references and index.

    ISBN 978-0-7864-3337-7
    softcover : 50# alkaline paper ∞

    1. American drama — 19th century — History and criticism.
2. Gothic literature — United States — History and criticism.
3. Literature and society — United States — History — 19th century.   4. United States — Intellectual life — 19th century.
5. Women in literature.   6. National characteristics, American, in literature.   7. Gothic literature — Great Britain — History and criticism.   I. Title.
PS343.A58   2008
812'.05270902 — dc22   2008027614

British Library cataloguing data are available

©2008 M. Susan Anthony. All rights reserved

No part of this book may be reproduced or transmitted in any form or by any means, electronic or mechanical, including photocopying or recording, or by any information storage and retrieval system, without permission in writing from the publisher.

On the cover: Abbey ©2007 Shutterstock; Mrs. Mary Ann Duff as Mary in *Superstition* (The Harvard Theatre Collection, Houghton Library)

Manufactured in the United States of America

McFarland & Company, Inc., Publishers
   Box 611, Jefferson, North Carolina 28640
      www.mcfarlandpub.com

For John D. Howard and
Alison Anthony Howard

Table of Contents

Preface	1
Introduction: "Gothic Mania": Gothic Plays and American Society, 1794–1830	5
1. "Gothic America": Dramas, Theatres, and American Society	15
2. "An Appetite for Gothic": Productions of Gothic Plays by City, 1794–1830	24
3. "The Senseless Brawl of Barbarians": Profane Plays and Patrons	33
4. The "Illustrious Spirit" Meets the "Sanguinary Monster": Characterization of Males in Gothic Plays	47
5. "Angel-Maids" and "Withered Flowers": The Gothic Heroine	61
6. "An Exquisite Treat for Feeling Minds": Acting and the Female "Stars" of Gothic Plays	79
7. "Dreadful Thunder" and "Lurid Lightning": Spectacle in Gothic Plays	95
8. "What Dreadful Place Is This?": Women and Dangerous Spaces	118
9. "A Plain Unvarnish'd Tale": Adaptations of British Plays for the American Stage	127

10. "This Sort of Thing": Reception of Gothic Plays in America	141
11. A Gothic View of America	150
Appendix 1	159
Appendix 2	160
Appendix 3	161
Appendix 4	162
Appendix 5	163
Appendix 6	164
Appendix 7	165
Notes	167
Works Cited	187
Index	193

Preface

In 1966, a television series entitled *Dark Shadows*, described as a "Gothic soap opera," premiered on American television. The show ran until 1971, for a total of 1225 episodes. The eerie introductory music, underscored by crashing waves, accompanied the image of an imposing manor house shrouded in mist. All of these elements combined to evoke a feeling of unease, a sense of undefined terror. That gloomy atmosphere and formless terror came to mean "Gothic" to me, and I suspect, to a host of others.

In the past few decades scores of scholars have written about Gothic literature, examining novels and short stories from the late 1700s up to the present day. Indeed, the term "Gothic" today is applied freely to literature, architecture, music, fashion, film, television shows, and makeup. But earlier, the term "Gothic" was used to describe a particular type of play that sought to inspire gloom and unease in its audiences. These plays, called by some the earliest form of melodrama, were included in the earliest repertories of the first permanent theatres in the United States, and they flourished on American stages between 1794 and 1830.

Gothic plays, particularly the earliest ones, in the late eighteenth century and early nineteenth century, shared many of the features made famous in Gothic novels and were extremely popular in England; however, these same plays proved just as popular in the young United States. This was a particularly critical period in American theatrical history, a time when anti-theatrical laws were finally repealed, but theatres still were viewed as places of vice; a time when theatres housed all classes, yet patrons proved particularly class conscious; and a time when Americans demanded respect for American artists but persisted in favoring

European works. In this same period, American women were glorified as superior beings ("Angel-maids") and simultaneously restrained in their public behavior. All of these tensions were played out in Gothic plays as presented in the theatres of Philadelphia, New York, Boston, and Charleston between 1794 and 1830.

In these turbulent years, Gothic plays reflected the ambivalence of Americans. On the one hand, Gothic plays featured a villain who freely transgressed legal and moral boundaries, and yet, as a form of melodrama, these same plays ensured the triumph of virtue, reinstating social order and conventional behavior. Theatres in the young United States, still fighting for respectability, could promote Gothic plays as particularly effective in instructing young men and women in appropriate moral behavior; however, the villain's profound wickedness encouraged patrons to enjoy vicariously his transgressions. These plays also highlighted ambiguity about our developing "American" characteristics; most of the Gothic plays were imported from England, and they sometimes contained positive sentiments about monarchy or, even more troublesome, villains who lasciviously described their physical longings; sentiments that were adapted by American theatre managers to better depict "American" virtues. Gothic plays also reflected the ambivalence about the place of spectacle in plays; as the scenery and special effects became ever more stunning in the early decades of the nineteenth century, they dazzled the audience but annoyed critics of the stage who complained that the theatres were ignoring worthy dramas for the sake of sensation.

This study uses productions of Gothic plays in four major theatrical centers of the newly formed United States as a way to examine American society, to better understand the conflicts surrounding the promotion and defense of American artistic endeavors and the artists who engaged in them. In addition, this study examines the representation of women in the dramas and compares that depiction with the lives of women in society of this period. The introduction and Chapter One describe Gothic plays and the rise of Gothic fiction and drama in the United States between 1794 and 1830. The second chapter discusses the demand for native talent and the country's simultaneous reliance upon Europe for direction in the arts. Chapter Three compares the repertory of the first permanent theatres in the four theatrical centers of Philadelphia, New York, Charleston, and Boston, and the fourth chapter relates accounts of audience behavior in these theatres. Chapters Five and Six examine characterization in the plays and compare attributes assigned to characters with those promoted in popular prescriptive literature. The seventh chapter discusses the careers and off-stage reputations of four leading actresses of the American stage who often portrayed Gothic heroines. Subsequent chapters address the changing role of spectacle, American adaptations of British Gothic plays, and critics' reactions to Gothic melodramas and other spectacular entertainments.

Although Gothic plays were popular with audiences in the United States, they were not so appreciated by critics, who contended that these works, along with other melodramas and extravaganzas, relied upon spectacle at the expense of characterization. Scholars, too, dismissed "melodramas" as unworthy of study. David Grimsted's 1965 groundbreaking *Melodrama Unveiled* challenged that view, arguing that an examination of melodramas, which proved so popular with American audiences, could perhaps offer insight into attitudes of the time. *Melodrama Unveiled* includes Gothic plays as a subset of melodrama but it does not treat them in great detail. Yet these plays possess some unique features not found in other forms of melodrama. A few scholars do focus specifically on Gothic plays: Bertrand Evans' 1947 *Gothic Drama from Walpole to Shelley* discusses themes in the dramas and provided a list of Gothic plays. Jeffrey N. Cox's excellent introduction to *Seven Gothic Dramas (1992)* discusses the development of Gothic drama and describes its life on the English stage. Paul Ranger's *Pity and Terror Reign in Every Breast* provides a full-length study of Gothic plays in England, with a particularly helpful section on stagecraft. These studies, however, confine themselves to the British stage. Consequently, no full-length study examined the productions of Gothic plays in the United States in the late eighteenth and early nineteenth centuries, a critical time in the development of the young country.

Much of this study rests on primary sources. The plays themselves were obtained through Readex, in the *Three Centuries of Drama* collection or the *English and American Drama of the Nineteenth Century* collection. Accounts of productions and of audiences at the theatre were obtained from theatrical memoirs and from contemporary periodicals, many of which I obtained on microfilm from Readex and from the *American Periodical Series*. I obtained playbills and engravings from The Harvard Theatre Collection, whose staff was knowledgeable and unfailingly gracious. The Free Library of Philadelphia and The Pennsylvania Historical Society also house collections of playbills, and their staff, too, proved most helpful.

I also am indebted to many others for their assistance. Dr. Patti Gillespie provided invaluable direction and critique; Dr. Edward L. Fink assisted with quantitative analysis in the early stages of this project, and Dr. Alan S. Jackson at Binghamton University provided materials from his own collections and offered his expertise in nineteenth century stagecraft. DePauw University generously provided time and financial assistance for the completion of this work. Finally, I am most beholden to Dr. John D. Howard, the ultimate Romantic, who shared his formidable knowledge of Romantic literature, provided unstinting (if sometimes terse) support and devoted many hours to editing the manuscript.

Introduction: "Gothic Mania"
Gothic Plays and American Society, 1794–1830

It was snowing on the night of January 4, 1803, in Philadelphia, according to the records of theatre manager William Wood. Still, many had braved the elements to see the lovely Miss Holman perform the role of Angela in *The Castle Spectre*.

The play was still new, having appeared on the stage in Philadelphia only once before, and it featured many scary elements popularized by Gothic fiction: a sinister castle, moldy dungeon, beautiful, virginal heroine pursued by a thoroughly evil, aristocratic villain. Lovely Angela, recently arrived at an isolated castle, finds herself a prisoner of her uncle and guardian, the Earl of Osmond, who intends to marry her — by force if necessary. While in the castle, Angela is visited by the ghost of her murdered mother and learns, eventually, that her wicked uncle killed her mother and imprisoned her father in the dungeon of the castle.

As the audience, sitting in box, pit, and gallery, peers through clouds of cigar smoke at the dimly lit stage, delicate Angela cautiously creeps through "a gloomy subterraneous Dungeon, wide and lofty," searching for her imprisoned father.[1]

Suddenly, Angela cries, "Hark! Twas the clank of chains!" A figure slowly approaches her, a "dreadful form." Horrified, Angela gazes upon the apparition, murmuring, "How sunk his eye!— How wildly hangs his matted hair on his pale and furrowed brow!"[2] Angela soon learns that the seeming apparition is really her father, long incarcerated by his brother, the evil Earl of Osmond. Their joyous reunion is cut short by the appearance of the evil Earl himself! As the Earl prepares to kill Angela's father, Eveline, the ghost of Angela's mother, materializes and, as the Earl stands transfixed with horror, Angela stabs him. The Earl "falls with a loud groan, and faints." At this, the ghost "vanishes in a flash of fire and a loud clap of thunder is heard, and Angela and Reginald rush into each other's arms."[3]

Several of the elements present in the *The Castle Spectre* — gloomy, uneasy atmosphere, an innocent young woman fleeing a mesmeric, sophisticated villain, an unabashed use of supernatural events — have come to be known as "Gothic." The term itself changed its connotation over the centuries; originally a name for Germanic tribes, it later became synonymous with "barbarous" and still later acquired a more neutral connotation of "medieval." With the publication of Horace Walpole's *Castle of Otranto*, subtitled "A Gothic Story," supernatural elements became associated with the term as well.[4]

Gothic tales of the eighteenth century often were set in decaying castles or forbidding abbeys of distant centuries, remote from contemporary life. However, despite their ancient settings, the literature reflected contemporary anxieties: fears of political revolution, the impact of industrialization, challenges of urbanization, changes in women's roles, and changes wrought by scientific discovery.[5] Gothic fiction featured passion; in Gothic fiction of the eighteenth and nineteenth centuries, "imagination and emotional effects" triumphed over reason, and "passion, excitement and sensation transgress[ed] social proprieties and moral laws."[6]

Gothic fiction enjoyed its first wave of popularity in the late eighteenth and early nineteenth centuries, but it remains popular today. Indeed, today the term "Gothic" is often used to describe works by twentieth and twenty-first century authors: Shirley Jackson, William Faulkner, Stephen King, Anne Rice and others have been described as "Gothic."[7] The term also is applied freely to areas other than literature, very frequently as a descriptor for films. Moreover, the term has inspired a multitude of web sites that address literature, fashion, music, and other elements of popular culture.[8]

Critical studies of Gothic literature have flourished in the past few decades, and scholars have utilized various approaches in attempting to define the genre. David Punter, in *The Literature of Terror*, surveyed critical studies written in the twentieth century and identified five major approaches to a definition of Gothic. The first approach, which encompassed many of the earliest critical studies, viewed the Gothic revival as a "recognisable [sic] movement in the history of culture, with recognisable [sic] socio-psychological causes."[9] A second approach claimed that Gothic fiction could be defined by the type of plot. Punter grouped other studies of Gothic literature under a third approach that took an opposite view, contending that Gothic was better defined by its "narrative difficulty" than by its "narrative achievement." A fourth approach characterized Gothic literature by its "particular antagonistic attitude towards realism," and Punter's final group of studies attempted to define Gothic by its themes, arguing that some were particularly "Gothic." After outlining these approaches, Punter cautioned that his summary still did not represent all approaches.[10]

One particularly important approach to Gothic literature emerged in the twentieth century as scholars began to assess "female powerlessness" in Gothic works.[11] Feminist studies of Gothic literature have proved especially popular, especially those that studied works by women writers. Gothic fiction had long been considered a "feminine form," not a part of mainstream literature, and, as such, an inferior genre, unworthy of serious critical attention.[12] Ellen Moers, in *Literary Women*, coined the term "Female Gothic" and identified it as "work [of] women writers ... that, since the eighteenth century, we have called the Gothic."[13] Juliann Fleenor argued that "Female Gothic" employs the usual symbolism from Gothic fiction, such as the ruined castle and the inner room, to symbolize "both the culture and the heroine," and that this literature "provokes various feelings of terror, anger, awe and sometimes self-fear and self-disgust directed toward the female role, female sexuality, female physiology, and procreation."[14] Fleenor identified several themes in Gothic literature including the use of interior space to suggest "repression, segregation, and dichotomy" and the relegation of women as either "pure and chaste, or as impure and corrupt," a key feature of the Female Gothic.[15] Another theme prevalent in Gothic literature, whether written by women or men, was a fear of female sexuality.[16]

Although many feminist literary critics have deliberately placed texts written by women at the heart of the Gothic tradition, some acknowledged that characteristics identified as part of Female Gothic could be found in works written by men.[17] Consequently, this study

Frontispiece from *Raymond and Agnes* depicting Agnes escaping from the convent, disguised as The Bleeding Nun. The Harvard Theatre Collection, Houghton Library.

examines depictions of women and men in Gothic plays written by women and men.

Gothic plays enjoyed their first popularity in the 1790s, when "gothic drama became a mania, as did the gothic novel."[18] In this period, in England, the reading population increased from one and a half million to between seven and eight million, the years in which Gothic stories enjoyed great popularity.[19] Although early Gothic works, such as those by Mrs. Radcliffe, still proved too expensive for most readers, cheaper books soon became available as publishers found new ways to produce and distribute works; between 1790 and 1830, for example, William Lane's Minerva Press churned out thousands of Gothic tales.[20]

The widespread popularity of Gothic fiction puzzled its earliest critics, and over the years, scholars have tried to account for its hold: some claimed that Gothic literature was particularly appropriate for the times in that it "challenged the limits of the predictable, the natural, the possible"; whereas others argued that Gothic literature reflected the "uncanny dualities of Victorian realism and decadence." However, one of the most compelling arguments for the popularity of Gothic literature between 1794 and 1830 was its seeming celebration of transgression. Gothic literature often depicted characters who engaged in illegal and illicit acts and who exhibited violent passions.[21] Women may have found Gothic fiction particularly titillating, for although it did threaten the heroines with violence, it also promised "adventurous freedom." The heroine, then, served both as a victim and a heroine.[22]

Many Gothic plots featured transgression: transgression of law as well as transgression of "the stronger barriers of taboo."[23] Naturally, these elements in Gothic fiction of the late eighteenth and early nineteenth centuries worried critics, who feared that such literature might corrupt readers.[24]

Readers in the United States certainly embraced Gothic fiction when it first appeared. During the early 1800s, Americans enjoyed a sudden increase in publication of Gothic fiction, mostly reprints of British books.[25] The increase probably was linked to two sources: the declining cost of books in the 1790s and the rapid growth of circulating libraries. Whatever the reason, novels were particularly popular in the period, and educated men in America feared the effects of a "new intermediate cultural world" that was developing between the well educated and those who were barely literate.[26] In this period, the most popular genres were the Gothic terror romance and the novel of seduction.[27]

The enormous popularity of Gothic fiction in the United States during the eighteenth century seemed contradictory, in that the United States was an "optimistic country founded upon the Enlightenment principles of liberty and the 'pursuit of happiness.'"[28] Leslie Fiedler, in *Love and Death in the American Novel*, observed that "the generation of Jefferson was pledged to be done with ghosts and shadows, committed to live a life of yea-saying in a sunlit, neo-classical world."[29] Although critics (especially clergy) objected to these "morbid" and "nasty" works, many Americans in the eighteenth century enthusiastically welcomed the fiction.[30] Despite regular denunciation by the clergy, the novels "stubbornly flourished" in the new country, and Americans began to write their own.[31]

Gothic literature may have held a special appeal for citizens of the United States in the late eighteenth and early nineteenth centuries precisely because of its element of transgression. During this period, citizens of the United States were bombarded with prescriptive literature, advice manuals, and sermons aimed at controlling their behavior in the wake of social upheavals. Young women in particular were recipients of stern warnings from these sources, especially sermons, and were increasingly advised to remain quiet and safe within the confines of the home. In the midst of these constraints, readers may have found the emotional excesses evoked by Gothic fiction particularly appealing. Consequently, Gothic fiction was welcomed enthusiastically in North America "despite — or possibly because of regular denunciation from the pulpit."[32]

Gothic novels also proved very popular when adapted for the stage. These plays were so popular in Britain that a critic in 1790 commented that Gothic dramas were "threatening to drive all other plays off the stage."[33] Gothic plays proved just as popular in the United States. Several of Mrs. Radcliffe's novels became successful stage plays, including *The Romance of the Forest* and *The Italian*. Although Matthew G. Lewis wrote *The Castle Spectre* for the stage, his famous work *The Monk* became the less-than-successful stage play *Aurelio and Miranda*. The novel *Caleb Williams* became the very successful production of *The Iron Chest*; Mary Shelley's *Frankenstein* received several stage adaptations, Lord Byron's "Fragment of a Novel" and John Polidori's subsequent *The Vampyre* inspired several stage versions in the 1820s. Even Charles Maturin's *Melmoth the Wanderer* was transformed for the stage by American Benjamin West. Although most of the plays originated in England and often appeared in the United States without alteration, several were adapted by Americans and a few were written by native playwrights.

These plays that sought to inspire feelings of unease and terror were labeled "Gothic" by various historians in the nineteenth century because they shared some features of the fiction. Although many studies have examined Gothic fiction, few have examined Gothic plays, and yet such a study should provide valuable information about society of that time because of the public nature of theatre-going. The very act of experiencing a text as part of a public group implies that the spectator condones the presentation. The public nature of presentation also suggests that theatrical managers believed that their offerings would be acceptable, as theatres had to please to survive. Consequently, adaptations and changes made to texts prior to their public presentation on the stage assume a greater significance.

Many texts described as "Gothic" were produced for the stage, but specific description of these plays is difficult because, despite frequent use of the term, no clear, generally accepted definition of "Gothic plays" exists.[34] Critics and historians did not agree on the use of the term; many did not use the term at all, whereas others used it to describe plays that seemed similar to narrative works acknowledged as "Gothic": an oppressive atmosphere, an ancient tragedy, a beautiful and virginal heroine, a suavely evil villain, and a powerful feeling of foreboding.[35]

Given the confusion surrounding the meaning of the general term "Gothic," it should be no surprise that the phrase "Gothic drama" was variously understood. The problem of definition was further complicated by the close association of "Gothic" plays to melodrama. "Melodrames" as a specific genre were introduced in theatres at the turn of the nineteenth century, and "Gothic" plays shared many of their conventions, such as the use of music to enhance mood. In 1803, an advertisement in *The Charleston Courier* alerted audiences to this musical innovation:

> The Melo-drame, being new to the English and American stage, it may be necessary to observe, that in this species of dramatic composition, instrumental music is introduced occasionally during the pauses in the dialogue, with a view of heightening the effect, and aiding the expression of those passions which occupy the scene; the present admirable piece may be considered as the first experiment to introduce a new species of drama. On the English stage it has succeeded beyond calculation; and it is presented to the public of Charleston, under the strongest impression, that it will contribute, in an eminent degree to their rational pleasure.[36]

Gothic plays shared other conventions commonly associated with melodramas: contrivances in plot, stock characters, and the inevitable triumph of virtue. Their similarities to other melodramas has prompted some scholars to assert that the so-called Gothic plays of the eighteenth and nineteenth centuries, most of which were similar in form to melodramas, should not be termed "Gothic" at all.[37] However, others argued that these plays should be described as "Gothic" because they shared characteristics with fiction acknowledged as "Gothic," such as "settings, machinery, character types, themes, plots, and techniques selected and combined to serve a primary purpose of exploiting mystery, gloom and terror."[38]

In spite of their similarity to Gothic narratives, Gothic plays differed from the fiction in several critical ways.[39] Unlike the novels, the plays did not typically build suspense or terror through narrative; instead they represented the terror visually. Dramatists tried to heighten the emotional impact of the story; where the novelist "suggested" horrors, the playwright "made a satisfying physical show" of them.[40] In addition, some Gothic plays, by adhering to a melodramatic structure, deviated "from the Gothic in [their] optimism"; thus, even if a play were based on a Gothic narrative that ended tragically, the play would follow a melodramatic structure and provide a happy ending in which the virtuous triumphed.[41] Most importantly, though, Gothic plays combined the clear distinctions between good and evil characters with particularly graphic ways of showing the consequences of sin. As a result, these plays were particularly effective in offering moral instruction for patrons.

Gothic plays proved immensely popular in each theatrical center of the United States, comparing favorably with other genres, including works by Shakespeare. They were included regularly in the repertories of major theatres.[42]

The undeniable success of Gothic plays in the United States between 1794 and 1830 was particularly interesting in light of the social turmoil of this time. During these years following the Revolution, the new country sought to forge its own identity apart from Europe, yet, because of the ideals of the Revolution, many contradictory forces emerged and were played out in the theatres, either on the stage or in the audience. At this time, populations were booming from the influx of immigrants and working-class young people, which changed the composition of audiences in the theatres. Gothic dramas reflected such changes in demographics by invariably depicting the villain, who ultimately is destroyed, as an aristocrat. Yet the heroes or heroines seemed representative of the middle classes, spouting the same sentiments as those promoted in prescriptive literature. Moreover, though Gothic plays featured the downfall of the elite, they still promoted patriarchal control by white middle-class men over youth, women, and black Americans. And, though perhaps the rising power of the middle-class and popularity of Enlightenment ideas conflicted with the "old exclusivity of the genteel code and the patriarchal control of youth and women," characters in the popular Gothic plays continued to reflect this older model, modeling deference to middle-class older males.[42] Other tensions that were played out in the theatres involved the role of women in the new society. For example, women in the new republic were encouraged to read but simultaneously warned to avoid too much education. In addition, they were instructed to aspire to matrimony and motherhood and yet sternly enjoined to avoid any contemplation of physical love. Another tension concerned the development of a uniquely American culture. In the early Republic, Americans celebrated "American" virtues and yet clung to British traditions, especially in drama and theatre. Finally, in this period before separate theatres catered toward specific classes, all classes attended the same theatre, and clashes among these classes erupted in the theatres themselves. Individual theatres attempted to please all classes with their repertory, which necessitated increasing spectacle and special effects. Simultaneously, however, they had to counter charges from middle-class critics who decried the decline of drama and the poor taste of the lower-class patrons. In addition, theatrical managers had to appease the clergy, who periodically condemned particular plays and patrons.

Gothic plays were effective in surmounting the challenges in these decades after the Revolution as illustrated by their continued popularity. Their very structure is contradictory, combining Gothic moral chaos with melodramatic resolution, a Gothic sense of unease and ambiguity with a rigid formulaic structure. In such a time of conflicting impulses, confusion about nationality, and changing social roles and expectations, these plays provided structure and comforting guidelines. Gothic plays successfully negotiated the contradictions of the age by ostensibly instructing young men and women in appropriate moral behavior and American virtues, while thrilling audiences with spectacular scenery, supernatural effects, and the opportunity to enjoy, albeit vicariously, serious transgressions of acceptable behavior.

Chapter 1

"Gothic America"
Dramas, Theatres and American Society

The evil Marquis de Montault is cornered but defiant; he sneers as his accusers confront him with damning evidence that implicates him in the murder of his sister-in-law, the imprisonment of his brother, and the attempted seduction of his young niece. At this moment in *Fountainville Forest*, the British version of the play, the Marquis grabs a dagger and cries, "I will not yield me to your torturing ruffians, nor, like a slave, expire upon a scaffold. This way alone, does not degrade ambition." The Marquis then stabs himself and dies. However, in the American version, *Fontainville Abbey*, as the Marquis grabs the dagger and attempts to stab himself — he is seized. The Marquis, wrestling against his captors, cries, "Curses o'ertake ye all, ye servile crew! Now fortune hath denied me means of life, Ye, too, would wrest from me the choice of death!" At this point, the American playwright William Dunlap gives the judge a speech, not present in the British version, that suggests a new attitude toward automatic privilege of a rigid class system:

> It is not fit a wretch so black with guilt
> should die but by the sentence of the law.
> A public expiation shalt thou make
> To that society thy deeds have wrong'd.
> Thy ill bought trappings stripp'd from off thy back
> And in their place foul shame and infamy;
> Thus shalt thou die, to men a fearful warning
> Of Heav'ns avenging, swift pursuing justice.[1]

In this new world, Dunlap's speech suggests, rank and privilege will not protect a man from just punishment.

In the years following the American Revolution, citizens in the newly formed United States wrestled with questions of equality, cultural dependence, and national identity, and many of these tensions were played out in the theatres.[2] Plays adapted for American theaters often inserted speeches about equality, yet slavery still existed, even in northern states.[3] Debates about our national identity also appeared in the theatres themselves—in the choice of particular dramas, defense of particular plays as promoting "American" virtues, and ongoing tensions among patrons about appropriate and "respectable" behavior.

Gothic plays, despite, or perhaps because of, their faithful depiction of such contradictory tensions in American society, appeared regularly between 1794 and 1830 in the major theatrical centers of the United States: Philadelphia, New York, Charleston, and Boston. During this period, theatres had to adjust to rapidly changing audiences as more working class patrons swelled audiences, and yet most cities before the mid-1820s had only one or two major theatres in which all classes mingled, often to the alarm of more elite patrons.[4] In addition, theatrical managers also had to placate audiences who simultaneously admired British plays and actors and yet resented the United States' continued cultural dependence upon England. The continued popularity of Gothic plays in the nineteenth century indicates that these plays had broad appeal for audiences of all classes.

By the 1790s, each of the major theatrical centers had populations large enough to sustain a permanent theatre. At this time Philadelphia was considered to be the most important theatrical site; the Chestnut Theatre had a reputation of excellence. Other major cities that had anti-theatrical laws on their books began to repeal them and quickly became theatrical centers in their own right. In 1792, Charleston repealed its Vagrancy Act of 1787 which had prohibited theatricals; in 1793 the Charleston Theatre opened. In 1793 Boston repealed its Act of 1750 which had prohibited theatrical entertainment; in 1794 the Federal Street Theatre opened. New York's Park Street Theatre opened in 1798.[5]

The first appearance of Gothic plays also coincided with a particularly turbulent time in the history of American society. Described as a period of "social disequilibrium," the years between 1790 and 1830 featured rapid urban growth and a booming population; between 1790 and 1830, for example, New York City and Boston more than tripled their populations, and Philadelphia and Charleston nearly doubled their size.[6]

Most of this growth resulted from immigration, particularly from England and Ireland. The fact that these immigrants outnumbered those from other countries undoubtedly exerted some influence on the theatres, which already tended to feature British acting companies and plays by British playwrights.[7]

The composition of the population also was changing. In the early 1800s, only nine percent of the population was between the ages of forty-five and sixty-five; in 1810 over half of the white males were under the age of sixteen.[8] This masculine segment of the population was particularly transient; by 1821 the nation had added nine new states that contained over twenty-five percent of the population, and many of those who migrated west were young.[9] Thus between 1790 and 1830, the potential audiences for theatres were exceedingly young and probably more male than female. Theatrical managers, in an effort to please this new segment of the population, doubtless attempted to provide plays that would appeal particularly to this group.

Economically, too, the nation was changing rapidly; by the 1790s, many large fortunes, founded in "overseas trade and urban land speculation," had established America's "first truly wealthy urban elite. At the same time, the number of propertyless urban dwellers also increased, creating a "growing economic inequality."[10] True, more Americans found opportunities for wealth between 1793 and 1807, when an increase in foreign trade and internal trade, accompanied by improved transportation and means of credit, afforded many ordinary people riches and the chance to rise in the world.[11] Then, around 1820 and for several subsequent decades, a time of early industrialization, there occurred another period of wealth redistribution which increased the gap between the very wealthy and the very poor of urban society and left the bottom half of society "little more than ten percent of the community's assets."[12] This disparity of wealth seemed to be reflected in theatres; for example, several new theatres sprang up in the major theatrical centers, particularly in the 1820s, to compete with the established ones; these new theatres often began as circuses and appealed directly to lower-class patrons.[13]

With economic change came social change. As urban centers increased in size, social segregation increased and geographic dividing lines between rich and poor became more distinct. Workers, immigrants, and poor people occupied older housing in the center of cities, and these urban centers, with their huge numbers of poor and homeless, became areas of "the highest mortality, criminality, and poverty rates ever known on the Eastern seaboard."[14]

Though American society in this period saw increasing geographic segregation of economic classes, it simultaneously witnessed a relaxation of social distinctions between classes. With the economic shifts in America between 1790 and 1830 came a breakdown in ties to community and a breakdown in deference to an established elite; "words like 'gentleman' and 'lady' were becoming less specific."[15] At this same time, free African Americans, especially in New York, were challenging the old authority, and consequently, the "old deference accorded whites was well and truly crumbling everywhere."[16] Such developments must have proved threatening to upper class Americans, whose previously unquestioned superiority was now challenged.

The middle classes in particular attempted to exhibit refined sensibilities to separate themselves from the lower classes. In the years between 1794 and 1830, the "line that once divided gentry from the rest of society" now moved lower and divided those in the middle class from "workers and marginal people."[17] Even as America separated from Britain and celebrated its republican government, the middle classes "embraced gentility."[18] Simultaneously, however, some Americans recognized a conflict between their "commitment to aristocratic gentility" and their "devotion to republican equality."[19] This conflict was apparent in Gothic plays, and particularly evident in adaptations made for American audiences.

During these same years, Protestantism in America grew to be especially powerful, partially as a result of that series of revivals known as the Second Great Awakening.[20] The clergy continually warned the public, particularly the young, against the many vices surrounding them, and one of the greatest vices that they identified was the theatre. Many renowned clergymen denounced the theatre as a place of iniquity, noting that theatrical managers permitted strong drink in the galleries, and, infinitely more damning, permitted prostitutes in the third tier.[21] Evidently some managers even arranged for free passes to be delivered to the prostitutes at their place of employment.[22] Managers found themselves in a dilemma; if they denied access to the prostitutes, they lost business, yet if they admitted them, they outraged various segments of the population. Despite the clergy's public outcries against the presence of liquor and prostitutes in the theatre, the managers continued these practices for several decades.[23]

It is probably significant that Gothic plays appeared in the theatres when the theatres themselves were battling anti-theatrical prejudice, particularly from the clergy.[24] Then, as now, theatres needed to please audiences in order to survive. That theatrical managers included Gothic plays in the repertories in such tenuous times suggests that they believed these plays would be acceptable to their diverse audiences, that certain elements in Gothic plays would appeal to the ever-increasing number of less affluent patrons as well as to their more established, and perhaps more conservative, patrons.

Understanding American Gothic plays and the audiences that saw them is complicated by the then intimate relationship between the British and American cultures, including their arts. Despite the nation's political independence, it remained culturally dependent. Throughout the period of Gothic drama's greatest popularity, Americans relied upon "British literature, British art, British plays, and British actors."[25] Some Europeans of the period went so far as to argue that Americans had no culture of their own: "In the four corners of the globe, who reads an American book? or goes to an American play? or looks at any American picture or statue?"[26]

Even some Americans alternated between hostility to and uncertainty about the existence of genuine American culture and art. For example, some Americans decried the developing American language:

> Mr. Webster's Dictionary is intended to be a complete assylum [sic] for fugitive words, no doubt the idiotisms of his countrymen will here find refuge: thus, her's and your's will be changed into hern, and yourn; fetch and catch into fotch and cotch; and roof and hoof into ruff and huff ... novelty will characterise [sic] the Dictionary of Mr. Webster.... Americans boast of their independence in policy, and why should not this independence extend to language also? As Washington was the hero of American liberty, so Webster will become the defender of the American language.[27]

Yet an article in the *Boston Spectator* of 1814 claimed that many "publick documents" were "rendered almost unintelligible by their mock sublimnity," and argued that "our national character has suffered much by this foppery of words. It is a serious injury to ourselves and it makes us ridiculous abroad."[28]

That a number of Americans feared the sting of European disparagement as suggested by an 1822 newspaper article: "Let native talent, by all means, be encouraged; but let it have fair play. We have already been sufficiently sneered at by foreigners."[29] Despite the very real possibility of inciting scorn from European critics, many Americans seemed intent on forging an identity apart from Britain. One such patriot wrote in 1807,

> I am not one of those who decry every thing that is American. I love my country, and I delight to contemplate that noble spirit of perseverance which had enabled the laborious husbandsman to climb the loftiest mountain, and to change the rude garb of nature for the rich habiliments of cultivation.[30]

By the 1820s, more critics recognized that developing a uniquely American culture depended on cultivating American audiences as well as American artists. A fervent appeal in an 1825 newspaper called for citizens in the United States to encourage their own artists:

> When will the intrepidity and perseverance of independent America, enable us to command a literature of our own! When will the liberality of our countrymen make it an object for authors to write for us! How long must our poets yet sing, before we will listen — How long must our painters labour, before we will admire? — How many years must yet pass away before we can criticize for ourselves! — and why have we not the mental courage to defy the tyranny of foreign ridicule, and foreign censure?[31]

Of the myriad British influences on American culture between the 1790s and the 1830s, two in particular were important to any understanding of Gothic plays in America: the English novel and the English theatre.

As early as 1795, too, American playwrights had joined their literary counterparts in complaining of their fellow citizens' disparagement of native literary efforts. William Dunlap commented that he did not publicize his Gothic play *Fontainville Abbey* as the work of an American, because "such an avowal at that time would have been enough to condemn the piece."[32]

This prejudice obviously continued throughout the 1810s as suggested by one complaint in 1813: "if a poet should attempt to portray American manners, to celebrate American achievements, or to record American events, in the form of a dramatic piece, he literally becomes 'a fixed figure for the time of scorn to point his slow unmoving finger at.'"[33]

This situation did not seem to be improved by 1825, in that published complaints as late as 1828 confirmed that, despite some American successes in other forms of literature, no American dramatist had yet been accepted by American audiences:

> It is but a very short time since we released ourselves from British leading-strings in relation to the other walks of letters, compelled to do so by the genius of an Irving, a Cooper, a Bryant, a Halleck, and the like; and until some great dramatic writer shall arise among us ... to draw, by the magic power of his genius, the tribute of applause from our hearts ... we shall be afraid to encourage native dramatic bards ... and shall be obliged to depend on England for our plays, as, till very recently, we did for our players and managers.[34]

The writer (and others) attributed the seeming "lack of dramatic talent among Americans" to a "lack of encouragement" by audiences who still did not trust their own judgment about dramatic works until they learned the opinion of English critics. Another American critic growled that American audiences required all new plays to carry the "certificate of having been performed a hundred nights, with unbounded applause" in London, and only admired those plays that "had received the stamp of a London audience."[35]

Although some Americans complained of the lack of dramatic geniuses and others of the lack of audiences, in fact there were both; however, as an account in 1827 explained, each was "ignorant of the very existence of the [other]." In fact, as the report observed, America could boast possession of "nearly sixty American dramas, consisting of tragedies, comedies, operas, serious and comic, melo-dramas and farces, besides others that baffle all our attempts at 'codification.'"[36]

America's cultural dependence upon Britain was evident in theatre as well as drama, as illustrated by the routine practice of the American theatre's using British actors, perhaps because many of the theatre managers were themselves born and raised in Britain. For example, in 1806, citizens in New York feverishly awaited the arrival of Thomas Cooper; one notice commented, "The public are so impatient in regard to Mr. Cooper's arrival, and so anxious are they to assure themselves of witnessing his performances that all the lower boxes are already engaged for the five nights of his appearance."[37] And as late as 1823, published notices advised Americans of the superior quality of British actors, even suggesting that the reputation of a theatre depended upon such importations: "The liberal and enterprising managers of this establishment, have ... drawn over from England, from time to time, those who stood high there in the profession ... and [have] 'given our theatre a good standing and a good character.'"[38] Although some Americans objected to importing actors and called for theatres to "bring forward a few from our own country, to show that we can in America produce as ingenious, active men and boys, as can be imported," their objections seemed to carry little weight, for British stars outnumbered homegrown ones until the Civil War.[39]

The idea that "all is good and delightful that comes from Britain" carried over even into criticism.[40] For example, Philadelphia's *Port Folio* frequently reviewed plays appearing in British theatres instead of those appearing in Philadelphia. It explained,

> Though for some years we have declined inserting in the *Port-Folio* a regular critique upon the plays represented on the Philadelphia Stage, yet from time to time we wish to give an outline of the fable, and characters of every drama of merit. Local criticism interests only a few, but an occasional analysis of a Tragedy or Comedy will probably be delightful to many of our readers.[41]

Despite (or perhaps because of) British influence on the plays, actors, and criticism of the American stage and despite journalistic carping about local productions, Americans did attend their own theatres. Moreover, they attended in increasing numbers, as suggested both by the regular expansion of major theatres in Philadelphia, New York, Charleston, and Boston and by the erection of rival theatres in these cities.[42] And despite the economic inequality evident in urban centers, most working people could have afforded a ticket, particularly for a seat in the pit or the gallery. In 1794, a ticket for a box seat cost one dollar; for the pit fifty cents, and for the gallery, twenty-five cents.[43] These prices varied only slightly between 1794 and 1823.[44] Although the price of the pit and gallery may have fluctuated, the established theatres continued to charge the same price for boxes even when faced with competition from new theatres or circuses that charged only fifty cents for any ticket. After 1823, however, established theatres evidently had to cut prices to compete for audiences; in New York, the Chatham Garden opened in 1824 with a price of only fifty cents for a box seat and offered serious competition for the Park Theatre. The Chatham also was unusual in that it continued performances throughout the summer; a notice in *The New York Mirror*, and *Ladies' Literary Gazette*, observed, "Notwithstanding the thermometer has risen to one hundred and twenty in the sun, and ninety-nine in the shade, this theatre continues nightly to attract a crowded and fashionable audience."[45]

In sum, then, Gothic plays enjoyed their greatest popularity at a time when the country was experiencing tremendous changes in population and social structure. Despite the radical changes that occurred between 1795 and 1830, these plays enjoyed steady popularity at both the established and the new theatres. Thus, it seems clear that Gothic plays appealed across classes of the population. Furthermore, these plays flourished at a time when the new country was attempting to fashion an identity apart from England. Yet in spite of America's vehement insistence upon political independence, its citizens continued to cling to British culture. This partiality was especially apparent in theatricals; Americans preferred British plays and performers well into the 1820s.

Gothic plays appeared regularly in Philadelphia, New York, Charleston, and Boston between 1795 and 1830, although different ones proved popular in each city.[46]

CHAPTER 2

"An Appetite for Gothic"
Productions of Gothic Plays by City, 1794–1830

Sir Edward Mortimer, a gloomy, mysterious man, isolates himself from society because of his dreadful secret. Although basically a good man, he once made a terrible error. As his young male secretary Wilford begins to unravel Mortimer's mysterious past, Mortimer grows more agitated. At the climactic moment of *The Iron Chest*, Sir Edward, in a frenzy of emotion, faints begins to suffer convulsions, and shrieks,

> Where is my honour, now? To die! To have my ashes trampled on, by the proud foot of scorn! Polluted! Hell! Who dares to mock.... Is't you — or you? Wrack me that grinning fiend! Damnation! Who spits upon my grave? I'll stab again![1]

The role of Sir Mortimer, with its emotional extremes and passionate speeches, was a favorite of leading men in the early years of the nineteenth century. On the night of December 19, 1820, audiences in New York were treated to Edmund Kean in the role. Kean, a star on the English stage, had made his first appearance in the United States approximately three weeks before, and the box office receipts were staggering. Theatre manager Edmund Simpson reported that Kean averaged $1,000 a night.[2] Kean premiered in New York as Richard III. On subsequent nights, he portrayed Othello, Shylock, Brutus, Hamlet, Hamlet, Macbeth, Giles Overreach — and Sir Edward Mortimer in *The Iron Chest*.

Kean then traveled to Philadelphia in January of 1821, and again performed in Shakespearean roles, but he again included Sir Edward Mortimer in his repertoire. On the night he performed in *The Iron Chest*,

William Wood, theatre manger, reported that the box office took in $727.25, more than the theatre received for Kean's portrayals of Shylock and Hamlet.³

Several Gothic plays featured characters that appealed to major tragedians of the day. The presence of these stars drew patrons who may have been more interested in acting than in spectacle. Gothic plays, however, were able to provide both — and thus appeal to varying tastes. As a result, productions of Gothic plays appeared regularly in each of the major theatrical centers in the United States between 1794 and 1830. They were included in the earliest seasons of the first permanent theatres in each city and then won renewed popularity with newer theatres or circuses built for working-class patrons.

Philadelphia, the leading theatrical city in the 1790s, produced Gothic dramas regularly. They first appeared at the Chestnut Street theatre, and this theatre increased the number of Gothic plays as the population expanded in Philadelphia, peaking between 1817 and 1823, times of competition from the Olympic, a theatre that began as a circus.

The Chestnut Street theatre, opened by Thomas Wignell in 1795, served as the major theatre in Philadelphia and soon gained a reputation of excellence, for both its acting company and its audiences.⁴ In the 1790s, leading actors included James Fennell and Thomas Abthorpe Cooper, and actresses included Mrs. Robert (Anne Brunton) Merry, Mrs. Marshall, and Mrs. Oldmixon.⁵ That the audience remained fashionable into the 1820s is suggested by a notice in the *Theatrical Censor and Musical Review*, which stated, "A brilliant and overflowing audience attended Mr. Sloman's benefit this evening. The fashion and beauty of the city graced the dress circle, and such was the crowd that many ladies were obliged to take seats in the back boxes, and others in the second tier."⁶

In the 1820s, however, the increase in the number of working-class patrons, which accompanied industrial development, presumably altered the composition of audiences. The cost of a ticket to any theatre was affordable for working people. The average wage for laborers in the Philadelphia area between 1794 and 1830 was about a dollar per day.⁷ Rates for common labor on the Erie Canal even as late as 1828 averaged 71 cents a day.⁸

A comparison of prices for common household necessities with the price of a ticket to the theatre indicates that, although a seat in the boxes probably would have proved too expensive for a working man or woman, a seat in the pit (for men and escorted women) or a seat in the gallery (for men) would have been affordable. At twenty-five cents, a gallery seat in Philadelphia between 1795 and 1830 would have equaled a quarter of a day's wages.[9]

Working-class patrons, then, could have afforded a ticket to the Chestnut and probably did attend in increasing numbers. Despite this probability, though, the managers of the Chestnut decreased the number of Gothic plays produced after 1823, at the very time that more working-class patrons would have attended the theatre. This decrease in Gothic plays at this time seemed particularly peculiar in that they proved very popular with working-class audiences and were regular features of new theatres built specifically for this segment of the population. One possible reason for the decrease was the Chestnut Street Theatre's new competition, the Walnut Street Theatre, which opened in 1822 under the management of Stephen Price and Edmund Simpson. Simpson, also manager of New York's Park Theatre (long associated with the upper classes), apparently sought to attract more elite patrons.[10] Perhaps the Chestnut decreased offerings of Gothic plays, which were becoming ever more popular with working-class patrons, to compete with the Walnut Street Theatre.

New York produced more Gothic plays than any other city from 1794 to 1830 and also sustained enormous increases in population during these years, averaging a 50 percent increase every ten years.[11]

The Park Theatre was erected in 1794 and was the major theatre in New York City at that time, existing without much competition until the 1820s. The Park gained the reputation of attracting upper-class patrons, and class distinctions within the theatre were apparent, as suggested by an article in 1807 by "Theatricus," who observed that the actor Mr. Twaits was "an uncommon favourite with our pit and gallery, and although he sometimes raises a laugh among the genteeler part of the audience, the boxes, it is uniformly at the expense of nature or modesty."[12]

Gothic plays appeared regularly in the repertory at the Park. Between 1798 and 1806, the number of Gothic plays increased, undoubtedly because William Dunlap, manager of the Park, wrote two plays, *Fontainville Abbey* and *Ribbemont*, and produced them. However, managers of the Park sharply increased the number of Gothic plays between 1825 and 1830. The Park continued to produce several of the most popular Gothic plays throughout the 1820s, often producing the same plays in the same months as its rival theatres. Despite its efforts, by 1825, the Park was losing to the competition, as suggested by this lament in *The New York Mirror and Ladies' Literary Gazette*:

> We would say something concerning the performance at the Park Theatre, but we really believe the spirit of the actors is damped, by the "beggarly account of empty boxes." ... it is singular to us that the very meritorious actors now on this stage do not awaken more of the public interest. The manager is about to produce another splendid melo-drama; and as the Chatham Garden will close on the 26th instant, we hope the performers will meet with a patronage more worthy their deserts.[13]

Despite the growing class distinctions present in the audiences of the different theatres in New York, the behavior of these patrons seemed uniformly disrespectful of the acting. In 1807, a newspaper observed "We are satisfied, the Manager has not yet to learn, that all the visitors of a theatre do not attend *solely* to witness the stage exhibition."[14] The situation was not particularly improved even by the 1820s as suggested by a notice in *The New York Mirror and Ladies Literary Gazette:* "Before we conclude this brief notice, we must suggest one improvement to the proprietor. There is too much light on the stage, and too little in the boxes. It would be difficult to recognize a friend across the house. This defect can easily be remedied, and no doubt will be."[15]

Although the attention of the audience certainly fluctuated according to play and featured players, such contemporary accounts suggest that actors had to compete with many potential distractions. Gothic plays, with their emphasis on suspense and their growing use of special effects, may have been particularly successful in maintaining the interest of theatrical patrons.

In Charleston, the (Thomas Wade) West company opened the Charleston Theatre in 1793 but soon encountered competition from the French (City) Theatre Company, which featured novelty. The West company failed in 1796 and the French Theatre Company, now under the management of Henry Placide, moved to the more spacious Charleston Theatre in 1800 and began offering regular productions of Gothic plays. The years between 1801 and 1808 saw a relatively large number of Gothic plays, due at least in part to the presence of John Hodgkinson, who specialized in many Gothic roles and portrayed them frequently.[16]

Productions of Gothic plays increased again between 1819 and 1821. This increase perhaps occurred in response to a sudden increase in the city's population; Charleston added more people between 1810 and 1820 than in any other decade between 1794 and 1830.

In the early 1790s, Boston was served by the Old American Company, which also served New York.[17] Then, in 1794, Charles Stuart Powell and a company of unknown English actors opened the Federal Street Theatre. The season failed and Powell was replaced. In the 1796–97 season, Powell opened the Haymarket Theatre to compete with the Federal Street. Perhaps in competition for audiences, Federal Street increased its number of Gothic plays. The Haymarket failed in 1803, leaving Federal Street without serious competition for twenty-four years until the Tremont Theatre opened in 1827.[18] During these years, however, the acting company at Federal Street was not always perceived at particularly strong. A column in the *Boston Weekly Magazine*, in January 1817, derides the company for "not having in PERMANENT possession, at least one leading male and female performer of undisputed and superior professional accomplishments." The critic concluded, "with such a company, is it all surprising that managers find it difficult to fill the theatre by the performance of standard dramas?"[19] The Federal Street theatre continued to offer Gothic plays throughout the 1810s and 1820s.[20]

An analysis of the production of the plays in this sample reveals that the Gothic plays receiving the greatest number of performances in the major theatrical centers were *Bluebeard, The Castle Spectre, A Tale of Mystery, Bertram,* and *The Iron Chest.*

Bluebeard, sometimes subtitled "Female Curiosity," was the story of Fatima, who was forced by her greedy father to marry the rich, but evil, Abomolique instead of her true love, Selim. Abomolique had been married many times, but his wives always disappeared. He always tested each new wife by giving her a key to the Blue Chamber, a magic room, and then warning her not to enter it on pain of death. Unfortunately, each wife had succumbed to her curiosity and opened the door, and consequently, had been beheaded. Abomolique gave the key and the usual warning to Fatima and left the castle. When Fatima toured the castle, she came upon the Blue Chamber, and, after some vacillation, opened the door. There she discovered a chamber of horrors, complete with walls streaming blood and an animated skeleton. When Abomolique returned and learned of Fatima's offense, he condemned her to death and dragged her off to the chamber. But before he was able to behead her, Selim and his army crashed through the back wall. Selim fought with Abomolique, and, in the course of the struggle, the animated skeleton killed the villain.

2. "An Appetite for Gothic"

The second most popular Gothic play, *The Castle Spectre*, by Matthew Gregory Lewis, featured a memorable villain: the Earl of Osmond. The Earl has fallen in love with his niece Angela, taken her away from her lover, Percy, and confined her to his castle. Angela, however, rejected his advances, and the Earl, enraged, threatened her with rape and then locked her in her chamber. There, Angela saw the specter of her mother and learned that her father, supposed dead, actually still lived in the dungeon of the castle. A friar helped Angela find her father, but before they could escape, the Earl discovered them and threatened to kill Angela's father (his brother) on the spot. At that moment, the specter of Angela's mother appeared; this so horrified the Earl that he was rendered momentarily helpless, and Angela, taking advantage of his confusion, stabbed him.

The third most produced play, *A Tale of Mystery*, was most famous for its position as the first melodrama. In the play, Count Romaldi visited Bonomo to demand the marriage of Bonomo's ward Selina to Romaldi's son. Bonomo, however, knew of Selina's love for his own son, Stefano, and so refused the match. Angered at Bonomo's resistance, Count Romaldi sent a letter to Bonomo proving that Selina was not his niece, but instead the daughter of Francisco Bianchi, a mysterious mute who had been staying at Bonomo's house. After receiving the letter, Bonomo evicted both Selina and Francisco, and they were forced out into the wilds. Soon after, however, authorities informed Bonomo that Count Romaldi had been revealed as an assassin, who had authorized the murder of his own brother eight years before in order to gain his estates. Moreover the Count's real name was Bianchi — and the brother he attempted to kill was Francisco. In the final scene, Romaldi, disguised, was attempting to flee archers who had been sent to execute him. But as they closed in upon Romaldi, Francisco and Selina appeared and shielded his body from the archers.

Bertram, by Charles Maturin, depicted the story of Imogene and Bertram, two young lovers separated by treachery and deceit, who were reunited after many years. Imogene, told that Bertram had died, married his rival. Although Imogene married her husband for financial security, she acknowledged him as a good man and a good father. However, she never loved him. When Bertram was shipwrecked near Imogene's castle, he learned of her marriage and angrily accused her of betrayal. Imogene, frantic for his love, agreed to meet him for a romantic tryst, but afterward, she was horrified at her infidelity. Worse, Bertram scorned her and soon after murdered her husband. After her husband's death, Imogene ran with her child into the forest. When found, she was insane, and her child was dead. Upon seeing Bertram, she managed to reproach him for his cruelty but then abruptly died. Bertram, in remorse, stabbed himself.

The Iron Chest featured another popular villain, Sir Edward Mortimer, who lived in isolation in a lodge in the forest. Sir Edward shunned society because of his guilty secret; he had killed the father of his ward, Helen. Though he had been publicly acquitted of the crime, Sir Edward knew his own guilt and his conscience tortured him. He kept a damning confession locked in an iron chest in his study, and one day, after catching his young secretary, Wilford, examining the chest, he feared discovery and so arranged to have Wilford framed for theft. When the assembled company examined the case against Wilford, however, they found the confession and realized Sir Edward's guilt. Sir Edward promptly descended into madness.

Although all major theatrical centers produced all of the most popular Gothic plays, each found a different favorite.

In Philadelphia, the play receiving the most productions between 1794 and 1830 was *A Tale of Mystery* by Holcroft. *Bertram*, assessed by Wood as "highly attractive … despite of a merciless attack upon its alleged immoral character," received the second greatest number of performances.[21] Philadelphians also enjoyed another play not so popular in the other cities: *Marmion*, a romantic tragedy based on the tale by Sir Walter Scott. Philadelphia audiences, more than those in other cities, seemed to prefer Gothic plays with less supernatural effects.

The most popular plays in New York were *Bertram* and *The Iron Chest*, followed closely by *The Castle Spectre*.[22] That these pieces were favorites is somewhat surprising in that both of these plays rely on language more than spectacle. However, New York also produced several Gothic plays that did not appear in any other city, and these plays were particularly noted for their lavish spectacle: *The Mountain Torrent, The Rose of Arragon, Melmoth*, and *Presumption; or The Fate of Frankenstein*. Of this last play, one critic observed:

> Our countrymen are in a great degree, matter-of-fact men, not much inclined to romantic enthusiasm. Nevertheless, they relish occasionally a touch of the horrific, though, and this drama has enough to satisfy the most voracious appetite. It is dramatized from Mrs. Shelley's story of the modern Prometheus.[23]

The Gothic plays most frequently performed in New York did not rely so much upon spectacle, and New York offered a greater number of Gothic dramas than did other cities.

The most popular Gothic drama in Charleston between 1794 and 1825 was *Bluebeard* with 27 performances, followed closely by *The Castle Spectre*, plays noted for their special effects. Yet Charlestonians also appreciated those plays that relied more on language, as suggested by the popularity of *Bertram* and *The Iron Chest*. Indeed, A column entitled "Dramatic Criticism" in 1803 bemoaned "the fondness for modern ghost novels, which, however contemptibly written, have laid such a complete hold on susceptible hearts as to have superseded in request all the more rational ones of the old school." The same article condemned "Monk" Lewis's sensational play *Adelmorn*: "It is astonishing what a total absence of wit, humour, and poetical merit there is in this play."[24] Charleston theatricals seemed to strike a balance between those Gothic plays that relied more upon language and those that relied more heavily on special effects.

Boston audiences exhibited an "appetite for gothic melodrama" and exhibited more performances of the popular Gothic plays than any other city.[25] Boston especially favored spectacle, as suggested by the popularity of *The Castle Spectre* and *Bluebeard*.[26] A 1799 advertisement in the *Massachusetts Mercury* enthusiastically promoted one of the first productions of *The Castle Spectre* in the city:

> The public are respectfully informed that every attention has been paid to bring out *This Magnificent Spectacle* in order to make it an object worthy [of] general attention and patronage. No piece ever produced in London has attracted such curiosity and brilliant houses, and it is probably more calculated to interest the feelings of an audience, to surprise and astonish than any Dramatic representation ever seen in America.[27]

That Bostonians appreciated spectacle is further suggested by the popularity of *Adelmorn*, a play by Matthew Gregory Lewis that featured a lavish supernatural scene; this play was not as popular in any other city. Some Boston critics publicly decried the presence of novelties in Boston theatricals: "novelties in the Drama are deserving of as little encouragement as novelties in Religion — they are in both instances too often insidious innovations in established excellences."[28] Despite their objections, however, Gothic plays, particularly the sensational ones, flourished in Boston.

In summary, Gothic plays appeared in each of the major theatrical centers between 1794 and 1830, beginning at the established theatres that served a heterogeneous audience. These theatres increased the number of Gothic plays when competing with new theatres or circuses that catered to working-class patrons, and, in the case of the Chestnut, decreased the number of Gothic plays when competing with a theatre that catered to upper-class patrons.

The five most popular Gothic plays were performed regularly in each theatrical center; however, a different play proved the favorite in each city. Philadelphia preferred those plays less dependent on supernatural effects; *The Castle Spectre*, for example, so popular in other cities, was not one of the five favorites there. Moreover, Philadelphians, unlike audiences in other cities, included *Marmion* among their most frequently performed Gothic plays. Possibly the theatre, relatively free from competition for much of its existence until 1830, did not need to emphasize spectacle to attract new audiences as much as did theatres in other cities.

Audiences in New York, although fond of those plays that resembled tragedies, also were receptive to new works; New York frequently produced plays not offered in any other city, particularly those more dependent upon spectacle and horrific special effects such as *Frankenstein* and *Melmoth*. However, these two plays did appear in the 1820s, at a time when several theatres in the city competed for audiences. That competition, perhaps, accounted for the popularity of those two particular dramas.

Audiences in Charleston seemed to enjoy a mix of Gothic plays: the three most popular plays—*Bluebeard, The Castle Spectre*, and *A Tale of Mystery*—were noted for their special effects; however, Charlestonians also favored *Bertram* and *The Iron Chest*, both plays more noted for their story than their spectacle.

In Boston, audiences clearly favored those Gothic plays that featured novelty. Not only did Bostonians prefer the three plays most noted for special effects, *The Castle Spectre, Bluebeard*, and *A Tale of Mystery*, but they also excluded *Bertram* and *The Iron Chest* as favorites and instead substituted *The Wood Daemon* and *Adelmorn*, plays famous for their novelty. Perhaps audiences in Boston particularly liked novelty in the plays because their acting company was, at various times, considered relatively weak. Plays that emphasized spectacle, then, would not have required the same level of acting skill as plays that featured more complex characters like those in *Bertram* or *The Iron Chest*.

CHAPTER 3

"The Senseless Brawl of Barbarians"
Profane Plays and Patrons

In the harsh moonlight, Imogene clings to Bertram, her long-lost love, for whom she has just violated her wedding vows and dishonored her husband. As she combats her desire for him, she sobs, "I am desperate to say I'll met thee, but I will — will meet thee; No future hour can rend my heart like this — Save that which breaks it. —" But just as she finishes this pledge, her child runs in and cries, "my father is returned, and kissed and bless me." When Imogene hears these words from her innocent child, she reels with horror at her infidelity, and moans, "What have I done, my child; forgive thy mother." At her change of heart, Bertram, "surveying her with stern contempt," hisses, "Woman, oh woman and an urchin's kiss rends from thy heart thy love of many years — Go virtuous dame, to thy most happy lord, and Bertram's image taint your kiss with poison."[1]

On December 9, 1816 in Philadelphia, the Chestnut Theatre offered the premiere of *Bertram* by Charles Maturin, followed by the afterpiece *The Agreeable Surprise*. William Wood, manager of the theatre, recorded in his log that the ticket sales for the evening were good: $820.50, the highest amount for the week.[2] A patron attending this performance could have chosen a seat in a box, the pit, or the gallery.

In 1816, a dollar bought a patron a seat in the fashionable lower tiers of boxes; seventy-five cents allowed a seat in the less desirable but more affordable pit, sometimes so crowded that it appeared to be just a "great ocean of all sorts of heads."[3] A fifty-cent ticket relegated a person to the gallery, where the "cheek of Decency crimsoned with the profaneness, obscenity, and senseless brawl of barbarians."[4]

Box seats in the two lower tiers were traditionally reserved for people of fashion.[5] Women in these seats were referred to "respectable" in contemporary accounts. Although these fashionable patrons themselves were criticized occasionally for their loud talking and apparent indifference to the plays, their sins were overshadowed by those patrons in the upper boxes, the infamous third tier, in which sat women assumed to be prostitutes.[6] Despite American society's "strong Puritanical bias," prostitutes comprised a part of "every theatre audience of the eighteenth century" and, in some cities, they continued to sit in sections assigned for them well into the nineteenth century.[7] That those in the lower boxes were conscious of the "noted public impures" and their clients, is suggested by one observer who complained, "The pleasure imparted by the scene performed on the stage is very much diminished by some which pass in the boxes ... abandoned, shameless, profligate men in good clothes, sitting with the most notorious of the impure sisterhood ... in the very eyes, and within ear-shot of virtuous ladies."[8] In Charleston, a column called "The Moralist" chastised the young men of the city for leaving the "society of elegant and virtuous women to attach themselves to those impures ... unhappy, miserable women ... who flock to the upper boxes arrayed in all the wantonness of attraction." According to "The Moralist," "there is not in nature a greater happiness to man of feeling and morality than enjoying the society of an amiable and virtuous Woman — And there is not in nature as great a brute, as he who forsakes them to associate in public with the most abandoned of their sex."[9]

If a patron chose to sit in the pit, described by some as the place for serious playgoers, he may well have been pelted from above with "scraps of apples, nutshells in handfuls, and perhaps something worse."[10] He also would have peered at the stage through clouds of cigar smoke, and strained to hear the orchestra through the "cat-calls of the gallery."[11] Of course, a respectable woman, unescorted by a man, would not venture into the pit at all; to do so would seriously jeopardize her reputation, a lesson learned too late by several ladies, whose reputations were "entirely lacerated" by their actions.[12] As a notice in *The Cynick* stated, a respectable woman would meet a "promiscuous assemblage" in the pit, and thus the "proper fastidiousness of the female character" would keep her from sitting there.[13]

Patrons in the gallery were characterized as working-class rowdies. Blacks, too, were "relegated" to the gallery, "distant from all but the most disreputable whites."[14] The "gallery gods" often were accused of disrupting the performances with crude behavior and drunken routs.[15] According to William Wood, however, disorderly conduct actually occurred more often in the boxes because these "larger and more divided spaces" allowed more "unruly" patrons to "stealthily mingle themselves with the respectable," so as to escape detection. Wood concluded that in all of his years as a theatrical manager, he recalled "*only two instances of a necessity to remove disturbers from either the pit or the gallery.*"[16]

On this particular night, the production of *Bertram* proved memorable; unlike most Gothic plays, it incited angry responses from some critics and members of the clergy because in the play, Imogene, wife and mother, commits adultery with her long-lost love Bertram.[17] Even though Imogene, as a result of her heinous mistake, lost her husband, her child, her sanity, and her life, she evidently did not lose enough to satisfy the clergy. A review in the *Boston Weekly Magazine* contended that Imogene, "blest with every personal accomplishment, the adored wife, the believed mother" plummets "with the facility of a harlot, from the nuptial couch of matrimony, to grovel in the adulterous embraces—not of a gallant, gay Lothario, but of an out-lawed rebel, a cut-throat robber."[18] Not only was the play decried in print as morally unacceptable ("as a performance, it neither can nor should be beheld without disgust"), but the actress who portrayed the guilty character was denounced in church as she herself sat in the congregation.[19] However, others defended the play and argued that it was "the production of no common mind," and that it was "the successful effort of a powerful fancy" to paint "the wildest extreme of physical and moral desolation."[20]

Although the play certainly inspired controversy, it probably did not enthrall the audience to respectful silence. Instead, even as the wretched Imogene wailed on stage, "a company of ten or so" might have, as on other nights, turned "the boxes into a grog shop ... and brought "jug and bottle, and glass, and tumbler into the front seats."[21] Or perhaps, on this night as on another, a "finished vagabond" in the gallery spoke "smut" and roared it "out loud, directing it to the ladies in the boxes."[22] In addition, ladies may well have been troubled by noises from the upper boxes, particularly the "titter of the impure, and the dull chatter of her stupid wooer"; indeed the "clack of these abominables" may have drowned out the voices of the actors."[23]

Engraving of Edmund Kean as title character in *Bertram*. The Harvard Theatre Collection, Houghton Library.

Despite the apparent problems existing in theatres of this time, patrons continued to flock to them; *The Mirror of Dramatic Taste and Censor* in 1811 estimated that there were, in Philadelphia, "two to three thousand people" in "the constant habit of attending the theatre."[24] Theatres in other major cities enjoyed the same popularity at this time; New York, Charleston, and Boston all had at least one major theatre by the mid-1790s, and more opened in the early 1800s. Indeed, between 1800 and 1810, theatres in these centers in the United States apparently enjoyed unprecedented popularity, as indicated by a letter published in 1807:

> As a taste for the Theatre has lately become so very prevalent in all parts of the United States, and theatrical intelligences sought after with such avidity by all ranks of people, we, in order to gratify this ruling propensity, have been induced to give such a sketch of the New-York performers, as we presume will not be altogether uninteresting to your readers.[25]

In addition to confirming the popularity of theatre in all cities, this article suggested that, though permanent theatres had existed in the major population centers of the United States since the mid-1790s, they only recently had began to enjoy widespread popularity. This rising popularity also suggested by the appearance of several periodicals devoted exclusively to theatre: *The Theatrical Censor, The Thespian Mirror,* and *The Thespian Monitor* all premiered between 1805 and 1810. That the theatre's popularity was not a fleeting phenomenon was indicated by continued references to theatre throughout the early decades of the nineteenth century. As late as 1824, articles still remarked on the high degree of public interest in theatre: "Of all the subjects that occupy the public attention, none appear of more interest than the Theatre, whether the object of its votaries' praise, or its enemies' condemnation."[26] That theatres still inspired controversy as late as 1827 is indicated by a comment in the *Boston Spectator and Ladies' Album*:

> There may be among our readers, some who dislike equally, the profession and notices of it; who may think that we give an undue importance to what they call a vanity, if nothing worse. To them we would say, that truth and virtue can only be promoted by free discussion, and that so long as we search for abuses and strive to reform them, our labor and columns are devoted to a good end.[27]

Despite, or perhaps because of, the theatre's increasing popularity in the United States, critics were quite ambiguous about its value, boastful of its potential as moral teacher yet fearful of its perceived immorality of the dramatic presentations, the actors, or the patrons. In 1816, an article in *The Boston Weekly Magazine* noted,

> The notions which we entertained concerning the Theatre, twenty-five years ago, were, that it was an institution too abominable even for the momentary regard of the Christian;—that those who frequented it were no better than heretics—and those who played there were upon the very face of it, vagabonds. Legal war was therefore declared.... Having suffered the Drama to take revenge upon its ancient foe, we ... forget that unless restrained within proper bounds, it may, in its triumph over bigotry, involve more sacred principles ... we seem not to remember that morality has any thing to do with it.[28]

Periodicals appearing in America in the first decade of the nineteenth century frequently and painstakingly lauded the theatre for its instructive potential, perhaps to deflect any lingering doubts about its respectability. Such articles inevitably acknowledged first the dangers of the stage, as illustrated by this example published in New York's *The Cynick* of 1811:

> The theatre, in its best condition, is attended by so many evils of every description, that its toleration has been a subject of serious discussion; and many excellent and wise men have openly objected to it with all the strength of reason, and all the majesty of virtue.[29]

After conceding the potential dangers of the stage, such articles then cited the potential advantages, particularly the effectiveness of the drama in providing moral instruction and in keeping patrons from indulging in more harmful amusements:

> the rational and manly diversion it afforded to the mind, was allowed not only to have great effect in itself, on the moral character, but also to have been a beneficial substitute for dangerous and pernicious enjoyments.[30]

This device of promoting dramas as morally instructive was not a new one; as early as the 1750s in America, Douglass had publicized his production of *Othello* as a "moral dialogue."[31] Yet the frequency of articles defending the stage from criticism about perceived immorality in the early 1800s suggested that theatres were under renewed attack.

That these attacks were not concentrated only in one city was indicated by the publication of one particular defense of the stage, which appeared in three different periodicals in several different cities.[32] True to form, the article first cited the dangers of an unregulated stage:

> The stage is the direct School of Vice when it presents immoral scenes, when it utters base and corrupt sentiments, under the specious semblance of candour and truth. It becomes a nuisance to society, when a false taste presides over its representations; when the passions are caricatured, when manners are miscopied, when its language is barbarous, its pronunciation vicious, or its delivery vulgar.[33]

The article then glorified the potential benefits of a stage that was well-regulated:

> But, under proper management, the stage becomes the School of Virtue, the School of Manners, the great School of Society. In it is taught whatever is interesting not only to man, but to civilized man. It teaches all that ennobles [sic], all that embellishes human life. It teaches all the decencies of publick and private intercourse. It is the School of Morals; it is the School of Arts; it is the School of Language; it is the School of Piety.[34]

One frequently cited defense of the stage was its potential for reaching those who might ordinarily not be affected by moral instruction: even the hardened sinners, the "guilty creatures, with their hearts subdued by the cunning of the scene, have, it is said, proclaim'd their malefactions."[35] If the drama was able to reform even villains, it surely was capable of improving those ordinary folk who merely strayed from the path of virtue, as suggested by this observation in *The New York Mirror and Ladies' Literary Gazette*:

> The person who has listened attentively while the consequences of a single error have been portrayed before him, and has not found his resolution of pursuing honor and virtue strengthened, must be either more or less than a man.[36]

The same periodical implied that women were particularly susceptible to moral messages in plays:

> the female who hears the sigh and sees the unavailing tear shed at the shrine of honor lost, and does not more closely draw the cord of virtue round her heart, is unworthy the name of woman.[37]

Given the evident public interest in using the stage as an instructor of moral virtue, theatrical managers in the United States sought to appease any critical attacks by offering entertaining, yet morally acceptable, plays. One critic in 1801 applauded their efforts as an improvement over dramas of a previous age:

> without adverting to the licentious dramas of the age of Charles the second, it may be observed, that many of the earlier productions of the eighteenth century, would not be endured, without considerable alterations, by a modern audience. In general, profligate characters are no longer brought upon the stage, to fascinate us with the gaiety and splendour of their vices during the greater part of the drama and to be rewarded at its close. Virtue is, for the most part, represented in light at once amiable and respectable, and our laughter is excited by delineations of follies, not of vices.[38]

Concern about the morality of theatrical offerings revolved around its potential effect on "respectable" women in the audience. Even Shakespeare's works were accused of assaulting their sensibilities. An article in *The New York Mirror and Ladies' Literary Gazette* condemned a production of *The Merry Wives of Windsor*: "No performance should be produced on our boards that will cause the cheek of modesty to mantle with a blush, and no chord should ever be touched that vibrates unpleasantly upon the ears of our fair countrywomen."[39] Some months later, when the managers again produced the play, the same periodical assailed the piece as "exceptionable," and "indelicate" and observed that the production suffered from a sparse audience and notable lack of ladies in the theatre.[40]

Gothic plays, with their emphasis on rewarding virtue and punishing vice, did not suffer from "a lack of ladies" in the theatre. In this time of public attacks upon the theatre for perceived immorality of dramatic fare, Gothic plays generally were not targeted, probably because villains were male characters and because they were so severely punished for their transgressions. Although Gothic plays featured unabashedly evil villains who engaged in kidnapping, blackmail, fratricide, and possible incest, the plays in which they appeared were not attacked as immoral. The play *Bertram*, however, was attacked. Although the villain in the play did not commit crimes more heinous than those of the usual Gothic villain; the female character in the play did not conform to the usual depiction of Gothic heroines. Gothic plays depicted female characters as dutiful, pure, and pious. Moreover, these females were required to be completely passionless. Yet in *Bertram*, Imogene did transgress sexually. Although she was swiftly and severely punished, the play was attacked. Thus, charges of immorality against plays in this period seemed only to address women's sexual transgressions.

Most denunciations of the theatre in the United States addressed the immorality of theatrical patrons. Theatrical managers had to defend themselves against charges of laxity in their restraint of dissolute and profane deeds of the audience. Such charges followed the establishment of the major theatres in each theatrical center and continued through the 1820s with the opening of new ones. In New York, William Dunlap remarked:

> If the theatre is represented as the scene of licentiousness, the licentious will seek it. And if, as now in most theatres, they see a display of the votaries and victims of vice in one part of the house, and the allurements to inebriation in another,

they may have just grounds to believe that they are indeed in the place of Circe instead of the temple of the Muses.[41]

A letter in *The Mirror of Taste and Dramatic Censor* urged the theatre's managers to evict unruly members of the audience. One letter, signed "A Citizen," condemned "two evils" present at the Chestnut Street: men who lit up cigars and women of ill fame. The writer asserted that such men should be evicted, observing that "a man who is rude enough to annoy a whole theatre full of people, for his filthy gratification, will light his cigarr [sic] and smoke as long as he can, arguing thus with himself: 'I can only be made to put it out at last, in the meantime I shall have some smoking and so far get the advantage of them.'"[42]

Although annoying, the presence of cigar smoke in the auditorium was not as threatening as the presence of an "evil of a much more serious nature ... the immodest conduct of women of ill fame, and their companions in our upper boxes."[43]

Apparently all cities also had problems with prostitutes in upper tiers.[44] William Dunlap urged theatres to cease the "improper, indecent, and scandalous [sic] practice" of allotting "a distinct portion of the proscenium to those unfortunate females who have been the victims of seduction." Dunlap argued that "no separate place should be set apart, to present to the gaze of the matron and the virgin the unabashed votaries of vice and to tempt the yet unsullied youth by the example of the false face which depravity assumes for the purposes of enticing to guilt." Dunlap lamented that this provision for prostitutes continued in other cities even in the new theatres. He noted that at the Federal Street Theatre in Boston, "the boxes displayed the same row of miserable victims, decked in smiles and borrowed finery, and the entrance could only, by its separation from those appropriated to the residue of the audience, become a screen inviting to secret guilt."[45]

Philadelphia, too, missed its opportunity for reform, as Dunlap observed:

> The new theatre of Philadelphia gave an opportunity for reform, as did that of New York; but these opportunities were neglected, and those who wished to support, as a mode of improvement, the representation of good dramatic works, have been driven from the boxes by the spectacle presented, no on the stage, but on seats placed opposite to them, and attracting their attention *from* the stage.[46]

Others however, argued that without such special provisions, women of ill fame could "find their way into the lower boxes, where they gayly [sic] converse with the young men, and impudently confront the chaste part of the sex." Such critics hoped that these "unhappy marauders" would be relegated to a place "suitable to their degraded state."[47] Critics in Charleston, for example, urged such a separation; a notice in *The Courier* of 1815 urged that efforts be made to "ensure that ladies of character" were properly shielded from association with their fallen sisters by the "proper division of boxes." The article decreed "the 1st boxes with the pit" as "appropriate to the reception of Ladies of respectability exclusively."[48]

In all cities, public outcry about prostitutes in the theatre addressed not their presence but the possibility of their mixing with "respectable" women.[49] Yet theatrical managers were quick to assert that sinners should not be barred from theatrical audiences: Dunlap claimed, "It is not practicable to exclude the impure and the vicious from public resorts, neither is it to be wished. If the drama is such as a good government ought to permit, its influence cannot be ill on the immoral auditor, and may be good."[50]

Such "immoral auditors" evidently were of all ages. Not only young men were criticized for dallying with the "impures"; one letter remarked that "men who ought to be at home training their children and grand children in a very different kind of morality may be seen (a little more silly to be sure than the young) exposing their infirmity by awkward playfulness with those damsels, and luxuriating in prurient flippancy, when they would be, more appropriately, at home, wrapt [sic] up in flannel."[51] The author of this article, however, seemed most annoyed by the loudness of the prostitutes, noting that "instead of concealing their purposes or intimating them privately, by a wink, a significant look, a hem, or even the sultanic [sic] hint of dropping the handkerchief," these women seemed to "glory in the vile traffic" and spoke "so loud at times as to interrupt and annoy" those patrons who wished "to hear the play."[52]

Some accounts of patrons in the boxes suggest that some less respectable men were infiltrating the boxes. Occasionally, rowdy young men, described as "intruders," misbehaved in the boxes. Critics chastised the managers for their lack of control, noting that although it may have been impossible "wholly to exclude improper company from the boxes," the manager should have prevented "either by providing a greater number of constables, or by some other means."[53] The editor of one paper complained about some young men in the boxes who "converted the boxes into a grog shop" and "caroused" during the performance. The author concluded, "there are other grievances ... which would never occur if every one who can afford to wear such a coat as gentlemen wear, could imitate the manners of gentlemen as well as they can ape their dress."[54]

Patrons in the gallery also received criticism for bad behavior; one letter to the editor noted, "It is to be regretted, that the excellent music of the best orchestra in America should be drowned by the shoutings and cat calls of the gallery."[55] Another letter also singled out the gallery, complaining of "a finished vagabond" in the gallery, who "spoke smut and roared it out loud, directing it to the ladies in the boxes."[56]

In Charleston, young men, presumably those who would sit in the gallery, caused problems even outside the theatre:

> Whereas a number of disorderly boys and men are in the practice of assembling around the doors of the Theatre on the nights of performance, for the purpose of obtaining admission by force or fraud, to the injury of the building and the disturbance of the audience — the mangers hereby offer a reward of fifty dollars to the informer, upon the conviction of any person or persons, who shall be found destroying the Theatre, forcing an entrance, or any wise causing a riot.[57]

In contrast to those in the boxes and in the gallery, patrons in the pit seemed primarily interested in watching the play.[58] Charles Durang noted that "the intellectual taste and analytical judgment of our city congregated" at the pit in the Chestnut Street theatre of Philadelphia, "to listen — to follow the track of the actor's readings." In the pit sat "the elite of the literary young men of the town."[59] Unescorted respectable women, however, could not, with propriety, sit in the pit; moreover one source implied that even escorted women did not routinely frequent the pit:

> The admission of females to the pit in this town, as in the principal cities of America, would certainly tend to check that irregularity of conduct so often exhibited there.... If honest tradesmen were permitted by custom, for no regulation of the theatre is against it, to bring their wives and daughters with them, they would themselves be more cautious in their conduct.... Boys would be restrained from indecorums in which they are at present too liberally indulged, and ... the Boston Theatre would exhibit an audience less deviatory from the morality of the Boston Public.[60]

In general, however, those in the pit seemed to be more victims of rowdiness more so than perpetrators of it. Fictional accounts, such as those written by Washington Irving, describe the indignities visited upon these patrons, and contemporary letters corroborate these accounts.

When critics proclaimed their moral outrage at the behavior of patrons in theatres, they usually did soon behalf of the respectable women in the audience. One critic condemned the manager of one of the theatres, who, evidently, allowed boxes to be taken by friends for a whole season and then allowed these friends to sell the box at any price they pleased. This practice made box seats difficult to obtain and affected the convenience of female patrons. The author raged against the practice, blasting the perpetrators as men "who dare to call themselves and be called, the friends of rectitude and virtue." The writer then requested that, should such gentlemen choose to disregard the "safety and convenience of gentlemen," he should have hesitated at "insulting that most sacred charm of social life, the decoration of civil society, and the admiration of all ages, female delicacy."[61]

As a result of the dearth of boxes on one occasion, several female patrons sought seats elsewhere in the house and, as a consequence, suffered public humiliation. The article recorded,

> during the crowded houses of the last winter, several ladies, urged by the longings of curiosity, ventured into the pit, after finding it impossible to get seats in the boxes. For weeks afterwards, their indiscretion, or what was called their boldness, was bandied about from tea-table to the breakfast and from the breakfast to the tea-table, till it had completely run the rounds of scandal. Their reputation was entirely lacerated.[62]

Critics also voiced concern that respectable women might be tainted by constant exposure to unsavory patrons in the theatres: "Does it never occur to the fathers of families or to the matrons of this once virtuous city, that constantly witnessing the abominations I allude to must necessarily beget associations in the young female mind, which ... must sully that internal purity of thought."[63]

All theatres took pains to publicize the presence of respectable women in their audiences; however, critics writing about newer, less well established theatres seemed to include the reference to such women more often, probably to boost their image of respectability and help them compete with the more established (and therefore more respectable) theatres. One such reference concerned a production at the Olympic in Philadelphia:

> *Lodoiska* was repeated to such an audience as has not graced the theatre this season; in point of numbers it was not what might have been hoped, but there was a far greater number of ladies of the first rank, than have graced the boxes since

the commencement of the present theatrical season. We hope it is an [*sic*] earnest of better things.⁶⁴

Apparently, women of fashion did not attend the theatre on the first night of a production.⁶⁵ That ladies in Philadelphia and Boston stayed away as well, was suggested by this comment in 1807:

> the house on this occasion was respectably filled, and although there was no great assembly of fashion or beauty, *(a circumstance not remarkable on a first night's performance)* [*emphasis added*] the managers had not reason to be dissatisfied with the company they collected.⁶⁶

In general, however, theatres catering to all classes used the presence of respectable women a gauge as to measure their success.

In summary, theatres enjoyed a boom in popularity around 1805; simultaneously, they came under renewed attack for immorality — in their dramas, their actors, and their patrons. Defendants of the theatre pointed to theatre's potential as an effective instructor of morality, particularly effective for reaching those patrons who might not be amenable to more direct preaching. Theatrical managers had to answer to the press for productions that were perceived as indelicate; and such attacks were particularly vehement if women exhibited any signs of sexual interest. Actors were criticized in print for any appearance of immorality, such critiques of their character appearing in print along with critiques of their professional merit. Yet few actresses on the American stage in this period, 1794–1830, were accused of immoral behavior. Audiences too came under criticism for perceived immoral behavior. The mere presence of prostitutes in the theatres did not seem to cause much public outcry until they moved from their allotted place and mingled with respectable ladies or when they made their presence known through loud talk. The presence of respectable ladies appeared to be a barometer for gauging the morality of the theatrical offering — except on a first night, when ladies in Philadelphia and Boston, if not the other cities, made it a custom not to attend the theatre.

Theatrical managers in the United States soon took advantage of evident public interest in the stage as an instructor of moral behavior; they sought to forestall any critical attacks by offering entertaining, yet morally acceptable dramas, and Gothic plays, with their thrilling action, spectacular scenery, and clear-cut characters, fit the bill. Defendants of the theatre pointed to its potential as an effective instructor of morals; however, Gothic plays offered one more reason for their popularity: they permitted patrons to consider the possibility of engaging in immoral behavior — without ever condoning it. Patrons were able to enjoy the titillation of potential sin and yet retain their own sense of moral superiority when the villain was vanquished.

CHAPTER 4

The "Illustrious Spirit" Meets the "Sanguinary Monster"
Characterization of Males in Gothic Plays

The dashing Percy, heir of Northumberland, has stolen into the castle of the evil Earl of Osmond to save his betrothed from the Earl's lascivious intentions. Captured by the Earl, Percy confronts him boldly, crying, "Angela, thine? — That she shall never be! There are angels above who favor virtue, and the hour of retribution must one day arrive!" But the Earl, surrounded by his armed henchmen, interrupts, smiles coolly at the passionate young man, saying, "But long ere the arrival of that hour shall Angela have been my bride; and now farewell, Lord Percy!" Then, as he leaves the wretched Percy, the Earl, in an aside to the audience, ponders his own wickedness:

> If she refuse me still, the death of this, her favourite — his death! Oh! Through what bloody paths do I wander in pursuit of happiness! Yes, I am guilty! — Heaven! How guilty! Yet lies the fault with me? Did my own pleasure plant in my bosom these tempestuous passions? No! They were given me at my birth: they were sucked in with my existence! Nature formed me the slave of wild desires; and Fate, as she frowned upon my cradle, exclaimed, I doom this babe to be a villain and a wretch![1]

In his speech, Osmond attributes his "tempestuous passions" and "wild desires," to a congenital lack of self-control. Because he is a "slave to passion," Osmond concludes that he is predestined for wickedness.

The character's assumption that unchecked passions lead inevitably to evil acts was reflected in literature of the late eighteenth and early nineteenth centuries, which stressed self-control. One manifestation of this concern was evident in the proliferation of courtesy books, or guides to appropriate behavior. In the United States, readers imported books on conduct in record numbers; at least seventy-five works were printed or imported between 1738 and 1820.[2] Although these works were aimed at the "middling classes," they would have been available also through the new lending libraries; records show that conduct works were "repeatedly borrowed, recommended, referred to, and quoted."[3]

One particular book that enjoyed widespread and enduring popularity throughout the United States was Lord Chesterfield's *Letters of Advice to His Son*, first published in 1775. Although Chesterfield's letters originally were intended to raise his son "upon a pedestal so high that his lowly origin should not betray itself," the published work appealed to those who sought to improve their positions in the world.[4] It proved particularly popular in the United States; not only was it a best-seller in 1775, it was the "only Revolutionary-era work to be reprinted through 1860."[5]

In their original form, Lord Chesterfield's *Letters* met with some criticism. His advice to young men to "cultivate appearances—even, when necessary, to dissimulate," offended the sensibilities of some Americans.[6] One particularly troublesome passage counseled young men to flatter women but never to consult them on serious matters. Chesterfield first acknowledged the value of women to a man of fashion:

> As women are a considerable, or at least a pretty numerous part of company; and as their suffrages go a great way toward establishing a man's character in the fashionable part of the world (which is of great importance to the fortune and figure he proposes to take in it), it is necessary to please them.

After conceding their importance, however, Chesterfield dismissed women as unworthy of any serious regard: "women, then, are only children of a larger growth; they have an entertaining tattle, and sometimes wit; but for solid reasoning, good sense, I never knew in my life one that had it."[7]

Chesterfield subsequently counseled men merely to pretend to consult women on any serious matter:

> A man of sense only trifles with them, plays with them, humors and flatters them ... but he neither consults them about, nor trusts them with serious

matters; though he often makes them believe that he does both ... they almost adore the man who talks seriously to them, and who seems to consult and trust them; I say, who seems; for weak men really do but wise one only seem to do it.[8]

The popularity of Chesterfield's *Letters*, with its unflattering portrayal of women and its unabashed directive to merely assume the appearance of virtue, worried some Americans. Mercy Otis Warren warned her son against relying on Chesterfield's advice, noting that the author "sacrifice[d] truth to convenience, probity to pleasure, virtue to the graces, generosity, gratitude, and all the finer feelings of the soul, to a momentary gratification, we cannot but pity the man, as much as we admire the author."[9] Warren believed that Chesterfield would adversely affect the "youthful reader" and that "the honey'd poison, that lurks beneath the fairest flowers of fancy and Rhetoric, should leave a deeper tincture on the mind, than, even his documents for an external decency and the semblance of Morality."[10]

To address such concerns, several carefully edited American editions of Chesterfield appeared. Reverend Dr. John Trusler, who edited one such work, stated in his preface: "Much night have been said on the subject of indelicacy but as instructions on that head, to persons as possessed of a liberal education, must have been unnecessary, they are here purposely omitted." Moreover, Trusler noted that it had been "the editor's study, to make Lord Chesterfield useful to every class of youth."[11]

What, then, could a youth learn about gentlemanly behavior from Lord Chesterfield? In his Letters, Chesterfield continually urged moderation as a key virtue. In one letter, written in 1747, Chesterfield listed the "true pleasures" of a gentleman: "those of the table, but within the bound of moderation; good company, that is to say, people of merit; moderate play, which amuses, without any interested views, and sprightly gallant conversations with women of fashion and sense." Chesterfield added that these pleasures "occasion neither sickness, shame, nor repentance," but warned that "whatever exceeds them, becomes low, vice, brutal passion, debauchery, and insanity of mind; all of which, far from giving satisfaction, bring on dishonor and disgrace."[12]

The very excesses that Chesterfield identified: "low vice, brutal passion, debauchery, and insanity of mind," were those passions exhibited by Gothic villains. These villains, often aristocrats, were passionate, ruled by lust, jealousy, or avarice; they were creatures of excess, verbal and physical. The audience understood, however, that the villains' wild excesses would cause their destruction. If they could not control their own emotions, they could not long control their environment.

Gothic heroes, on the other hand, exhibited the moderation suggested by Chesterfield. If young, the heroes triumphed over the passionate villain and won the heroine and higher social status. Older heroes, who, like the villain, once struggled with controlling their passions, were required to master their emotions and publicly repent their former lack of self-control.

When heroes learned this valuable lesson, they were rewarded with a full restitution of their worldly goods and the return of their devoted spouses. The message from conduct literature about the importance of self-control was reinforced in Gothic plays: young men were warned to control their passions and respect women.

Despite the hero's eventual triumph in Gothic plays, the most interesting characters were undeniably those who violated these dictates. Gothic villains drove the action, lusted openly after younger women, and actively sought power.

Though Gothic plays ostensibly reinforced Lord Chesterfield's dictates of gentlemanly behavior, especially his emphasis on self-control, they also seemed to revel in the wickedness of the villain. Gothic plays encouraged members of the audience to identify with the villain, usually the most dynamic character, and through that identification enjoy the act of transgressing of the boundaries of gentlemanly behavior. These plays also reflected the ambiguity present in Lord Chesterfield's attitudes toward women, for in Gothic plays, young men praise women's beauty and piety; however they did not credit them with intelligence or self-sufficiency.

"Spare, Oh Spare That Maiden": The Hero

Like heroes in melodramas, Gothic heroes were generally ineffective in their actions. Although their words suggested their courage, they had little opportunity to prove their mettle; they usually were prevented from assisting the heroine in the climactic scene. In only two plays in this sample of Gothic plays did heroes resolve the action of the play, and in only seven plays did they even assist. Instead, heroes themselves were usually saved by a combined force of heroine, comic man, various other characters, or by an outside force.[13]

Because of their ineffectiveness, Gothic heroes seldom revealed their noble qualities through plot. Instead, the audience learned about their attributes through language — particularly through speeches by the heroes themselves. For example, through their speeches heroes revealed that they were stalwart in love and that they remained faithful to one woman despite adversity. In *The Man of Fortitude*, Sir Bertrand discovered his missing wife in the clutches of the villain. When told that his life would be spared if he encouraged his wife to accept the love of the villain, Sir Bertrand cried, "Renounce her! press thy suit! Oh never, never! Torture, and tear me; rack me joint by join! While sense of being in this breast remains, I firm shall stand and urge a husband's claim!"[14]

Heroes also used speech to proclaim their own virtue and their confidence that innocence would triumph over vice. Carlos, in *The Mysteries of the Castle*, proclaimed, "The goodness of our cause is more than armor to us — Let the guilty tremble — we have nothing to apprehend — Follow me."[15] In his courage and virtue, the hero was contrasted favorably with the comic man, who was cowardly and self-serving. For example, in *The Man of Fortitude*, Bertrand chastised his servant Carlos, saying, "Thou tremblest, lad; for shame, bear up," to which Carlos replied, "Sir, I can't bear up — I don't fear a coat, and I'm a lion at a petticoat — But one stands no chance with a ghost, for one never knows where to have him."[16]

Also through their speech, heroes revealed their great respect for women, whose spiritual qualities they discussed in elevated language; in this aspect too they were contrasted favorably with comic men, who often commented frankly about a female character's physical attributes. In the opening scene of *The Castle Spectre*, for example, the hero Percy enumerated the virtues of his fiancée, Angela, declaring, "I loved her for a person beautiful without art, and graceful without affection; for a heart tender without weakness, and noble without pride." Percy's servant Motley however admired only the physical attributes of a female, describing one as "a sweet smiling rogue, just sixteen, with rosy cheeks, sparkling eyes, pouting lips."[17]

Gothic heroes worried excessively about the virtue and the reputation of heroines. St. Valori in *The Carmelite* pronounced, "Perish the man who dares to breathe a doubt of her unspotted chastity."[18] In *The Mysteries of Castle*, Persiles pleaded with the villain, "tear out my heart, strew me on the earth — but spare, O spare that maiden!"[19] Sir Bertrand, in *The Man of Fortitude,* accosted the villain verbally, demanding, "What triumph canst thou reap by foul revenge; Or why revenge on female innocence? If manly reason is of no avail, On me pour out thy bitterness of soul — I've fortitude to meet and brave it all."[20] Perhaps Gothic heroes exhibited this concern for the heroine's virtue because they more frequently dealt with a villain who was sexually threatening the heroine.

"Noble Youth": The Young Hero

The first type of hero, young and idealistic, appeared in two-thirds of the plays in this study.[21] This type of hero was often an aristocrat, but he did not use his rank or wealth to attract the heroine. Such a hero was Aurelio *in The Rose of Arragon,* who, although a Prince of the region, disguised himself as a peasant to win the true love of Rosaline, observing, "As her equal have I gained her love."[22] Aurelio, like other Gothic heroes, employed elevated language when he spoke of the heroine: "I know her heart is mine; and shall I be that villain — No! here I swear, by the dimpled God that pure hearts worship, whose honied shafts are dipt by honour, and whose plumed pinions virtue guides, never will I crush the rose that blooms within my power."[23] Aurelio, like most Gothic heroes, exhibited filial loyalty, seeking the blessing of Rosaline's father even though he feared that the old man would not consent. Despite his qualms, he would not encourage Rosaline to elope with him against her father's wishes, saying, "Nay cheer thee, love! indeed I would not have thee do it, for by heaven! the man who tears a child from a parent's care, deserves a worse than death."[24] Like most Gothic heroes, Aurelio was incapacitated quickly by the villain; by this development he was able to be perceived as courageous and yet present no hindrance to the villain's full measure of wickedness. Count Laranda (the Conde) imprisoned the young hero so that he could steal Aurelio's throne and fiancée. Also like many other Gothic heroes, Aurelio offered his life to preserve the virtue of the heroine.[25] When the Conde informed Rosaline that unless she married him he would kill Aurelio: "this night thou'rt mine, willingly, or his blood — ," Aurelio begged Rosaline not to submit, saying "Nay, fear not love; I can defy death whilst thou art true to me."[26]

Finally, Aurelio, like other Gothic heroes, was unable to assist the heroine at the climactic moment; he could only watch helplessly as the Conde first prepared to stab Rosaline and then turned instead to kill her father.[27] In this play, as in several others, the hero watched his beloved resolve the action by killing the villain; Rosaline grabbed the dagger and plunged it into Laranda's heart. Only after the Conde dropped to the ground did Aurelio join Rosaline.

A Man of "Reason and Virtue": The Older Hero

Although Gothic plays usually presented the hero as a young man, they sometimes featured an older hero. This older man gained wisdom through suffering and usually acknowledged that he brought on his own misfortune through his rash action.[28] For example, in *Ribbemont,* the older hero believed that, in a fit of jealousy, he had murdered his long-faithful wife.[29] He confessed that, informed of his wife's supposed infidelity with his close friend, he challenged the friend to a duel, wounded him, and left him for dead. He then obtained poison from the monks and gave it to his unsuspecting wife. Later, Ribbemont began to question his hasty actions, musing, "No peace I've felt since gallant Narbonne died.... Peace! ... it has been hell! ... my poor Honoria too. And if I have been rash ... merciful heaven! The thought once entertain'd brings certain madness."[30] Predictably, Ribbemont learned that a vengeful peasant deceived him; his wife and his friend were innocent. He fell into deep depression and cried, "I am that wretch, that have, by passion urg'd, Passion, by vile and dev'lish malice rous'd, Provok'd my friend to mortal strife, unquestion'd.... Yes, monk, I slew my friend, nor told him why.... My wife I murdered too ... now join and curse me."[31] Ribbemont, like other older heroes, contemplated suicide as a solution to despair. He attempted to take poison when his grief becomes too much to bear: "Come forth, come forth, thou blest oblivious draught! Last refuge of the wretch; care's antidote."[32] Ribbemont's suicide was prevented by the appearance of his wife, who had only seemed dead. His friend Narbonne then appeared and informed him that after recovering from his wound, he had waited for Ribbemont to admit his error. Both wife and friend then forgave the now-humbled Ribbemont.

Like the other older heroes in Gothic drama, Ribbemont denounced his former passionate nature and declared that he had gained wisdom from his painful experience: "For what was lost thro' honor, falsely nam'd and False opinions of my fellow-men, Passions unbridled, and despotic pride; Has he thro' pure benevolence restor'd; and won my soul to reason and to virtue."[33]

The Sanguinary Monster: The Villain

In nearly all melodramas, the most memorable character was the villain. Gothic villains shared many of the characteristics of their counterparts in melodrama; like them, they rejected moral control, showed little compassion, sought revenge, and were defeated by the end of the play.[34] Gothic villains, however, also exhibited qualities not apparent in other melodramatic villains.

Villains in melodramas occasionally were portrayed as comic and inept, but villains in Gothic plays were serious. Usually aristocrats who lost everything by the end of the play, villains in Gothic dramas fell into two major types: the villain, who, although guilty of other crimes, did not harm the heroine, and the villain, who, in addition to his other crimes, physically threatened the heroine.[35] Although both types of villain suffered for their crimes, the second type suffered more from fear of retribution than from remorse.

An especially apt example of the first type of villain was Sir Edward Mortimer in *The Iron Chest*. Sir Edward, like other villains of this type, was gloomy despite his wealth and position. He was referred to as "his melancholy worship"; his servants talked of the "wild glare" in his eyes" and observed that he appeared to be "devoured with spleen and melancholy."[36] Sir Edward's melancholy, like that of similar villains, resulted from a guilty secret; he had murdered the uncle of the heroine. Even though he was publicly exonerated of the crime, Sir Edward withdrew from society to live a reclusive life in the forest, where he suffered from pangs of conscience; he recounted, "Oh I have suffered madness! None know my tortures."[37] Despite his suffering, Sir Edward, like other villains of this type, was unable to repent his crime: "Hurt honour, in an evil, cursed hour, drove me to murder; — lying; — 'twould again. My honest, sweet peace of mind, — all, all! are barter'd for a name. I will maintain it"[38]

The second type of villain also suffered in the play, but he suffered more from his fear of damnation than remorse. For example, Osmond, in *The Castle Spectre*, was described as "gloomy and ferocious," a man who "never utters a sound except a sigh, has broken every tie of society and kept his gates barred unceasingly against the stranger."[39] Osmond suffered from fear of everlasting torment for the murder of his sister-in-law, Evelina, and the supposed murder of his brother Reginald. Osmond compared his conscience to a serpent that "winds her folds

Robert Maywood as the villain Baron Trevasi in *The Mountain Torrent*. The Harvard Theatre Collection, Houghton Library.

round the cup of my bliss, and ere my lips reach it, her venom is mingled with the draught."[40] Osmond was particularly horrified by the thought of eternal damnation, at one point crying, "Let me not hear the damning truth. Tell me not, that flames await me, that for moments of bliss, I must endure long ages of torture"[41] Yet despite his fear of hell, Osmand could not repent his crime because he desired Evelina's daughter, Angela, and his repentance would mean losing her. Despite his fear of damnation, Osmond declared, "Mine she is; mine she shall be, though Reginald's bleeding ghost sit before me, and thunder in my ear — 'Hold! Hold.'"[42]

The second type of villain frequently devoted his time to menacing the heroine, and indeed the major conflict in the plays often derived from this relationship. In nearly half of the plays, these villains threatened the heroines' lives or virtue or both. One prime example was the Marquis de Montault in *Fountainville Forest* by James Boaden. In this play, the fugitive Lamotte, accompanied by his wife and son as well as the orphan Adeline, found refuge in a deserted abbey owned by the Marquis. Near starvation, Lamotte robbed a passing aristocrat who turned out to be the Marquis. When the Marquis later arrived at the abbey, Lamotte recognized him and begged him not to press charges. The Marquis agreed, but only if Lamotte agreed to aid him in seducing Adeline: "Well Lamotte, this fair one may heal the breach between us— She has beauty That struck me at first sight — I'll see her shortly."[43] Adeline, however, was repelled by the villain, especially when he boldly suggested a liaison: "This lonely place will rather fix a gloom For ever on your youth, that should be led To happier scenes of gay, voluptuous love."[44] Adeline fled from the Marquis, who declared, "She must be mine by kindness or by force." He then seized her, saying, "in vain this struggle! How lovely is this terror! By my transport It heightens the bewitching charm of beauty and lends ten thousand graces to that bosom."[45] But in the struggle, the Marquis saw Adeline's locket on which was a picture of her mother and realized that Adeline was his own niece. With this discovery, the Marquis feared that his long-concealed crime of fratricide would be discovered, and so he instructed Lamotte to kill Adeline. When Lamotte was unable to commit murder, the Marquis charged him with his past crimes. However, when the court was in session, the Marquis' murderous past was discovered, and he stabbed himself to avoid the gallows, exclaiming, "I will not yield to your torturing ruffians, Nor, like a slave, expire upon a scaffold. This way alone, does not degrade ambition."[46] The interaction between heroine and villain titillated the audience with the potential for seduction; the Marquis' periodic lustful remarks and Adeline's oft-expressed fears about preserving her virtue allowed the audience to contemplate the potential horrors of a sexual assault without ever condoning it.

The Gothic heroes and heroines, virtuous and caring, had their counterparts in other melodramas, but the popularity of Gothic plays suggest that the distinctive qualities of these characters may have especially appealed to audiences. What might these unique characteristics suggest about American audiences and their expectations for social behavior between 1794 and 1830?

In their characterization of males, Gothic plays seemed to reinforce tenets of prescriptive literature. Heroes were moderate in their habits, deferential and chivalrous to women, interested only in women of comparable age, and capable of strict self-control over their emotions and their actions. Yet, heroes were not the drivers of the action, nor were they particularly interesting characters. Their very self-control, so lauded by prescriptive literature of the day, rendered them boring, and worse, ineffectual against the passionate, wicked villain.

Young Gothic heroes, for example, exemplified many of the traits apparently prized by society of the early nineteenth century. They displayed deference to older males, whether these older male characters were heroes or villains. Young heroes obeyed their fathers and fathers-in-law and strove to please them. This deference may have indicated societal expectations for young men in America of the early 1800s. Following the Revolution, the proportion of young people to middle aged people in the population was unusually high, much higher than in the twentieth century. In fact, the median age of the American population in 1800 was only 16 years. At this time too, many young men and women were leaving their homes (and direct parental influence) for urban settings in search of work: after the War of 1812, the growth of commercial exports prompted the development of new businesses and industries, consequently "creating a demand for bankers, warehouse men, and insurance agents," and encouraging "a steady stream of young men and women from the country" to descend upon the cities.[47]

As young people flocked to cities, older people sought new methods to influence their behavior. One such method was prescriptive literature, treatises that offered "conduct-of-life instruction" especially popular for young men.[48] Lord Chesterfield's *Letters* urge his son to accept his counsel:

The young leading the young is like the blind leading the blind: "they will both fall into the ditch." The only sure guide is, he who has often gone the road which you want to go. Let me be that guide, who have [sic] gone all roads, and who consequently, can point out to you the best.... But if anybody, capable of advising me, had taken the same pains with me ... I should have avoided many follies and inconveniences which undirected youth run [sic] me into.[49]

Gothic dramas reflected this attempt to control the behavior of rash young men, and particularly advocated deference for older men, respect and chivalry toward women, and self-control. In these sentiments, they echoed public opinion.

Young heroes in Gothic plays, for example, exhibited automatic respect and deference for older men, specifically fathers or prospective fathers-in-law. This deference was sustained even when these older men were inconsiderate or rash. These young heroes did not exhibit the same deference for their mothers, however; whereas eight plays out of thirty-one featured a young hero who deferred to his father, only one depicted a young hero who showed similar deference to his mother.[50] Such devotion and unquestioning obedience on the part of young men for their fathers or prospective fathers-in-law constituted a powerful model of behavior that would have particularly satisfied societal expectations.[51] In their deference to older men, these young heroes reflected suggestions from prescriptive literature.

Both older and younger heroes in Gothic plays also reflected societal expectations for chivalry toward women. Younger heroes often worried about the heroine's virtue and were quick to redress perceived insults to her honor. That this attitude was not uncommon at the time is illustrated by an article in the Boston *Kaleidoscope* in 1818 entitled "Insults to Females":

> Scarcely a day passes, but we hear of the unmanly conduct of those pests of society, who nightly prowl the streets, with a view to insult those young ladies who may happen to be without a protector. A well dressed woman can seldom venture out alone after twilight, without being subjected to the impertinence of these "less than men." Is there no remedy for this growing evil? We think there is — and although it may be a summary mode of doing justice, we believe it will be found the effectual one. We mean an application of the horse-whip to every offender who may be detected in such a low and villainous practice.[52]

Older heroes in Gothic plays not only respected young women; they also revered older women in the plays. Even though they had succumbed to fits of jealousy in the past, they still loved their wives, and wanted only to win their forgiveness. They appreciated women of their own age and did not seek out younger women as sexual objects. In this, they, too, reflected contemporary sentiments that encouraged reverence and respect for older women. Lord Chesterfield, for example, encouraged his son to seek out fashionable older women of good sense as excellent teachers.[53] Yet these heroines never were depicted as sexually appealing, even to their husbands. No description of them ventured beyond their virtue, their patience, or their piety.

Out of all members of the audience, older men may have found characterization of older women in these plays most appealing, for these characters sacrificed their own lives for those of their families. Also, older female characters, praised for their virtue and piety, were not presented as sexual creatures. Therefore, older men in the audience did not have to consider women their own age in a sexual way and could instead focus on young, virginal heroines.

Although the Gothic hero reflected sentiments of prescriptive literature most effectively, advocating deference to older men, respect for women, and self-control, he was not an interesting character. Instead, the most memorable character in Gothic plays was the villain, who not only failed to exemplify these qualities but defied them. The Gothic villain was a hallmark of Gothic plays and undoubtedly was a major cause of their popularity. He certainly was the most complex character and consequently was considered the plum role, portrayed by the most popular leading actors.

The villain in Gothic plays was always an older man, and equally important, an active man; in most of the plays he drove the action and controlled the fate of other characters. Even though he suffered from his passions and was invariably defeated, he, unlike other characters, held power over all the other characters, at least for a time.

Gothic plays, then, presented living depictions of prescriptive literature. Through their depiction of young heroes, the plays implied that men who deferred to their elders, revered women, and controlled their emotions would triumph over evil, win the love of a beautiful young woman, and achieve prominence in the world. Yet they often were depicted as ineffectual in battle and often had to be rescued by others. Older heroes, too, echoed the teachings of prescriptive literature, praising piety and virtue as the most important qualities in a woman

Because Gothic plays seemed designed to please older men, it seems plausible to suppose that older men comprised a majority of theatrical audiences of this time. This conclusion is supported by other studies that argue that theatrical audiences between 1794 and 1830 in America were comprised largely of older men.[54] Moreover, these men seemed to come from the upper classes. Bruce McConachee, in *Melodramatic Formations,* observed that theatres of this time were themselves run by elite males; for example, when the Park Theatre in New York burned in 1820, it was quickly rebuilt by John Jacob Astor and John Keeman, wealthy men of the city. This same phenomenon occurred in other theatrical centers.[55]

Other sources support the suggestion that prosperous men comprised the majority of audiences in American theatres before 1830. Even after 1833, Tyrone Power, comic actor, commented in 1833 that "the well filled house" at the Tremont Theatre in Boston was composed "chiefly of men, as on my debut at New York."[56] The view that these males were upper class rather than working class is reinforced by the configuration of seats in the theatres; in almost all theatres of this period, box seats outnumbered all other types of seating combined. For example, in Philadelphia's Chestnut Street Theatre, thirteen hundred patrons sat in boxes, as opposed to only three hundred in the gallery and four hundred in the pit.[57]

Characterization in Gothic plays suggests a picture of societal expectations in America of the early 1900s. These plays reinforced a code of behavior proffered in courtesy literature of the day, behavior that encouraged self-control and deference toward women. Simultaneously, however, Gothic plays allowed males in the audience, particularly older wealthy males, to identify with the passionate, sexually powerful villain who triumphed physically over much younger men and pursued their sweethearts, much younger women. Moreover, the villain's lascivious designs on the protesting heroine allowed the older male to consider, albeit briefly, the possibility of sexual activity with a younger woman, while yet publicly condoning the moral order of the play. Finally, Gothic plays permitted older men in the audience to vicariously enjoy absolute control over the people and events in their lives—control not possible in the swiftly changing American society of the early nineteenth century.

CHAPTER 5

"Angel-Maids" and "Withered Flowers"
The Gothic Heroine

In *The Mysteries of the Castle,* by John B. White, Cornelia, the innocent young heroine, and her mother, Ellenora, have been imprisoned by the evil Fauresco. One day, Cornelia chances to find a door unlocked. She ventures outside and meets a man "beautiful" and "fair" who "throws himself" at her feet and utters "words of warm affection, tenderness and love." Later, Cornelia relates her adventure to her increasingly agitated mother: "And now he pressed his lips to mine: without well knowing what I did, I shrieked and fled." At this, Cornelia's mother cries out, "Thank Heaven! You then are safe! You have escaped the serpent in the shape of man!" When Cornelia objects, stating that this man could never have meant her harm, her harried mother retorts, "Infamous beguiler!— but had you hearkened to his insidious tongue — too late would you have sighed for your credulity — to the sequel."[1]

The Mysteries of the Castle by John B. White features two heroines often found in Gothic plays: the innocent virgin and the protective mother. Although heroines in Gothic plays shared some characteristics with heroines of melodramas, Gothic heroines appeared more diverse, for although they often were depicted as conventional young virgins, they also appeared as doting mothers, devoted wives, or even fallen women. The popularity of Gothic plays indicates that the usual depictions of these heroines met with public approval; indeed, when a heroine did not behave conventionally, as illustrated by the unfortunate

Imogene in *Bertram*, she was condemned, along with the actress who portrayed her. Such an outcry about the depiction of one single heroine suggests that heroines in Gothic plays generally behaved in conventional ways. Moreover, the vehemence of attack on the play indicates that such plays were viewed as potentially powerful models for behavior.

The most popular Gothic plays appeared in each theatrical center of the United States, and each featured at least one virtuous heroine who exhibited some qualities of "True Womanhood," identified by Barbara Welter as piety, purity, submissiveness and domesticity.[2] These characters were promoted as especially instructive for middle-class female patrons.[3] Women in the audiences at Gothic plays, however, may have recognized some contradictions in depictions of Gothic heroines, for though these characters pronounced their appreciation of all these qualities, they did not always behave in ways that reflected these sentiments.

In studies of popular Gothic fiction, feminist scholars have identified two approaches: in one, Gothic fiction is viewed as "an expression of rebellion and ambivalence toward the woman's sphere"; in the other, it is said to "confirm and clarify that function."[4] Such contradictory messages would have emerged in productions of Gothic plays as well. The speeches given to the heroine celebrated submissiveness and domesticity, dutiful sentiments that indicated her acceptance of her place in the "woman's sphere." Yet, the actions of a Gothic heroine were not wholly submissive or domestic. She was not submissive to all males, nor could she depend upon males to rescue her. She sometimes found herself in desperate situations in which she had to act independently and assertively. This heroine also did not exhibit qualities of domesticity. Even though her words often expressed a longing for domesticity, for home and hearth, her actions rarely reinforced these sentiments. She was not living with a spouse, nor did she inhabit a conventional home. Instead, the heroine routinely found herself alone and unprotected in a strange and dangerous space.

A middle-class woman in the audience at a Gothic play may have been struck by the obvious contrast between her life and that of the heroine in the play. Whereas the heroine was, admittedly, often threatened by danger in a frightening space, she also was out in the world, confronting powerful males in their own domains, and triumphing over them. By contrast, real women of the period were severely restricted in their lives outside of their homes. Indeed, women comprised a smaller percentage of the theatrical audiences before the mid–1820s, although their numbers undoubtedly rose as more working-class women moved into urban centers. As late as 1828, Frances Trollope, in her *Domestic Manners of the Americans*, reported that "the larger proportion of females deem it an offence against religion to witness the representation of a play."[5]

Women who were in attendance at theatres during this time would have been aware of another contradiction between sentiments expressed in Gothic plays and the realities of contemporary life. In flowery speeches, Gothic heroes, and even Gothic villains, praised women for their modesty and their chastity. Yet, in the theatres themselves, according to contemporary sources, men routinely sported with prostitutes in full view of ladies in the lower boxes. According to contemporary accounts of this time, women in theatrical audiences were divided into two groups: "respectable" women and "women of ill repute." "Respectable" women generally sat in the lower boxes and were escorted to the theatre by a man.[6] If any disturbance was expected in the theatre, women did not attend.[7] The other group of women, those that newspapers called "impures," were described as frequenting the upper boxes of the theatre, or the infamous "third tier." That prostitutes were indeed present is not contested. Many contemporary accounts of the audience, including those of Washington Irving, William Dunlap, and citizens who wrote irate letters to editors of newspapers, indicate that prostitutes were indeed present in the theatre on a regular basis. However, the many complaints about them seemed to be directed toward their unruly behavior rather than their mere presence. The angriest letters were written by men purporting to protect "respectable women" from contact with prostitutes.

Accounts of theatrical audiences in this period divided women patrons into two categories: chaste and corrupt, a division described in feminist studies of Gothic fiction as "the basic dichotomy in the Female Gothic."[8] However, the "pure and chaste" women would have been aware of those other women in the audience, women who openly flaunted their sexuality and obviously did not exhibit qualities of piety, purity, submissiveness, and domesticity.[9] They also would have recognized that though male theatrical managers and male critics decried raucous behavior on the part of "impure" women, they did not bar prostitutes from attending the theatre.

Some women may have been unfairly labeled as prostitutes when, in fact, they were working-class women, who fell victim to class distinctions and automatically were relegated to "non-respectable" status.[10] This misperception probably was more common after the mid-1820s, when more accounts discuss the presence of working women in the galleries. However, in these first decades of the nineteenth century, women were even more limited in their choice of seats; "respectable" women patrons were required to arrive with an escort and sit in the lower boxes. Women of ill fame, however, were provided with special seats in the upper tier of boxes, a practice described in detail by William Dunlap in his *History of the American Theatre*. Such a clear-cut division of female patrons, then, presumably made distinctions between "ladies of quality" and "impures" very clear. However, even in the first decades of the nineteenth century, some observers noted increasing difficulty in discerning the "respectable" from the "non-respectable" female patrons simply by dress. In an article in the *Mirror of Taste and Dramatic Censor*, one writer commented that he had seen a "troop of women of ill fame" seated in the lower boxes, but admitted that he did not know how to remedy the situation because "in different gradations from private concubinage, down to public prostitution there were many who could not be so distinctly known to come within the limits of a prohibition as to justify their expulsion."[11] The writer concluded that if such women were "not evidently such, their exclusion was not necessary; but that where they were notoriously of the trade, they could be distinguished from others by their dress and behavior."[12] Thus, even in this early period of American theatrical history, before women routinely sat in the pit or the galleries, their respectability was becoming less easy to determine. By contrast, however, distinctions between "respectable" and "not respectable" were painfully clear in the Gothic dramas themselves.

Heroines in Gothic plays, as in melodramas, were unfailingly virtuous and nurturing, serving old fathers, husbands, or children. Frequently they were described as angels. For example, in *A Tale of Mystery*, Selina was called "an angel"; Adelaide in *The Count of Narbonne* was described as "my best angel." Honoria in *Ribbemont* was "angel-wife"; Cornelia in *The Mysteries of the Castle* was "an angel in female form"; Hortensia in *The Man of Fortitude* was "sweet angel, saint"; Agnes in *Raymond and Agnes* was "the very angel I beheld from the hotel" and in *The Forest of Rosenwald*, she was "the very angel I saw quit the convent in Madrid."[13]

All heroines, regardless of age, were serious characters who used elevated language to express high-minded sentiments about love and never made any humorous references about men, matrimony, or motherhood. Here they were contrasted with comic women, who offered a cynical view of men and marriage. For example, Julia, the heroine in Miles Andrew's version of *The Mysteries of the Castle*, cried, "Oh, profane not thus the sacred appellation — a husband! honor'd name!" However, her servant Annette proposed a more cynical view: "don't mind a little confinement, ma'am, it's only a prelude to matrimony."[14]

Gothic heroines, depending upon their age, exhibited other qualities as well. Young heroines exhibited purity, piety, and submissiveness, in that they displayed deference for their fathers. They also spoke of their reverence for matrimony and motherhood. Older heroines were noted for their loyalty and deference to their spouses, their attention to duty, and their piety. Older heroines were not required to exhibit purity or obsess about their chastity; they never were prey for seducers. Finally, the third type of heroine, the fallen woman, did not exhibit any qualities of "True Womanhood"; however, she did promote a wariness of bad connections.

An "Angel Maid": The Young Heroine

Young, virginal heroines appeared in over three-quarters of these Gothic dramas, although they sometimes were accompanied by older or secondary heroines. These young heroines were noted not only for their virtue but also for their beauty. Like young heroines in melodramas, these women were inevitably fair; Julia was a "timid, fair one"; Isabel was "so fair, and yet so humble"; Angela was "fair Angela"; Rosalva was "the fairest maiden in Castile"; Una was a "fair, lovely maid"; and Agatha was described as "fairest Agatha."[15]

Although young heroines in melodramas were sometimes motherless, those in Gothic plays nearly always were, and they often commented wistfully on their loss: Adeline in *Fontainville Forest* told her surrogate mother, "I never knew the comfort of a mother."[16] Mary in *Superstition* related to a friend, "Methought I saw my sainted mother lean o'er the bright edge of a silvery cloud and smile upon her happy orphan girl."[17] Although usually motherless, Gothic heroines often had fathers, to whom they offer complete devotion.[18]

Young heroines in Gothic plays showed excessive deference to their fathers. They honored their fathers' wishes even when doing so prevented them from obtaining personal happiness. Frequently their fathers gave heroines to the villain in marriage, and although the young women pleaded with their fathers to spare them this fate, they inevitably submitted.[19]

Gothic heroines not only obeyed their fathers but also accepted harsh treatment without rebuke. In *The Count of Narbonne*, Adelaide's father was abandoning her mother to marry a reluctant young heiress. Adelaide, hurt by his behavior, nevertheless forgave him, observing, "And were he not my father, I could rail; Call him unworthy of thy wondrous virtues."[20] In fact, this same heroine did not blame her father even for accidentally killing her, saying, "I know not my offence, yet sure 'twas great, when my life answer it. Will you forgive me now?"[21]

Another feature unique to young Gothic heroines was their habit of dwelling on possible sexual assaults. One of the best examples occurred in *The Castle Spectre*, in which Adeline was imprisoned by the lustful Earl of Osmond, her uncle. Although Adeline privately was unable to contemplate the Earl's sexual interest, saying, "I dare not bend my thoughts that way," she was able to do so publicly; when the Earl threatened force against her, she shrieked, "Force! Oh no!—you dare not be so base!"[22] In *The Mysteries of the Castle*, Julia confronted the villain, saying, "To gratify a base, unworthy passion—knowing my soul was wedded to another, left no dishonourable means untried to force a wretched maid, heart-broken to your arms—had not disgusted nature made me shun thee!"[23] In *The Count of Narbonne*, Isabel cried, "The lord, the tyrant of this place ... for a detested purpose follows me."[24] Heroines then, despite their delicate sensibilities, often confronted the villain with his lechery.

Gothic heroines also professed a preference for death over dishonor; in these plays dishonor often took the form of marriage with a villain or sexual activity outside of marriage. For example, Hortensia in *The Man of Fortitude*, evidently believing that God would look more favorably upon her suicide than upon her union with the villain, prayed, "Oh pardon me, if through a desperate act, I use this weapon as a friend, And set my soul, while pure, at liberty—Spotless, to join its lord in realms of bliss."[25] Gothic heroines, through their private musings and their public confrontations with the villains, managed to keep the threat of seduction before the audience without ever actually experiencing it.

Although Gothic heroines depended upon their fathers and other males, they sometimes proved more self-reliant and aggressive than heroines in melodramas of this period.[26] For example, in two of the plays the heroine disabled the villain; in four of the plays she killed him.[27] In all of these cases, however, the heroine was fighting to save another, helpless character, usually an old father or a child. Only then did the Gothic heroine abandon her dependency on a male and exhibit assertive behavior.

"The Best of Women": The Older Heroine[28]

Some Gothic plays, particularly those performed before 1810, featured older heroines.[29] One such type of heroine was the devoted wife, a heroine married either to the older hero or the villain. Unlike younger heroines, dutiful wives were praised primarily for their virtue, not their attractiveness. Matilda in *The Carmelite* and Adela in *The Warlock of the Glen* both remained loyal to their husbands even though both men had been presumed dead for years. Matilda, "still a mournful widow," said of her husband, "They say 'tis twenty years ago he died, I cannot speak of time, it may be so; but I should think 'twas yesterday."[30] In *The Warlock of the Glen*, another character remarked of Adela, "Ah! puir leddy, it's a sair change wi'her now-a-days; she niver held up the head o' her, sin' her laird's departure for the wars, where he fell among the slain."[31]

Devoted wives of older heroes remained loyal even when their spouses acted rashly. For example, Eleanora in *The Mysteries of the Castle* and Honoria in *Ribbemont*, were "murdered" by their husbands who believed them to be unfaithful. The women waited until their names were cleared and then generously forgave their spouses' bad judgment. Honoria explained, "for I still must love him! He, who for so many years was all my bliss; my heart's first love and ever new delight."[32]

Wives often faced exile as a result of their husband's mistakes, but they bore their adversity cheerfully. In *Fontainville Abbey*, Hortensia La Motte stayed with her husband in a ruined abbey, saying, "Shall I quit thee now? No, no La Motte; I'll aid thee with my counsels, and if need, support thy virtue in the hour of trial."[33]

Occasionally an older heroine was married to a villain, and she stayed with him in spite of terrible treatment at his hands. For example, in *The Sicilian Romance* the heroine was chained to a rock, yet of her abusive spouse she said, "O harm him not — Tho he has wrong'd me — he's my husband still."[34] Likewise, both the Countess in *The Count of Narbonne* and "The Lady" in *The Sicilian Romance* were imprisoned by their husbands who wished to marry heiresses, yet the wives did not confront the men on their own behalf. Instead they simply waited — and hoped that the bad treatment would cease. As the hapless Countess told her young daughter, "Obedience is thy duty, patience mine."[35]

Some older heroines in Gothic melodramas were portrayed as protective mothers. Matilda, in *The Carmelite*, guarded her son so completely that she did not even acknowledge him as her child until he was grown. She then informed him, "Thou art my son, for thee alone I've liv'd."[36] In *The Mysteries of the Castle*, Eleanora was so determined to save her daughter Cornelia from the lascivious villain that she considered killing her, lamenting,

> Oft have I besought heaven to take her from my arms, to rescue her while yet spotless from this detested crew; but despair and madness have already armed me, they have driven me to conceive a deed, which makes the mother sink within me; yet — for sooner than comply with Fauresco's brutal wishes, I will myself become her executioner.[37]

If a heroine was both wife and mother, she chose her maternal role over her conjugal one if her child was threatened. The Lady in *The Sicilian Romance* finally turned on her husband only when he threatened their child; as he approached she cried, "Attempt to force her from me, by heaven, spite of my love, the instant you advance, I'll strike my dagger, mark me, to your heart."[38] The older heroine remained loyal to her husband despite mistreatment; only when a spouse threatened others did she oppose him.

"A Thing That Mothers Warn Their Daughter From": The Fallen Heroine[39]

A few Gothic plays featured yet another heroine: the fallen woman. Like other heroines, she was a serious character who used elevated language as a traditional heroine did. Yet, unlike them she had not retained her virginity, and as a consequence, she had to die by the end of the play. Such a fate befell Imogene, fallen heroine in *Bertram*, who, despite her position as wife and mother, committed adultery with her long-lost love Bertram when he suddenly reappeared after an absence of many years. Following her adultery, Imogene was consumed with guilt, and her misery was intensified when she realized that Bertram had no love for her. When her loving husband returned, Bertram, despite Imogene's pleas, killed him. Imogene became insane, lost her child in the woods, confronted Bertram with his villainy, and abruptly died of grief.[40]

Another such heroine suffered a dire fate in *Marmion*. Constance, a professed nun, fell in love with Marmion and became his mistress. When he tired of her, he simply returned her to the convent. Constance, realizing that her return would result in severe punishment for her, confronted Marmion with his hypocrisy, saying, "Scorn not the withered flower you yourself have rifled. From this faded cheek Marmion has chased the blood of innocence, lighted in these wild eyes despair and frenzy, and on my hardened brow stamped infamy!"[41] Constance's despair naturally increased when she learned that, as punishment for her fornication, she was to be bricked up in a wall. The function of these unhappy heroines was to warn the ingenue of the consequences of unwedded sexual activity. Their tragic fates justified the heroine's vigilance in guarding her virtue.

Young heroines in Gothic dramas were extreme in their obedience to their fathers. Gothic plays implied that daughters were to be dutiful to their fathers' wishes, regardless of their personal feelings. In all the plays in this sample the heroine obeyed her father explicitly, and in several plays her obedience saved her life. In fact, because the majority of young heroines in these plays were motherless, the father exercised sole control over the daughter and had no rival for her affections.

Although young heroines in Gothic plays sometimes appeared assertive, they inevitably were acting in such a way to rescue other, more helpless characters. Thus, they were not directly violating the social expectation that women were to be dependent upon men. That society did expect women to exhibit such dependency is illustrated by this observation by James Fordyce in his widely reprinted *Sermons for Young Women*: "No, my friends, you were not made for scenes of danger and opposition. I repeat it again; fearfulness to a certain degree becomes you ... a worthy woman shrinking from manifest hazard, or threatened violence, we [men] are always forward and proud to protect; while, on the other hand, an intrepid female seems to renounce our aid, and in some respect to invade our province. We turn away, and leave her to herself."[42] Fordyce did restrict this delicacy, however, to the middle and upper classes, observing, "any young woman of better rank, that throws off all the lovely softness of her nature, and emulates the daring intrepid temper of a man — how terrible!"[43]

Women also were warned against becoming too independent in

their thinking lest they become "female philosophers." Although women of this period, 1794–1830, were encouraged to read, many contemporary articles and prescriptive literature cautioned women about the dangers too much education.[44] A woman who prized education for itself (rather than valuing it as a means to enhance her attractiveness) was in danger of becoming too independent, and thus less desirable to men, as illustrated by this 1813 diatribe against learned women:

> But vivacity, that lovely ornament that sets off and makes efficacious the more sober virtues — good nature, that perpetuates the conquests of beauty — that facility of disposition that accommodates itself to the varying circumstances of life — and, above all, that conscious weakness that looks up the lover and husband for instruction as well as protection — what are to become of these?[45]

Another essayist, identified only as "A Friend to the Sex," also warned that too much learning made women unattractive to men:

> That women should pore out their fair eyes in becoming adept in learning, would be highly improper. Nature seems not to have intended them for the more intense and severe studies. The gaining of the laurels of literary fame would rob their brows of many of those charms, which to them are more valuable as they are men more esteemed.[46]

James Fordyce advised women to pursue studies suitable for their probably "destination in life." He reasoned that such studies would "not require reasoning or accuracy, so much as observation and discernment," because women's business is "to read Men, so as to make [themselves] agreeable and useful."[47]

John Gregory, in his best-selling book, *A Father's Legacy to His Daughter*, aimed at "middling and elite families," instructed his daughters to downplay their intelligence.[48] Gregory cautioned, "If you happen to have learning, keep it a profound secret, especially from the men, who generally look with a jealous and malignant eye on a woman of great parts, and a cultivated understanding."[49]

Some counter-arguments emerged; Mary Wollstonecraft's *Thoughts on the Education of Daughters*, and her later *Vindication on the Rights of Women*, were widely read in the United States; excerpts of the work appeared as early as 1792 in periodicals such as *Ladies Magazine* and the *Massachusetts Magazine*, and by 1795, three American editions had been made available.[50] Yet Wollstonecraft's arguments also inspired apprehension. William Dunlap recorded in his diary on June 19th 1797, "Reading Mrs. Woolstencroft [sic]; she has much strength of mind, tho' her piety and philosophy appear a little, or perhaps not a little, incongruous."[51]

An article in a periodical outlined two pages of domestic duties that should be performed by every woman and then commented, "Women, indeed, formed on the narrow unphilosophic plan here aimed at, would ... in some respects come under the description of what she [Mrs. Wollstonecraft] calls *domestic drudges*—but surely a more desirable state than being drudges to infamy and prostitution."[52]

Another characteristic of heroines in Gothic plays was their utter lack of wit or humor, particularly noticeable in their interactions with males. Unlike their servants, heroines in Gothic plays never tease or criticize the males in any way, nor engage them in any witty dialogue. This careful consideration of male's egos is reinforced in prescriptive literature. In one essay, published in 1790 in Philadelphia and written by "a Friend to the Sex," the author warned readers that a witty woman could intimidate men:

> Men of the best sense, however, have been usually averse to the thought of marrying a witty female.... Men who understand the science of domestic happiness, know that its very first principle is ease ... but we cannot be easy where we are not safe. We are never safe in the company of a critic; and almost every wit is a critic by profession. In such company we are not at liberty to unbend ourselves. All must be the straining of study, or the anxiety of apprehension.... To suffer this restraint at home, what misery![53]

In "A Father's Legacy to His Daughters," John Gregory also advised young women to view wit as "a dangerous talent," and cautioned that "humour is often a great enemy to delicacy, and a still greater one to dignity of character."[54]

Young heroines spent much of their time fighting to preserve their virtue, and through their struggles, audiences learned that illicit sexual activity inevitably resulted in tragedy. Audiences of this time would have understood the importance of virginity to an unmarried girl. A girl in the early 1800s was expected to marry; about ninety percent did, after all.[55] The prospect of being an "old maid" was loathsome to many. An article in the *Mirror* in October of 1810 decried the "prejudices" against "old maids," remarking that they were "generally considered as the most unfortunate and most miserable of human beings," and observing that "among boarding school girls, the condition of an old maid appears the most melancholy upon earth, and it is thought the highest affront to any young lady, to imagine that such a dreadful destiny is likely to befall her."[56]

Instead, most young women sought matrimony, described in 1806 as "the proper theatre of woman's glory."[57] A woman needed to retain an "unsullied purity" in order to compete on the marriage market; her virginity was considered an "indispensable asset."[58] As one article in 1816 declared, "Purity of mind and conduct is the first glory of a woman. What a degraded being would she be, deprived of both these qualities!"[59] To ensure that young women recognized the dangers of sex outside of marriage, frequent reminders, in the form of articles and poems, appeared in newspapers and periodicals. Such a reminder was published in the *Charleston Courier* in 1803:

> "The Prostitute"
> It was a drear cold winter's night,
> The snow 'twas on the ground
> The howling storm, the bleak north wind
> In icy blasts blew round.
> I saw a poor half-naked girl,
> Sit shivering in the snow
> She held a babe; her check was wan;
> Her looks were full of woe.
> I turn'd me to the poor forlorn
> "Why sit you here," I cried;
> she rais'd her eye, she look'd at me,
> She wept aloud and sigh'd.
> "Ah me, said she; my babe is dead,
> He's frozen to my breast —
> Poor little wretch! Thy soul, ere now
> In heaven above doth rest."
> She wept again, in anguish then,
> Her cries they pierced my heart —
> I bade her be of comfort, and
> To me her tale impart —
> A lover then said she, had I
> Alonzo was his name.
> He won my heart, he won my all,
> Then left me to my shame.
> My father, a proud hearted man
> My crime it vex'd him sore,
> He curs'd me in his wrath, and then
> He drove me from his door.
> She ceas'd to speak; her bosom burst
> At thinking of the past;
> Then sigh'd and sobb'd, and sobb'd and sigh'd
> Then sigh'd and breath'd her last.[60]

The poem implied that the girl's fate was inevitable; as soon as she engaged in physical love without benefit of matrimony, her fate was sealed. "The

Prostitute" was a popular poem; it first appeared in the *Boston Gazette* and was later imported to the Charleston newspaper, ensuring that many young women, or those who had care of them, would see it.

Virginity was the safest way of avoiding pregnancy and disease. The heroine's fear of sexual violation reflected a real fear of young women in society of this period, for if they engaged in sexual relations before marriage they risked censure, loss of health, and marriage.[61] Prescriptive literature on this subject abounded between 1794 and 1825. One particular essay was translated from the French and published in the United States as "Advice from a Lady of Quality to Her Children in the Last Stages of a Lingering Illness." In her essay, the author included a chapter entitled "On Female Conduct," in which she warned her daughter that "Your sex requires the utmost circumspection; what among men is reputed a venial fault is an absolute crime with us ... I would wish that a young woman should be silent and modest; and the world, dissipated as it is, expects the same. Its judgment of us is very severe; and it often fixes our character for life."[62] Fordyce, too, conceded that women's behavior was much more constrained than was man's: "The world, I know now how, overlooks in our sex a thousand irregularities, which it never forgives in yours; so that the honour and peace of a family are, in this view, much more dependant on the conduct of daughters than of sons."[63] This modest behavior seemed especially important in the years of the early republic, because women now had to fend for themselves on the marriage market. As fewer families arranged matches and as more children moved farther from home in search of employment, young women were more likely to find their own mates, without aid from their families.

Although prescriptive literature recommended that young women cultivate a modest demeanor, it also emphasized that young women should be able to socialize with young men. Thus, women of the Revolutionary period were advised not to show deference to men, as they had been instructed in the Colonial period, but instead to socialize with men without arousing them sexually. Consequently, women of this time "bore an unequal burden in the relationship"; they were to "both please men and fend off their advances." Moreover, they were expected to accomplish this delicate task gracefully, without a show of prudery or excessive shyness.[64]

Authors of prescriptive literature advised young women about the necessity of mastering these lessons, and those works particularly stressed the importance of exhibiting a modest demeanor.[65] James Fordyce especially promoted modesty not only as a sign of virtue but also as an alluring quality: "Virtue exhibited without affectation by a lovely young person, of improved understanding and gentle manners, may be said to appear with the most alluring aspect, surrounded by the Graces; and that breast must be cold indeed which does not take fire at the sight!"[66] Yet Fordyce repeatedly cautioned young women about assuming the appearance of virtue without attempting to acquire the actual quality: "If men discover that you study to captivate them by an outside only, or by little frivolous arts, there are, it must be confessed, many of them who will rejoice at the discovery; and while they themselves seem taken by the lure, they will endeavour in reality to make you their prey."[67] Even the "better sort of men," according to Fordyce, would not help a young woman who was so unwise as "to drop that nice decorum of appearance and manner."[68]

John Gregory also conceded that all men would not appreciate the beauty of virtue immediately: "The natural hardness of our hearts, and strength of our passions, inflamed by the uncontrouled [sic] license we are too often indulged with in our youth, are apt to render our manners more dissolute, and makes us less susceptible of the finer feelings of the heart."[69]

If all men, even decent ones, were subject to strong passions and a general love of amusement, how was a young woman to protect herself? Clearly, women of the revolutionary period were pressured to marry, and the acknowledged "paucity of sanctioned alternatives" for these women certainly made marriage even more important. A woman's future happiness depended upon her choice of husband.[70] Thus, young women did indeed have to guard against male advances, as their "capital on the marriage market" was dependent upon their behavior.[71] Consequently, the cautions trumpeted by the advice literature were important. Some scholars have suggested that a woman's "defensiveness" would become "passionless," which later served as the basis for claims of female superiority.[72]

With all of the dangers waiting for unsuspecting young women, they were in need of guidance, and Fordyce warned them against the dangers of novelists and the "common herd of Play-writers":

> such works lead to a false taste of life and happiness; that they represent vices as frailties, and frailties as virtues, that they engender notions of love unspeakably perverting and inflammatory, that they overlook in a great measure the finest

part of the passion, which one would suspect the authors had never experience; that they turn it most commonly into an affair of wicked or of frivolous gallantry; that on many occasions they take off from the worst crimes committed in the persecution of it, the horror which ought ever to follow them; on some occasions actually reward those very crimes ... is this a kind of reading calculated to improve the principles, or preserve the Sobriety, of female minds?[73]

Fordyce did concede that some "works of imagination" could prove instructive for women, because the "female mind" was "disposed to be particularly fond" of such literature. If these works were "blended with instruction," Fordyce reasoned, they could prove beneficial. He recommended "Fables, Visions, Allegories, and such-like compositions," where "Fancy sports under the controul [sic] of Reason." To this more desirable grouping, Fordyce grudgingly admitted "Dramatic Writings also, where truth of character and purity of thought are preserved," but added, "of these last how inconsiderable the number!"[74]

Gothic plays certainly promoted the qualities most encouraged by Fordyce, Gregory, and other writers of prescriptive literature. Young, unmarried heroines in Gothic plays exhibited deference toward males as well as dependence when they were not forced by circumstances to act assertively. These heroines were modest, pious, demure, and virtuous. They exhibited no sign of wit or humor; they appeared completely passionless, and they worried excessively about preserving their virtue.

Whereas heroines in melodramas were nearly always young and unmarried, several Gothic plays depicted heroines as loving wives. These characters were noted primarily for their loyalty, good works, and piety rather than their physical attractiveness. In fact, these female characters were not described physically, and they were never prey for lascivious villains even though villains and older heroines would have been around the same age.

Audiences in the early 1800s would have been familiar with the expectations and restrictions placed on Gothic female characters. Society expected wives to provide comfort and care for their husbands, which entailed the cheerful execution of innumerable household tasks. Wives received this message from sources other than plays. Articles provided plentiful advice; for example, an article in the *Mirror* in July of 1811 provided a list of duties for a useful wife, including making butter and cheese, serving swine and poultry, gardening, spinning, laundering, loading carts, making soap, helping with harvest, selling her produce (ensuring that she "make a true reckoning and account thereof to her husband") and various other chores. At the conclusion of the list, the writer observed,

> If a man had presumed to hint to the late Mrs. Wolstoncraft [*sic*] that a married woman, who followed these directions, might be as happy in herself, and as useful a member of society, as one formed upon *her* plan and exhibited in a certain singular and reprehensible book, published since her death, the bare supposition would probably have produced a sneer from the heroine.[75]

In addition to proving herself useful in the home, a wife was to exhibit a virtuous example and, above all, piety. An article appearing in 1823 suggested that a woman was meant to be "the comfort and ornament of the domestic habitation." Her duty was to care for her husband, who, "cast often by his duty into a tempest of cares and business," and "assailed by the passions of his nature," might have become depraved. A woman, by contrast, was able to "tranquilly number her days, and signalize them by a thousand acts of virtue." The article concluded: "to love all that is worthy, useful, good, and virtuous, and to fly all that is opposed to it—this is what society demands of woman."[76] In a similar vein, an article in the *Boston Spectator* emphasizes the importance of piety, particularly in an older woman:

> Piety communicates a divine lustre to the female mind. Wit and beauty, like the flowers of the field, may flourish and charm for the season; but let it be remembered that like the flowers of the field, those gifts are frail and fading. Age will soon nip the bloom of beauty ... in these gloomy seasons, PIETY will support the dropping soul, like a refreshing dew upon the parched earth.[77]

Wives were expected to stay with their husbands regardless of their personal unhappiness in the marriage.[78] A guide to morals and manners published in 1808 contained a section entitled, "Proper Conduct of the Wife Towards Her Husband," in which the author, a man, sternly enjoined "it is your interest to adapt yourself to your husband, whatever may be his peculiarities."[79]

Gothic plays also depicted some heroines as protective mothers, and in several of the plays, motherhood was glorified as the woman's greatest achievement. This aspect of characterization also reflected society of the early 1800s; during this turbulent time of change, motherhood was depicted as the "source of women's greatest power." As mothers assumed responsibility for educating their sons to be virtuous citizens, their importance in the family increased.[81] Fordyce endorsed this view:

> But lastly, let us suppose you Mothers; a character which, in due time, many of you will sustain. How does your importance rise! A few years elapsed, and I

please myself with the prospect of seeing you, my honoured auditress, surrounded with a family of your own, dividing with the partner of your heart the anxious, yet delightful labour, of training your common offspring to virtue and society, to religion and immortality, while, by thus dividing it, you leave him more at leisure to plan and provide for you all.[82]

Mothers in Gothic plays devoted themselves to their families, and motherhood in these plays was exalted as a woman's greatest achievement.

Older heroines in Gothic plays were not noted for their physical attributes, nor were they depicted as sexual beings. Whereas the young heroine could allude to the possibility of seduction, the older heroine was prevented from even contemplating such a scenario. Instead she was depicted as passionless.[83] These heroines were depicted primarily as dutiful, loyal wives and self-sacrificing mothers, women who identified themselves only by these roles.

A third type of heroine appeared in a few Gothic plays: a fallen woman. She was a serious female character who had lost her virginity to a villain and who suffered as a result. This particular character would have reinforced existing messages from literature of the period about the dangers of mixing with disreputable company. Fordyce warned young women "in the first place, to avoid Dangerous Connexions [*sic*]. If that be not done, what is there on earth, or in heaven, that can save you?"[84] Fordyce thundered, "What! Would you parley with the destroyer, when he gives you warning? Then you are not ensnared, you knowingly and willfully expose yourselves. If you be poisoned, if you be lost; your folly is without excuse, and your destruction without alleviation."[85]

"I Dare Not Bend My Thoughts That Way": Women in the Audience

The various characterizations of heroines in Gothic plays undoubtedly appealed to all members of the audience, but for very different reasons. Gothic plays, because of their contradictory structure, were able to adhere to a rigid moral code in their melodramatic structure, and yet their Gothic tendencies allowed female members of the audience to enjoy vicariously the experience of transgressing conventional behavior. Thus, the words of the heroines supported the lessons of popular prescriptive literature, but her actions did not.

Young women in the audience would have observed the young heroine displaying proper deference toward males, carefully monitoring her wit, and obsessively guarding her virtue. Yet at the same time, young women in the audience would have witnessed that heroine engaging in a terrifying but undeniably exciting adventure, worlds away from the safety, predictability, and restraints of a home. Moreover, some young women in the audience may have enjoyed the situation of a very young heroine attracting the attention of a much older, powerful male.

Older women in the audience probably applauded the older heroines' obvious devotion to their children and their loyalty to their spouses. However, these women, too, may have found a guilty pleasure in vicariously experiencing the older heroines' triumphs over their spouses, particularly when those spouses were unfaithful or abusive.

Women of all ages and classes would have witnessed the miserable consequences of unsanctioned physical love, as illustrated by the fallen heroine. Yet, even as they received this lesson from the stage, these "respectable" women could have seen lascivious activities in the theatre itself and also could have observed females who openly engaged in such activities, apparently without penalty.

The unlikely combination of the middle-class sentiments expressed in melodrama and the darker and more dangerous worlds of the Gothic allowed middle-class female spectators to condone publicly the words of the heroine and simultaneously enjoy her transgressions. The heroine's experiences in Gothic plays displayed a freedom from ordinary restraints of home and family and an opportunity to triumph over powerful males. Moreover, the sexuality to which the heroine alluded on the stage and that occurring in the theatre itself subverted the play's warnings about the importance of modesty and chastity. Though middle-class women of this period were expected to exhibit "passionlessness," the heroine's oft-expressed, baldly stated conjectures about the villain's intentions, and the very visible presence of prostitutes in the theatre, would have permitted "respectable" women in the audience to contemplate sexual activity without guilt.

CHAPTER 6

"An Exquisite Treat for Feeling Minds"
Acting and the Female "Stars" of Gothic Plays

In the year 1798 Mrs. Elizabeth Kemble Whitlock, sister of Sarah Siddons, portrayed Julia in *The Mysteries of the Castle* at Charleston; in that same year she also portrayed Matilda in *The Carmelite* at New York and Angela in *The Castle Spectre* at Boston. Mrs. Whitlock, along with other leading actresses of the period, such as Mrs. (Anne Brunton) Merry, Mrs. (Mary Ann) Duff, Mrs. (Charlotte) Melmoth, Mrs. (Elizabeth) Whitlock, Mrs. (Georgina) Oldmixon, and Mrs. (Elizabeth) Snelling Powell, performed often in Gothic plays.

Although the careers of Anne Brunton Merry and Mary Ann Duff have been examined in some detail, other leading actresses of the early American stage, stars in their own right, have not received as much attention. Mrs. Melmoth, Mrs. Whitlock, Mrs. Oldmixon, and Mrs. Snelling Powell, all lauded as extremely accomplished actresses in their era, regularly included Gothic heroines in their repertoire and often chose Gothic plays for their benefit nights. All of these actresses had favorable reviews from stage in Europe and then enjoyed great success in the United States, where they often "starred" in other American cities as well as in their "home" theatres. They all enjoyed economic success and several of them successfully managed their own careers, including their salary negotiations, without the assistance of a spouse. Most impor-

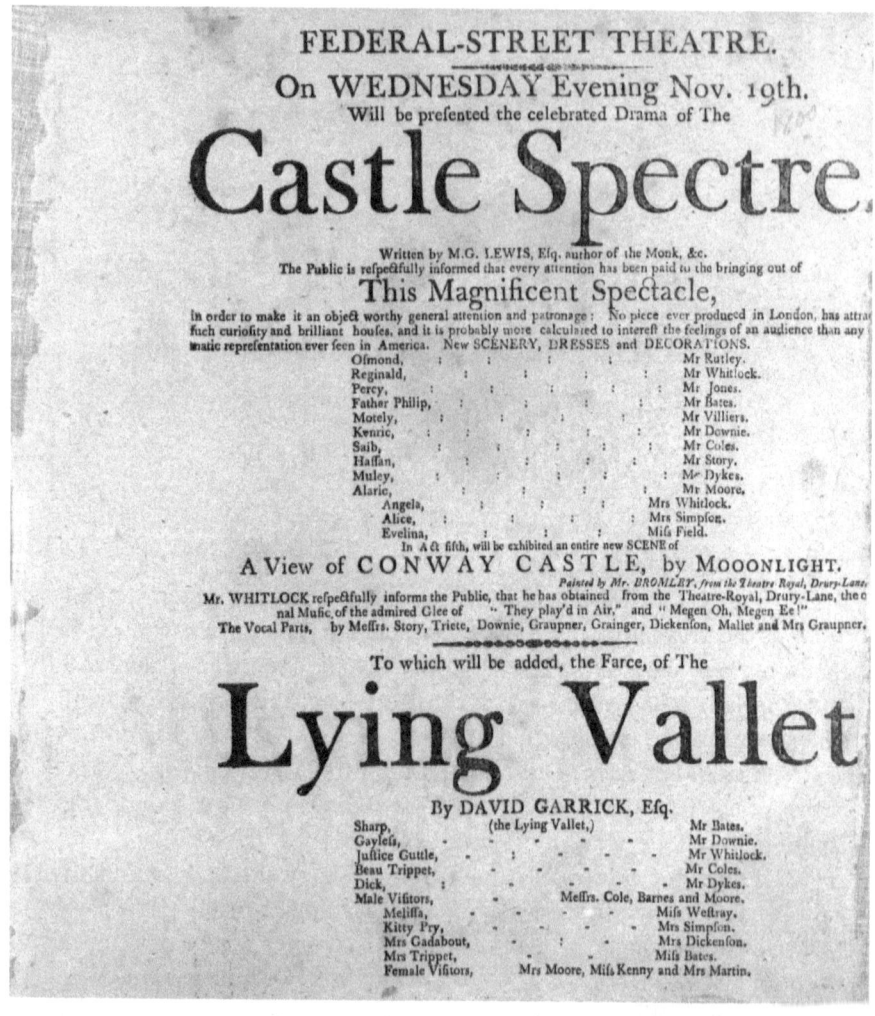

Playbill for Boston's Federal Street Theatre's production of *The Castle Spectre* featuring Mrs. Elizabeth Kemble Whitlock as Angela. The Harvard Theatre Collection, Houghton Library.

tantly, all of these actresses received public commendation for their virtue as well as their talent. This public expression of esteem is particularly interesting in that Americans of the early nineteenth century often objected to the stage and its performers, especially actresses who did not follow the usual rules of conduct. Yet these actresses received no condemnation for their unconventional lives, even though they were exhibiting themselves on a public stage, engaging in activities not of the domestic sphere and sometimes involved in unconventional marriages. These performers' frequent portrayals of virtuous Gothic heroines certainly aided their popularity on the stage and arguably promoted their reputations as virtuous women off stage.

Their appearances as Gothic heroines increased the marketability of these early actresses and enabled them to make a good living from the stage. Mrs. Melmoth, Mrs. Whitlock, Mrs. Oldmixon, and Mrs. Powell were members of a profession that paid well in a period of very limited employment for women. In *American Actress*, Claudia Johnson includes the results of a study of working women in 1840; the study found that even by 1840, half the women workers in New York City earned less than $2.00 a week.[1] Yet in the first decade of the nineteenth century, many actresses, even those who were not considered leading players, earned more than that.[2] Bernard, writing of actors in the 1790s, observed, "the supply of talent was not beyond the demand, and consequently incomes maintained a fair level ... there was no salary at this period under four pounds a week, while many reached as high as twelve and fifteen, and as benefits occurred at least twice a year, these ordinarily added one third to that amount."[3]

Not only did actresses earn a good living on the stage in the years between 1794 and 1830, they often earned the same salaries as male performers. Even in the 1790s, actresses received comparable compensation for their work, as indicated by William Dunlap's account of the 1798–99 season. Mr. Hallam and Mr. Cooper, stars of the company, received twenty-five pounds per week and Mr. Johnson, Mr. Tyler, and Mr. Jefferson earned twenty pounds. Leading actresses Mrs. Hallam and Mrs. Johnson earned twenty-five pounds per week, and Mrs. Melmoth earned twenty pounds. Of particular note is Mrs. Oldmixon, who earned thirty-seven pounds per week, more than any other player.[4]

Despite the obvious possibility of good wages in the profession, some contemporary sources assert that Americans, both men and women, avoided the stage for fear of harming their reputations. *The Polyanthos* observed in 1813, "It is not often that a native American is willing to encounter the odium attached ... to the profession of a player, by venturing before his countrymen on the stage."[5] Certainly, some accounts damning playhouses and the acting profession appeared in periodicals.[6] As one writer remarked in 1811, "Let morality raise her forbidding tones; let her inform us that few know her that still fewer are her friends, that a player's life too frequently proclaims him unacquainted with, and inimical to her."[7]

Disapproval of actors even may have increased in the 1820s in the United States, as suggested by an article in *The New York Mirror, and Ladies' Literary Gazette* in which the writer observes that though the "present age is enlightened and refined," there exists more "ancient bigotry and groundless prejudice" as indicated by "the present absurd antipathy to the company of actors."[8] The author complains that the New York public refused to believe in a performer's virtue, even that that performer behaved in an exemplary manner:

> No matter how noble may be their hearts, how refined and high-minded their sentiments, it is enough that they are actors, and bigotry or ignorance, or error, closes against them the doors of fashion, and bids them stand aloof from the superior domains of their fellow man.[9]

Defenders of the theatre complained that actors were erroneously believed to be idle and prone to "free-living." William Wood, manager of the Chestnut Street Theatre, retorted that "the charge of 'idleness' and dissipation can be made only by those who have no more knowledge of an actor's daily habits, than they have of those followed by the Circassians or Esquimaux."[10] A more humorous account about the difficult life of an actor, entitled "Professional Miseries," appeared in an 1825 edition of the *New York Mirror and Ladies' Literary Gazette*. The writer, supposedly an actor, observes, "I used vainly to imagine that the business of an actor was all play, but I have found to my cost, that no trade, no profession on earth, is so laborious to mind and body." The actor proceeds to recount the requirements of his day; he must go to rehearsal at ten in the morning, "to study and arrange all the nonsense which the manager chooses to accept from the wretched play-writer ... liable to be fined forty pounds for refusing to play a part which I know does not suit me." After rehearsal, the actor must spend time on wardrobe "to ascertain which combination of grotesque habits will ... produce the greatest portion of laughter in the one shilling gallery." Although the actor goes home for supper, he recounts that he must leave his home just as he is getting warm and comfortable and return to the theatre for the evening's performance, and plod through a rainstorm and streets "ankle deep in mud." As a result of his miserable journey, he contracts a fever and a tooth-ache. When his silly dance is "encored by some boys in the gallery" he must stand humbly before them, "a set of senseless brutes." He is then hit in the head by an apple. The actor finally finishes the performance, changes his clothes, and rubs his face with "grease and pomatum to get the paint out of the pores." Wearily, he slogs home through the mud down the "same wretched streets," where he is "hustled by three tall females of a certain description," who, after pulling him about, leave him abruptly "when they discover by the light of a great starry gas lamp, that, after all, it's funny — the actor man!"[11]

Despite the undeniable trials of the acting profession, William Dunlap, theatrical manager, historian, and playwright, maintained that actors in the early decades of the nineteenth century fared better in the United States than in England. Dunlap maintained that actors enjoyed more respect in the newly formed United States and accordingly conducted themselves with more decorum:

> We see those who have submitted to the disgrace of a stroller's life in England take a higher stand in this country, and maintain it. They feel that they are not degraded by a privileged order ... having thrown off the stigma which the law of their own country had affixed them, they feel bound to assume, with the more elevated character, a more elevated deportment and conduct.[12]

Dunlap's position is supported by a letter from "A Citizen" published in the October 1811 edition of *The Cynick*, which argued, "I look upon a playhouse to be a very good thing, often keeping young men from worse places, and young women from worse employment."[13]

A few decades later, however, the tone changes; another account, written in the 1820s, contests the view of American liberality. An article in *The New-York Mirror, and Ladies' Literary Gazette* in 1824 argued that performers in the United States received far less respect than performers in England, and the writer chastised Americans for their attitudes:

> It is with regret that I confess we are surpassed in this instance, by the English, in liberality. There is not half the disgrace attached to the profession there as here, in a land of freedom, of science, of religious toleration, and republican sentiments.[14]

These seeming contradictory accounts of the public's perception of actors in the United States suggest a increase in antipathy toward the stage in later decades of the nineteenth century. Actors seem to have been more respected in the last years of the eighteenth century and the first decade of the nineteenth and then suffered from mounting suspicion as the century progressed.

The limited number of actors and actresses in the United States during the 1790s and early 1800s may have ensured them a more favorable reception from the public than actors of a later period. As John Bernard argued in his *Retrospections of America*, salaries in the 1790s were high because demand for actors was great. However, this situation altered when actors began to be more numerous, and Bernard drew a direct link between decreasing salaries and decreasing respectability of players:

> When actors grew abundant this level [of comfortable salaries] was broken and their reputations in consequence began to decline. We seldom think how much morals depend upon means. If the rich struggle to be virtuous, how much more must the poor. When salaries sank, owing to the increased competition, characters sank also.[15]

In any period actors were scrutinized closely; most attempted to present a virtuous character to the public, and the press publicly lauded performers for their virtue. In 1806, one periodical remarked of Mr. Barnard, "It is with great satisfaction we have to add that the person of whom we are now treating is not less estimable for his moral, than respectable in his professional character.... He is a constant and serious attendant on religious worship."[16] Such references to a performer's respectability were especially prevalent in accounts of actresses.

Leading actors and actresses on the American stage in the 1790s and early 1800s usually were imported from England. Often these actors and actresses had performed at Covent Garden or Drury Lane, and their professional credits were well publicized to the public in the United States. Theatrical patrons in the United States clamored to see these performers, who had already been approved by a London audience.

In these same years, American periodicals and newspapers uniformly praised the virtue of leading actresses on the American stage, which suggests that these actresses working on American stages before 1830 were able to overcome public suspicion about their virtue. This attitude is particularly interesting because in this same period, English actresses seemed to suffer from poor reputations, possibly because of the requirements of their craft: "the public nature of acting and the absolute necessity of putting oneself up for general scrutiny led to an intellectual association between actress and prostitute."[17] Though such a connection between actress and prostitute may have become more prevalent in the United States later in the nineteenth century, it was not featured in contemporary accounts between 1794 and 1830.

Not only did periodicals of this period rarely criticize leading actresses, they actually discussed an actress's virtue and respectability as frequently as her talent. For example, an article in the *Philadelphia Repository* rejoiced that Mrs. Whitlock had returned to the theatre in that city and concluded, "Talents so conspicuous, certainly receive an additional luster when accompanied with an unsullied reputation, a demeanor amiable, virtuous, and polite."[18] This trend is particularly interesting in that several of the actresses who portrayed Gothic heroines, Mrs. Melmoth and Mrs. Oldmixon, did not lead conventional married lives and yet suffered no criticism in the press. In addition, two of these actresses, Mrs. Melmoth and Mrs. Whitlock, were not considered particularly attractive. Yet all of these actresses enjoyed their greatest popularity in the 1790s and early 1800s, a point when permanent theatres were new, and employment options for women were very limited.

One of the most famous actresses of the late 1790s was Mrs. Charlotte Melmoth, who performed the tragic roles in the earliest Gothic plays, the matrons in *The Carmelite, Ribbemont,* and *Fountainville Forest*. She had been born into a farming family in Surrey, England and eloped (or perhaps was tricked into a false marriage) when she was still at boarding school. She eloped with Mr. Pratt, who was known in the theatrical world as Courtney Melmoth. They parted company after a few years but she continued to use his name for the rest of her life.[19] Despite the potential for scandal, Mrs. Melmoth engendered no comment in the press about her absent husband. Instead, she regularly received comments about her talent.

According to Dunlap, Charlotte Melmoth first appeared in the United States on Nov. 20, 1793, and was considered the "best tragic actress the inhabitants of New York, then living, had ever seen; unless it were those who had traveled, and they were at that time few.[20] Mrs. Melmoth had been a favorite on the Dublin stage and had played for one season each at Covent Garden and Drury Lane. Of her professional life in the United States, Ireland noted that "no actress of tragedy in New York could at this time at all compete with her."[21] Mrs. Melmoth also appeared on stages in other cities; her 1803 benefit performance at Charleston brought in a profit of over one thousand dollars, and a newspaper reported that the theatre "was crowded with the most brilliant audience ever witnessed at Charleston and every circumstance connected with Mrs. Melmoth's performance, in that place, was of the most pleasing nature."[22] Despite her acknowledged status as a leading actress and despite critical acclaim for her "exquisite feeling of the pathetic," Mrs.

Melmoth had difficulties in her dealings with theatrical managers, who disparaged her personal appearance.[23] Dunlap observed, rather pitilessly, that the actress was "now past her prime, her face still handsome, her figure commanding, but not a little too large. Her dimensions were far beyond the sphere of embonpoint."[24] William Wood remarked, "in size she greatly exceeded any performer I have ever seen."[25] Ireland asserted that "she was past the prime of life, and her unfortunate bulk adapted her to a very limited range of parts."[26] Bernard quipped, "her misfortune, in latter years, was to expand to a size that no tragedy and black velvet had power to subdue."[27] All contemporary critics, however, agreed that her portrayals of matronly characters, where her size was not so not noticeable, were impressive.

Mrs. Melmoth's situation was aggravated by the changing depiction of heroines in Gothic dramas; the earliest plays, such as *The Carmelite*, *The Count of Narbonne*, *Ribbemont*, and *Fountainville Forest*, featured strong older heroines, and Mrs. Melmoth was considered the finest actress in these matronly roles. An 1805 review for *The Carmelite* raved, "her voice is "melodious, her gesticulation dignified, her countenance expressive. The Lady of St. Valori was all that we could wish."[28] However, after 1800, most Gothic plays featured younger female characters, and any older women were comedic, secondary characters. This development led to a dearth of roles for more mature tragic actresses. Mrs. Melmoth did attempt a comic role; in Charleston, she appeared in the role of Fiametta, a comic servant in *A Tale of Mystery*. Under Mrs. Melmoth's name, the advertisement reads, "being her first appearance in that species of character."[29] Evidently, Mrs. Melmoth performed the part well; a critic in the *Courier* commented:

> The character assigned to Mrs. Melmoth, which we consider as *intirely* [sic] *original*, was performed in a manner that to be conceived must be seen — we scarcely know a character of the same length in the whole round of the drama, more difficult to be hit off — and we venture to pronounce, that every one of taste or feeling ... will readily acknowledge that the performance of that character alone, by Mrs. Melmoth, was well worth the money paid for the whole night's entertainment.[30]

Despite the rather cryptic critique, Mrs. Melmoth apparently succeeded in this role, and, although she did not perform it often, she chose it for her final performance on the stage at the Olympic theatre in 1812.[31]

Mrs. Melmoth, recognizing that she did not appear to advantage in roles that required younger actresses, approached theatre manager

William Dunlap to request some changes in her situation, as Dunlap recorded:

> On May 24, 1798, Mrs Melmoth called on me. She wished a continuation in the company: promised to do every thing in her power: would give up all the young parts in Tragedy if required ... & saying she never wished to be made love to on the Stage. She talked of having a salary as high as Mrs. Johnson: I told her I would not bind myself to regulate one person's salary by another, that if I raised Salaries I could not expect success: She said she should not insist on the salary but she did not choose or think it just that she should pay at her benefit a higher salary than she received.[32]

Although Dunlap did not agree to all of Mrs. Melmoth's requests, he did acquiesce to one. In an entry dated June 27, 1798, Dunlap wrote: "Attend to business. Mrs. Melmoth call'd on me by appointment. Circumstances had prevented my send [sic] the letter to her concerning her business. She agrees with me to exert & accommodate ... I agreed to allow her $25."[33]

Mrs. Melmoth was so well known that in 1812 she merited a notice in several newspapers when she was involved in an accident in a stage coach and mistakenly thought to be dead. On May 28, 1812, in its obituary section, the *Boston Gazette* reported her death: "at New Brunswick, N.J. in consequence of the injury she received by the overturning of the stage, Mrs. Melmoth, a celebrated actress, formerly of the New York Theatre."[34] On the same day, however, *Poulson's Daily Advertiser* wrote, "It is with great pleasure we learn, that the report of the death of Mrs. Melmoth, in consequence of the accident of the stage being overset near Princeton, is without foundation — she is recovering very fast and will shortly be able to resume her journey."[35]

Mrs. Melmoth apparently managed her career quite successfully until "age forced her to abandon the stage"; she then embarked on another career as a teacher. Melmoth had "prudently saved enough" to purchase a small house on Long Island "with land enough to keep some cows, whose milk contributed to supply the New York Market." The money that she made from this trade along with money obtained from some boarding scholars "occupied her latter years profitably."[36] Ireland observes that throughout Melmoth's sojourn in the United States she "sustained an unblemished repute, and won the regard and respect of all who knew her."[37] Charlotte Melmoth died September 28th, 1823, at the age of seventy-four, and was buried at St. Patrick's Cathedral.[38]

Another famous actress of Gothic plays was Mrs. Elizabeth (or Eliza) Whitlock. Mrs. Whitlock was born in 1761 into the famous Kemble theatrical family; she was a sister to the famous Sarah Siddons. Elizabeth Kemble married Charles Whitlock and came with him the United States in 1793.[39] According to Clapp, "Mrs. Whitlock was a striking and pleasing resemblance to her sister, possessing a full share of her noble air and elocutionary powers, with more amusing powers of conversation."[40] In England she had appeared at Newcastle and at the Haymarket, and in 1794, appeared in Philadelphia with Wignell's troupe. Ireland notes that in 1800, she played again in London, and was afterwards at Boston, and then came to New York in 1802 as the leading lady at the Park theatre, however she never seemed to outshine Mrs. Melmoth, Mrs. Johnson, or Mrs. Merry. Mrs. Whitlock seemed to enjoy the greatest success in Boston, where she performed the leading roles in many Gothic plays between 1798 and 1801, including Adeline in *Fountainville Forest*, Matilda in *The Carmelite*, Adelaide in *The Sicilian Romance*, and Hortensia in *The Count of Narbonne*.

Like Mrs. Melmoth, Mrs. Whitlock enjoyed a solid reputation as a very talented actress. Of her prowess, Bernard praised "Mrs. Whitelock [sic], an admirable actress, who was in no way unworthy of her illustrious sister."[41] She evidently quite outshone her husband, who, according to Clapp, "was even then past the meridian of life, and dependent upon his wife's attractions."[42] She won praise for her simplicity in performance. As "Roscius" commented in the *Philadelphia Minerva*, Mrs. Whitlock was "still the female constellation" in a company that evinced "affectation, bombast, and unnatural grimace" in a season that "dragged heavily along, involved in clouds of ranting dullness."[43] "Theatricus," in an article in the *Philadelphia Gazette*, asserted that "no performer," "not even excepting the far-famed Mrs. Siddons," had been able to incite in him "such highly pleasurable emotions."[44] When Mrs. Whitlock came to the Philadelphia Theatre in 1801, "Mercutio" in the *Philadelphia Repository* exulted that "lovers of the drama, have reason to congratulate themselves upon the reappearance of Mrs. Whitlock, after so long, and so regretted an absence." The critic added that "this celebrated actress, is indeed an acquisition to our boards," and concluded "in the tragic walk, Mrs. Whitlock stands unrivalled, at least, in this country."[45]

Although Mrs. Whitlock enjoyed general approbation for her acting, she also was subject to frequent appraisals of her physical appearance. Dunlap described Mrs. Whitlock as "a fine-looking woman" and observed that she possessed some of the "Siddons and Kemble physiognomy"; but she was "fairer of complexion, and not so towering in stature."⁴⁶ Bernard, however, took a different view, commenting, "Her defects were her person, which was short and undignified, and her heavy, thick voice.⁴⁷ Even when the actress received gushing reviews for her talent, she suffered slights for her appearance. "Theatricus" in *The Philadelphia Gazette* commended Mrs. Whitlock as the "first actress in America," and noted that she had "an unlimited command over the feelings of the spectators." Theatricus went on at length about Mrs. Whitlock's prowess:

> To conclude, Mrs. Whitlock has a graceful carriage — her pronunciation is animated; her voice and her countenance are capable of every inflexion necessary to express the most opposite emotions and passions, with the utmost promptitude — her memory is so good and her application so assiduous, as to leave her little in debt to the prompter's aid.⁴⁸

Unfortunately, however, this lengthy list of attributes was not enough to secure Mrs. Whitlock unquestioned status in the profession, for the critic concluded his lengthy tribute with the phrase "and except for her person which approaches toward the masculine, she has every qualification desirable in an actress."⁴⁹

Throughout her career in the United States, Mrs. Whitlock enjoyed the reputation of a virtuous woman. As Ireland commented, the actress was considered "to have borne an exemplary character and to have graced society as well as the stage." Bernard asserted "this lady was an honor to her profession in every sense.⁵⁰ Dunlap commented that Mrs. Whitlock was "of great value in her profession, and out of it an honour to her family."⁵¹ She retired to England and died in 1835 at the age of seventy-four.⁵²

Another leading actress who performed in Gothic plays, Mrs. Snelling Powell, was particularly popular in Boston. She had been born in England in 1774 as Elizabeth Harrison and had acquired a strong reputation in London.⁵³ Dunlap commented that "her beauty and talents soon placed her at the head of her profession in the theatres of New-England."⁵⁴

Mrs. Powell appeared as Angela in *The Castle Spectre*, Innogen in *Adelmorn*, Agnes in *Raymond and Agnes*, Hortensia in *The Man of Fortitude* and Helen in *The Iron Chest*; the breadth of roles indicates her versatility. An examination of Boston repertory indicates that Mrs. Snelling Powell began performing Gothic heroines in 1806; she still was the main actresses depicting them in 1816. She was able to play tragic roles as well as roles that required more sprightliness. That she was loved in Boston was indicated by the amount of money collected at her benefit: Clapp remarked that "the annual benefits of the actors, in those days, were in reality benefits. That of Mrs. Powell was always honored by a full house.⁵⁵ At the benefits for 1805, Mr. Snelling Powell's brought in $1,100; John Bernard's $1,050, Thomas Cooper's $1,050; and Mrs. Powell's, $1,163, the most money for any performer in that season.⁵⁶

Mrs. Powell also differed from the Gothic heroines that she portrayed so often in that she did not seem to depend upon her husband. Bernard recounts a situation in the first decade of the nineteenth century in which he and a small band of actors, including Mrs. Powell, performed in Concord, Vermont. An angry mob had assembled outside the theatre, apparently intent upon stopping the actors from performing. The mob began "abusing and vilifying" the actors because they were English, calling them "spies and montebanks." Bernard recalled that Mr. Powell was "intimidated and would not go on with his character, but his wife, with a courage that that I could not but admire, persevered like a heroine."⁵⁷

Mrs. Powell was lauded enthusiastically for her spotless reputation, more than any other of the actresses who performed in Gothic plays. A newspaper article claimed, "She is an ornament to society, and her character is an illustration of the maxim of Solomon, that 'a virtuous woman is a crown to her husband.'"⁵⁸ In May of 1813, The *Boston Daily Advertiser* wrote of Mrs. Powell, "Those abilities which have acquired her a deserved reputation among the lovers of the drama, are, however, among the least of her merits. She is not less exemplary as a mother and a wife, than distinguished as an actress."⁵⁹ Mrs. Powell and her husband were even credited with elevating the profession of acting as indicated by the obituary of Mr. S. Powell:

> It is not too much to attribute to the private worth and respectability of Mr. and Mrs. Powell, the credit of having dissipated much of the prejudice which characterized our puritanic townsmen in 1795. They have at least proved that actors do not *necessarily* belong to the inferior ranks of society; for they have been examples of industry and prudence, rising from a depressed condition to affluence and respectability.⁶⁰

After the death of her husband, Mrs. Powell took over the management of the Boston Theatre. She died at age 70 in 1843.⁶¹

One of the most famous actresses of the period was Mrs. Oldmixon, apparently born as Georgina George, who appeared at the Haymarket and Drury Lane in London as a comic singer.⁶² Dunlap noted that she was such a favorite in London in 1785–86 that her portrait was exhibited at Somerset House.⁶³ Though she married Sir John Oldmixon, she did not use the title "Lady Oldmixon," because, as Dunlap commented, "as Lady Oldmixon, a stage player would appear rather incongruous, and unsanctioned by custom. ... the lady was called universally Mrs. Oldmixon."[64]

Mrs. Oldmixon, like Mrs. Melmoth, had a rather unconventional marriage. Her husband, who had been "the most elegant person in the most elegant city of England," now lived in the United States, and his wife was the main breadwinner.[65] Dunlap recorded that "Sir John did, with the earnings of his wife, purchase or hire a cottage at Germantown, and drove vegetables to market in a conveyance which would allow of his wife's going to town to attend her professional duties, and return when they were over the time."[66] Though she was married, and though she referred Dunlap to her husband for his signature on her contract, she herself apparently was a skillful negotiator. According to Dunlap, he was advised by another manager to be "very exact and very tight" in any negotiations with Mrs. Oldmixon, and "to specify the characters she must do."[67] Although Mrs. Oldmixon referred Dunlap to her husband for his signature on her contract, she negotiated on her own behalf, as noted in Dunlap's records of April 12, 1798:

> Mrs Oldmixon was waiting for me at Carr having been informed at my desire, by him, of my wish to engage her. We talked over the business: she said she had received offers from Whitlock for Charlestown [sic] very great — that her benefit was here insured to her & her salary 7 guineas per week — that she was willing to do the best old women in Comedy, the Comic Singers & occasionally a serious one, and the best chambermaids — she referred me to Sir John & I am to see him tomorrow.[68]

The actress and Sir John eventually separated; when recording the split, Dunlap cautioned, "what broke up this Germantown establishment, and separated the family is not for us to enquire into ... in 1816, Sir John was living obscurely at Sag Harbour, Long Island."[69]

Mrs. Oldmixon was considered a major draw; as indicated by her salary for 1798–99 season; Dunlap paid her $37 per week, the highest salary in the company, higher even than that of the major tragedian Thomas Cooper, who received $25 weekly.[70] Her agreement with Dunlap offered her a measure of control over her roles, as indicated by conditions of her contract:

> Mrs. Oldmixon engages for the ensuing season at NY: the first line of Opera, or such characters as she has given in a List of, the best of comedy Old Women, the best of the hambermaids ... a benefit free of the Charges on benefits. Stipulating

not to sing in choruses, unless in certain circumstances of the company she may herself choose so to do.[71]

This actress also displayed versatility in her roles; in addition to her operatic roles and comic portrayals, she also depicted several Gothic heroines including Clara in *A Sicilian Romance,* Barbara in *The Iron Chest,* and Fatima in *Bluebeard.* She also evidently was a hardworking member of the company; for on Dec. 7, 1798, Dunlap recorded, "Attend to business prospect of a good House. Evening Mrs. Oldmixon taken ill in her dressing room, goes home & is brought to bed of a daughter."[72]

Mrs. Oldmixon's reputation for excellence, especially in her singing, was known to Charlestonians, and her arrival in that city caused a flurry of excitement.[73] Her schooner from Philadelphia arrived in Charleston shortly before a benefit concert for the children of Mr. and Mrs. John Hodgkinson, who had both died: Hodgkinson of yellow fever, and his wife, Frances, of consumption. Mrs. Oldmixon's reputation was so well established that she was greeted "immediately upon her landing" by the benefit organizers who begged her to sing in the concert that very night. Mrs. Oldmixon's response to the gentlemen ensured that her reputation for brilliance on the stage would be enhanced by reports of her compassion and selflessness. The *City Gazette* related the account:

> She displayed the most anxious desire to contribute every thing in her power to serve the children; but at the same time expressed her doubts whether, exhausted as she was with fasting, sickness and fatigue, during a tempestuous passage of many days, she would have strength enough to meet the Charleston audience, for the first time, without manifest disadvantage. Her earnest wishes to serve the little ones, and to oblige the managers and the public however, soon over-ruled her apprehensions, and she generously consented, saying that she would rely upon the liberality of the company to make allowance for her situation. She accordingly sings this evening.[74]

Evidently, Charleston audiences knew of Mrs. Oldmixon's prowess, even though she had not previous performed in that city, and anticipation was high:

> When the time approached for the appearance of Mrs. Oldmixon, expectation was on tiptoe — the hum of conversation was hushed into silence, and all were anxiously solicitous to hear if report of her great vocal talent had outstripped her merits.

According the report in the *Courier* on November 1, Mrs. Oldmixon enjoyed a rousing success:

> She was several times interrupted by bursts of plaudits, which could not be restrained and when she had concluded, such a continuation of applause followed as testified an admiration and astonishment never before witnessed in that concertroom [*sic*].[75]

Like the other actresses, Mrs. Oldmixon enjoyed a long career on the stage; in her latter years she was known for her comic old women, which she played with "peculiar effect."[76] According to William Wood, she died at sixty-two years of age.[77]

These four actresses, though perhaps not as famous as some others of the period, enjoyed widespread renown during their careers. Moreover, they managed professional careers at a point in American history where most work for women was considered socially unacceptable, and work on the stage was perceived as particularly onerous. Yet, none of these women encountered public condemnation for their lives on the stage. Even those actresses who lived more unconventional lifestyles, without benefit of husbands, did not suffer slights in the press.

All of these actresses enjoyed success in the last decade of the 1790s and the first decade of the nineteenth century. Although coverage of the stage in this period was, admittedly less prolific than coverage later in the century, newspapers and periodicals still criticized performers for their conduct off-stage. But Mrs. Melmoth, Mrs. Whitlock, Mrs. Powell, and Mrs. Oldmixon did not incite any criticism or even speculation, although their lives were not necessarily conventional. In fact, they seemed to enjoy more acceptance in these early years of theatre in the United States than actresses would in later years of the nineteenth century. Several factors may have contributed to this popularity: first, proficient performers were not as plentiful in this period and so salaries and situations were comfortable; and such a situation, as Bernard noted, allowed actors to more easily maintain their good reputations, both on and off the stage. Second, each of these four actresses had performed in England before coming to the United States, and several had been very well-known. Their on-stage reputations, already established in London, may have aided their off-stage reputations in this country, whereas an unknown talent from the United States might have encountered less ready acceptance.

Though these earliest actresses of Gothic roles probably benefited from a limited amount of competition and from their reputations abroad, they also took care to present themselves to the public as virtuous women. Predictably, they all retained the title of "Mrs." even though two of the four did not live with a husband. Mrs. Melmoth, Mrs. Whitlock, Mrs. Hodgkinson and Mrs. Oldmixon traveled to other cities, increasing their base of supporters. In addition, each of these actresses was associated with particular Gothic heroines, and each continued to perform the role for years. Mrs. Melmoth was noted for her depiction of the stately matron in *The Carmelite*; Mrs. Whitlock and Mrs. Powell gave numerous performances as the young heroine in *The Castle Spectre*, and Mrs. Oldmixon was noted for her singing roles in the Gothic plays. Throughout their careers, these actresses depicted Gothic heroines, characters who were selfless, nurturing, humble, and unfailingly virtuous. Not surprisingly, the very words used to describe the characters were employed to describe the actresses themselves. Their public personas benefited from their close association with the virtuous Gothic heroines.

CHAPTER 7

"Dreadful Thunder" and "Lurid Lightning"
Spectacle in Gothic Plays

In *Fontainville Abbey*, written by William Dunlap in 1795, the heroine, Adelaide, gropes her way through the darkness. As she tentatively moves through the abbey, she vocalizes her fears about the dreadful dangers that surround her. In *The Wood Deamon*, written in 1808, Una, the heroine, also ventures into dangerous territory; however, the audience is able to view exactly what amazes and terrifies her: animated portraits of dead royalty; a sinking bed that takes her to the Necromantic Cavern; a giant bearing a clock; and Sangrida the terrible Wood Demon, who "appears in a car surrounded by dragons" and who "ascends in a shower of fire."[1]

Although both plays, *Fontainville Abbey* and *The Wood Daemon*, featured a young, innocent heroine who ventured into a dangerous space, the plays differed in their degree of visual reinforcement of the terror. In *Fontainville Abbey*, the terror was formless, enhanced by Adeline's narration as she stumbles through the ruins. In *The Wood Daemon*, however, the horrors were prominently displayed in the Necromantic Cavern. The difference in the degree of spectacle and special effects in the two plays emphasized the increasing importance of visual stimulation, a trend that would continue throughout the nineteenth century. Moreover, the scene painting and use of special effects exhibited in theatres in the United States during this period only emphasized a dependence on British models. In spite of America's efforts to

After which, (THIRD TIME) M. G. Lewis' Grand Romantic Drama, (taken from the German) in 3 acts, called the

WOOD DÆMON;

Or, the Clock has Struck.

The new Scenery and Decorations, designed and executed by Messrs. H. Warren, J. Jefferson, I. Darley, and Renaud.

Hardyknute,	Mr. H. WALLACK.	Leolyn, a Dumb Boy,	Miss H. HATHWELL.
Guelpho,	Mr. BURKE.		
Willikind,	Mr. JEFFERSON.	Una,	Mrs DARLEY.
Oswy,	Mr. JOHNSTON.	Clotilda,	Mrs. ANDERSON.
Rolf,	Mr. HATHWELL.	Ghost of Alexina,	Mrs. GREENE.
Ghost of Ruric,	Mr. PARKER.	Paulina,	Miss HATHWELL.
Spirit of Holstein,	Mr. GREENE.	Sangrida, Wood Demon, Mr. WHEATLY.

Act 1, Scene 1—The Stage filled with Brilliant Clouds.

The Guardian Spirit of Holstein

Discovered sitting on a Cloud in the centre, extending his Spear towards Una, who is sleeping on a bank—

The centre of the cloud beneath the Spirit opens,
Leolyn is seen kneeling and chained to a pillar—near him stands

SANGRIDA, WITH A BLOODY DAGGER:
The Ghost of Ruric and Alexina on each side—THE CLOUDS OPEN ABOVE, and shew on each side the Spirit—*four Children* in white and crowned with flowers, each pointing to a wound upon his heart.

ACT TWO, SCENE SECOND,

A Magnificent Banquet—Grand Pageant.

SUMMER---he is drawn by Reapers and surrounded by Green Wheat---which *Turns Yellow* as he passes.

AUTUMN---Drawn by Wood Nymphs, above her is an arbour of Unripe Fruit, which *Ripens* as she passes over the stage.

WINTER---Is drawn by *two white Bears*, and sits hovering o'er a *Flaming Altar*---*Icicles around his Car.*

SPRING---Represented by Leolyn, is drawn by Zephyrs---he lies asleep in a frozen grotto---he wakes and starts up---the *Birds* sing and flutter---the snow disappears, and the *boughs are covered with leaves and flowers*. The act ends with

Sangrida, the Wood Dæmon, ascending on a Dragon, fire issuing from his mouth.

Act 3, Scene 2, THE STATE BED CHAMBER:
Hardyknute sinks with Leolyn on the bed to the *Mystic Cavern*---Una secures the key and also sinks.

SCENE 3, A NECROMANTIC CAVERN,
Lamp hung in the centre---in the centre is an altar

Round which curl two Large Serpents—on one side an open Pedestal, on which lies the **BRAZEN FIGURE OF A GIANT,**

Who supports a clock on his left shoulder---on the other side is a rock with an entrance below—on the top lies *Leolyn* fastened to a Pillar by an enormous chain and padlock, near him his Guitar---Leolyn escapes with the assistance of Una---climbs on the shoulders of the *Giant*---Una hands him a wand, with which he changes the hands of the clock---It strikes ONE!

The Wood Dæmon stabs Hardyknute.

The ALTAR, &c. SINK and Leolyn acknowledged as the Heir of Holstein, &c.

Mr. Cooper will appear on Wednesday, as ZANGA, in the Revenge.

Due notice will be given of the next performances of *Damon & Pythias*, and *Virginius*.
In preparation, a new Tragedy, (*never acted here*) called EVADNE; or, the Statue.
Lord Byron's celebrated historical play of the TWO FOSCARI, will be produced shortly, with new Dresses, &c. Also, JULIUS CÆSAR, KING JOHN, &c. &c.
In rehearsal, a new Farce, (by a Gentleman of this city) called the PHRENOLOGIST.
Places in the Boxes may be taken of Mr. Johnson, at the Box Office, from 10 until 1; and on days of performance from 10 until 4 o'clock.
Checks not transferable. Proper officers are appointed who will rigidly enforce decorum.
The Doors will be opened at a quarter past 5, and the curtain will rise at a quarter past 6, precisely.
Box, One Dollar—Pit, *Seventy-five Cents*—Gallery, *Fifty Cents*—Children under 12 years, half price—
Thirty-five Seats in the Orchestra, for Sale nightly, at Box price.

Playbill for *The Wood Daemon*. Chestnut Street Theatre File, Historical Society of Pennsylvania, Philadelphia, PA.

separate itself from Britain in the Revolutionary War and the War of 1812, Americans still preferred British artistic efforts to those of their own countrymen. Not only did American audiences prefer British playwrights and traveling stars, they also preferred, or at least theatrical managers thought they preferred, British scene designers and painters.

In the early years of professional theatre in America, theatrical managers like Lewis Hallam arranged to have the actual scenery sent from England.[2] As American capabilities improved, theatrical managers instead sent for "models and designs of English productions ... usually pirated from productions at Drury Lane and Covent Garden."[3]

Designers too were imported between 1794 and 1830, at the time when Gothic plays peaked in popularity. When Wignell and Reinagle opened the Chestnut Street Theatre in Philadelphia in 1794, they not only purchased scenery, costumes, and furniture from a private theatre in England, but they also hired an English scene painter, Charles Milbourne, who had assisted at Covent Garden. After Milbourne departed, Reinagle hired Joseph Holland, another English scene painter, who had apprenticed at the Haymarket. Similarly, the Charleston Theatre hired Audin, a "talented French and English trained artist."[4] The practice of using English and English-style scenery in Philadelphia outlasted Reinagel: as late as 1820, when the Chestnut Theatre burned, William Wood recorded that "the most irretrievable part" was the "splendid English scenery, presented to Wignell in 1793."[5] American dependence on English theatrical scenery appears to have been substantial and theatrical audiences in America probably saw much the same spectacle as seen by audiences in England.

Discerning the effectiveness of spectacle presented in Gothic plays is difficult because of the ephemeral nature of theatre; little physical evidence of productions exists for American stages. We can, however, grasp details of physical productions from a combination of evidence, all of which presents problems. For example, text and stage directions can suggest what the playwright (or first production) intended; however, often we cannot tie a text to a specific production, and we cannot know if the suggestions in the script were realized on stage. Contemporary theatrical reviews are another source; they provide accounts of scenery and effects; unfortunately, such reviews were not written routinely for American productions between 1794 and 1830. Prompt books, an excellent source, provide evidence of how spectacle was produced, but again, for American productions of this time, prompt books are scarce. Another contemporary source, plates for Toy Theatres, can provide insight into scenery and special effects of theatrical productions because they were famous for their resemblance to actual productions; however, these too have a drawback in that they imitated plays performed on the British stage. Each type of contemporary evidence, texts, reviews, prompt books, and plates for toy theatres, is far more available for British productions. However, in that American scenery and special effects derived from British plays, we may be able to apply our evidence of designs and designers and apply evidence of spectacle on the British stage to that of the American.

Most of the early Gothic plays (1794 to 1800) utilized scenic elements associated with the word "Gothic," as popularly defined in the late eighteenth century, that is "medieval," or "antique." Of the nine plays first performed in this period, five unfolded in castles; two occurred in abbeys and two in halls.[6]

The popularity of these settings supports the suggestion that these two building types, the "mediaeval [sic] castle and the conventional church," were "lasting models of 'pure Gothic' architecture."[7] Such scenic buildings fostered the gothic atmosphere described in gothic literature, for the castles and abbeys of Gothic drama and novels were not splendid and imposing buildings but rather dark, oppressive, often decaying places.[8] In Gothic fiction, these oppressive places provided a "specialized form of 'inner space,'" that often entrapped the young heroine. These spaces, then, proved especially dangerous to young females in Gothic fiction; if they could avoid the "treacherous cave — tunnel, basement, secret room —" they would "usually be safe."[9] Angela in *The Castle Spectre* visited the dungeon; Adelaide in *Fountainville Forest* discovered the secret chamber.

The actual representation of the castle or abbey on the early American stage was not elaborate. Most of the scenes transpired indoors, within the castles or chapels.[10] Indeed, one early play's spectacle was so modest that a contemporary reviewer noted that "the tragedy of *The Carmelite* is one of those productions which depend for their interest entirely on the merit of the performers."[11] Similarly, stage directions in *The Count of Narbonne* noted that each act should take place in either a "Hall" or a "chamber." Aside from these brief descriptions, no other scenic instructions were given. Other plays of the period, although sometimes offering more specific scenic description in the stage directions, still used mostly simple interior scenes.

Setting most scenes inside a castle or chapel could have enhanced an atmosphere of gloom and oppressiveness in that the space could appear old, dark, and confining. Interior scenes were also interchangeable, easily reconfigured to represent various chambers, thus allowing for quick scene changes. Finally, these interchangeable settings were relatively inexpensive, in that they were almost certainly drawn from stock.

Few of the interior scenes of this period required the building of new scenery. In a letter written to the trustees of the rebuilt Federal Street Theatre in 1798, John Hodgkinson, who planned to manage the theatre, requested them to obtain the following scenic elements that he deemed "necessary for the performance of all old stock plays":

Five chambers varied	Two sets of wings one plain & one furnish'd will answer for the whole.
One Library	
One Wood	Wood wings for the whole
One Grove	
One Garden	
One Cut Wood	
One Village	
One Camp Flat	
Two Streets	Wings wanted
One Palace	Same wings for all
Two Palace apartments	
One Castle with gates	No wings wanted
One Kitchen	Same wings for both
One Rustic chamber	
One interior of Cave	Wings wanted compleat [sic]
One Prison and Arch	
Horizon, waves, etc.[12]	

If Hodgkinson's list represented the stock possessed by the theatres in the major cities, then these theatres had the necessary scenic elements to perform Gothic plays of this decade: general interior scenes probably were adapted from generic chamber settings, as were specific settings, such as the library and the "rustic chamber" specified in *The Iron Chest*, *Raymond and Agnes*, and *The Forest of Rosenwald*.

Available stock scenery also sufficed to mount most exterior scenes in plays of this period. For example, Hodgkinson's list noted a wood and a grove as standard stock pieces; these appeared in *Fontainville Forest*, *Fontainville Abbey*, *The Man of Fortitude*, *The Mysteries of the Castle*, *The Sicilian Romance*, *The Castle Spectre*, *The Forest of Rosenwald*, and *Raymond and Agnes*. A cut wood from stock as well as a street setting were required for *Raymond and Agnes* and *The Forest of Rosenwald*. A castle with gates would have proved most useful, as it was called for in *Raymond and Agnes*, *The Forest of Rosenwald*, *The Man of Fortitude*, and *The Wood Daemon*. A cave or cavern appeared in *Raymond and Agnes*, *The Forest of Rosenwald*, and *The Man of Fortitude*. Finally, a horizon and waves were required for *The Carmelite*. These set pieces, all listed by Hodgkinson, therefore, sufficed to mount most scenes in most Gothic plays of this period.

A few unique settings were not included in Hodgkinson's letter. A convent or abbey setting was required for scenes in *The Carmelite*, *The Sicilian Romance*, *Fontainville Abbey* and *Fontainville Forest*, and seven of the nine plays required a hall, yet Hodgkinson's list did not specify such settings.[13] Theatres probably adapted stock pieces, perhaps chamber settings, to represent these locales.

These early dramas almost certainly used common painted wings and drops rather than profiled and complex layers of ground rows and wings. For example, *The Mysteries of the Castle* by Andrews called for two drops, one with a "View of the City of Messina, the Bay, Mount Aetna, etc., etc." and another "the ramparts of Messina, with a view of the quay and harbour, where a vessel is seen at anchor, with sails bent— on one side near the front, the gates of the city with a centry [sic] box."[14] *The Castle Spectre* required "a view of the river country, with a fisherman's hut" and "a view of Conway Castle by Moon-light."[15] *The Carmelite* required "A rocky shore, with a view of the sea at break of day."[16] Downstage drops generally appeared at the top of an act, probably to allow scenery for upcoming scenes to be arranged behind them.[17] Plays first performed between 1794 and 1800 did not use many special effects. Storms were popular: *Fontainville Forest*, *The Man of Fortitude*, and *The Mysteries of the Castle* by Andrews all called for violent thunder and lightning, effects well known in theatre since at least the Renaissance. Only two of the plays of this decade featured supernatural events, and these required the skill of actors, rather than machinists.[18] For example, in *The Castle Spectre*, a specter suddenly appeared in "white and flowing garments spotted with blood," upon whose bosom "a large wound" was visible, and in *Fontainville Forest*, the phantom of the murdered Marquis walked across the stage. One effect in *The Mysteries of the Castle* by Andrews may have required the help of backstage personnel: a boat with lighted lanterns on board was to approach the shore.[19]

Lighting effects were necessarily simple in this period because candles were still used for illumination (gaslight would not be installed in American theatres for another decade). But by 1790, some modest control of the intensity of the lighting was possible: at the very least, theatres in England and the United States, could simply have turned the lamps in the wings away from the stage or used a footlight trap to lower the footlights to decrease the illumination. Another type of lamp, obtained by Garrick for Drury Lane in the 1760s, possessed a metal shield that could be drawn over the lamp, "affording a gradual diminution of illumination."[20] In addition, established theatres in the United States also used the Argand or patent lamp, first employed at Drury Lane in 1785; Argand lamps produced a "more brilliant and less flickering light" for the scene.[21]

Generally, the plays indicated time of day by the presence or absence of candles or lanterns. For example, in *Fontainville Forest*, stage directions call for a character to enter a chamber with a "lamp"; in *The Castle Spectre*, one holds a "torch."[22] Lanterns, or "lanthorns," were used to indicate night.[23] In several plays, stage directions specified that the lanthorn was to be dark.[24] For example, in *The Mysteries of the Castle*, stage directions noted that "a person with a dark lanthorn, muffled up, looks out a turret window, and then retires." Later stage directions called for Carlos to enter, "with a dark lanthorn."[25] Similarly, the villain in *The Sicilian Romance* carried a "dark lanthorn."[26]

Two plays can illustrate well the scenic requirements of this period. The British play *Fontainville Forest*, and the American play *Fontainville Abbey*, were both taken from Anne Radcliffe's novel, *The Romance of the Forest*.[27] Both versions told of Lamotte (or La Motte), his wife, and their new ward, Adeline, who took refuge in a ruined abbey owned by the wicked Marquis of Montault. Adeline discovered a secret passage leading to a secret chamber wherein she found a dagger, a parchment, and a skeleton. The parchment revealed that the skeleton was that of the rightful Marquis, Adeline's real father.

Both *Fontainville Forest* and *Fontainville Abbey*, as other plays of the period, used mostly interior scenes, occurring in an "apartment in the abbey," a "dark and antique apartment," or a "large hall of a Gothic abbey." The only exterior scene transpired in a forest.

The British play provided a single special effect: a phantom, the specter of a murdered man who walked across the stage. For this effect, the British production used an actor skilled in pantomime who walked behind a gauze curtain.[28] Although warned that audiences would not accept a phantom on the stage and that such a character would evoke laughter, not fear, the playwright insisted that the specter remain. In the epilogue, he even punned that he would "die rather than give up the ghost."[29] His perseverance paid off; the phantom proved popular with audiences.

Although William Dunlap, author of the American version, would have known of the successful phantom in the British version, he declined to include one in his own play. Instead, in the American version, as in the novel, Adeline saw no specter, and all seemingly mysterious events were explained away. Because Dunlap avoided writing in any supernatural elements in his play, he did not have to worry about providing such effects on stage. *Fontainville Abbey* did offer one lighting effect not noted in the British play; in one exterior scene, stage directions required "daylight breaking by degrees."[30] This effect, occurring as it did before installation of gaslight, probably was achieved by turning the candle fixtures towards the stage.

During the Gothic's second decade, 1800 and 1810, the popularity of castles and abbeys continued, but the complexity of both interior scenes and special effects increased. Of the representative plays, seven featured a castle as part of the set; one used an upper-class home, and one a cottage.[31] Six of the plays used the term "Gothic" in describing the setting.

As in the previous period, many of the interior scenes relied on simple sets easily assembled from stock. Barnard Hewitt confirmed this dependency on stock scenery in his description of the 1809 season at the Park Theatre in New York, noting that the plays of this season "required little more than the standard interior and exterior wings and shutters drawn from the accumulated stock."[32] Many of the exterior scenes still used painted drops for distant views. For example, the opening scene of *Foscari* called for representation of a "scene in Venice," and instructed readers to "see Dr. Moore's View of Society in Italy — Vol. 1, Letter 14."[33]

Special effects in this decade reflected a trend toward supernaturalism; five of the plays introduced such effects, including specters that ascended into the air.[34] For example, the ghost of an old man ascended into heaven in *Adelmorn*; the Bleeding Nun rose to heaven in *The Forest of Rosenwald*; and Sangrida ascended into the air in a car pulled by dragons in *The Wood Daemon*. Processions too were becoming popular in America; these were borrowed from Kemble, who had employed them so frequently at Drury Lane for "spectacular impact" that he was criticized in print.³⁵ Processions were featured in *The Wood Daemon* and in *Bluebeard*.

Despite the fact that scenery in most plays still was primarily interior, the scenery in a few Gothic plays between 1800 and 1810 was lavish—and such scenery was emphasized in playbills. Two American plays renowned for their spectacular scenery and special effects were *Bluebeard*, adapted by William Dunlap from the original by George Colman the Younger, and *The Wood Daemon*, adapted by John Turnbull from a prospectus by Matthew Gregory Lewis, entitled, *One O'Clock; or The Knight and the Wood Daemon*. Both American plays are very similar to the British originals in plot, characters, scenery, and special effects, and both proved extremely popular on American stages.

In fact, *Bluebeard*'s continued popularity made it a valuable reper-

Toy Theatre scene for appearance of Sangrida in a British production of Lewis's *One O'Clock; or The Knight and the Wood Daemon*. Collection of Allan S. Jackson, Vestal, New York.

tory piece. Dunlap's *Bluebeard*, "being got up with great care and expense, was successful and yielded a support to the theatre for time."[36] A critic from *The Philadelphia Magazine*, who described the play as a "melo dramatic romance: its very name is almost enough to condemn it," nevertheless acknowledged it as "one of the endurables of the class."[37] Odell confirmed that the play was revived in New York after a five year absence, and that it "tided the company through the storms of early January."[38]

The popularity of *Bluebeard* was due in large part to its spectacle, particularly the transformation of the Blue Chamber.[39] In Colman's original, stage directions specified that when the heroine puts the key in the lock,

> the door instantly sinks, with a tremendous crash and the Blue Chamber appears, streaked with streams of blood ... the interior apartment ... exhibits various tombs in a sepulchral building; in the midst of which, ghastly and supernatural forms are seen; some in motion, some fixed.—In the centre is a large skeleton, seated on a tomb, with a dart in his hand, and over his head in characters of blood, is written, "the Punishment of Curiosity."[40]

Dunlap's stage directions did not provide such detailed scenic description; instead they merely noted, "the door ... sinks, and discovers the interior apartment ... the inscription over the skeleton's head is now, 'The Punishment of Curiosity' ... the blue chamber undergoes the same change."[41] However, despite Dunlap's cryptic instructions, the effects were probably very similar to those of Colman's version, as suggested by a Harvard playbill of the seventh performance on March 24, 1802, which described the transformation in the production as follows:

> on Fatima's putting the Diamond Key to the Door, the Pictures all change to scenes of horror, the Walls of the Apartment are stained with Blood, and the Door sinking discovers the internal of the Sepulchre, with its ghastly inhabitants; a moment after, all resumes its former appearance.[42]

The effects promised in the playbill indicate that sloats and cassettes were used in the American stage of this period. Odell observed that the advertisement promised "new Scenery, Machinery, Decorations, Dresses, etc.," and that the scenery as described "probably vouched for something like actuality in the Park production."[43] That the scenery in the American production of *Bluebeard* impressed audiences was certain, for the critic from *The Philadelphia Magazine*, despite his evident distaste for the play, conceded that "the scenery of the piece, as exhibited this evening, surpassed any we have ever seen in other theatres."[44]

Special effects in *Bluebeard* seemed particularly innovative, especially the manipulation of mechanical figures in the procession. Odell observed that *Bluebeard* used artificial figures in the procession to give the effect of people marching in the distance; the figures corresponded in size to the "trees which crown the summits of the mountains." Then, the music became louder and the first part of the procession reappeared on the side of the stage opposite to that where it first was seen, closer to the audience, and appeared to be winding down a hill. At this point the figures were no longer artificial; instead they were represented by children, dressed as grown persons in Turkish costume and passing in the same order as seen previously. When the march reached the foot of the mountain, the point closest to the audience, the figures were represented by adults, who wore the same costumes and appeared in the same order as in previous passes.

The animals evidently were artificial also, and perhaps not very sturdy, for Odell noted that in an evening performance, one of the camels broke its neck. Although Odell referred to the presentation of the procession as a "childish device," the contemporary reviewer called it "the most striking scene we have ever seen." That the procession was challenging for the machinists was suggested by the same reviewer who noted that it "suffered much from the want of dexterity and readiness in the scene shifters, and those who had the arrangement of the machinery."[45]

Turnbull's *The Wood Daemon* differed only slightly from Lewis' version in characterization and was nearly identical to the British play in scenery and special effects.[46] Like most Gothic plays between 1800 and 1810, *The Wood Daemon* used a castle as the main setting; however, this castle differed from those of earlier settings in that it had to be practicable; not only did actors stand in front of the gates, they also entered the castle itself. Odell noted that newspaper advertisements of the time "worked up the curiosity of playgoers who hear with their eyes" and that they stressed the "new scenery, machinery, decorations, and dresses" in the production.[47] *The Wood Daemon* was "one of the most blood-curdling of musical mysteries and monstrosities," according to Odell, who added, "what pother and shifting of scenery!"[48]

Like *Bluebeard*, *The Wood Daemon* differed from earlier plays in its emphasis on and advertisement of spectacular scenery and special effects. For example, the stage directions described the opening scene as a vision that appeared to Una the heroine, which featured "bright clouds, a part of which disperse, and discovers Auriol standing on the highest part …

the clouds open and discover a child chained to a pillar, and the Wood Daemon in her magic robes holding a dagger as in the act of stabbing the child."⁴⁹ A Philadelphia newspaper advertisement described the same scene as,

> The Stage filled with Brilliant Clouds — The Guardian Spirit of Holstein discovered sitting on a Cloud in the centre, extending his Spear towards Una, who is sleeping on a bank — the centre of the cloud beneath the Spirit opens, Leolyn is seen kneeling and chained to a pillar — near him stands SANGRIDA, WITH A BLOODY DAGGER.⁵⁰

That these accounts were similar suggests that the production provided the special effects dictated by the stage directions.

A New York newspaper, describing a procession in *The Wood Daemon* that represented the four seasons, echoed the description provided in the stage directions. Both called for the first season to be Summer, represented "by a Girl seated on a Car, overshadowed by an Orange Tree," followed by Autumn, "represented by a Girl decorated with ripe Wheat and Vine Leaves, in a Car covered with a Vine, drawn by vine dressers ... preceded and followed by infant Bacchus's [sic] bearing bunches of Grapes." Winter came next, represented by "a boy dressed in furs, in a car covered with Ice ... drawn by White Bears." Finally, Spring appeared, "represented by a boy sleeping amid flowers on a car drawn by Cupids."⁵¹

Another scene in the play featured Sangrida the Wood Daemon appearing to demand her sacrifice. Stage directions in the British version specified "thunder again — the great window bursts open, and Sangrida appears in a car surrounded by dragons ... and ascends in a shower of fire"⁵² Stage directions in the American version had Sangrida appear "above the eminence of the back scene, seated in a car, drawn by Dragons — dreadful thunder and lightning ... and the Demon mounts into the air."⁵³

The most spectacular scene in *The Wood Deamon* is set in the "Mystic Cavern" (in the American play) or "Necromantic Cavern" (in the British play). Stage directions described the scene as including a sacrificial altar and a giant bearing a clock.⁵⁴

Other Gothic dramas of the decade, although less supernatural, were nonetheless visually spectacular. Storms remained popular, with thunder and lightning in four of the nine plays; however new natural effects, such as fires, collapsing walls, and raging rivers, appeared in several plays. Such elaborate scenic elements and special effects certainly would have challenged the ingenuity of machinists and the stamina of backstage personnel far more than effects required for earlier Gothic plays.[55]

During this decade in America, too, came from England that effect that soon became standard: the use of music to heighten the emotion or mood in the scene. *A Tale of Mystery*, adapted by Thomas Holcroft from a play by Pixerecourt, used music in this way and identified itself as a "melodrama" on its title page; this was the first play so designated in England. Stage directions in the play provided detailed instructions for how the music was to enhance the emotional impact; at various times the music was to be "expressive of horror," "confused," "loud and discordant," or "expressive of terror."[56] Other Gothic plays that followed this play incorporated music as a part of the action.

Although American dependence upon British scenic innovations remained strong, certain differences in the American treatment of spectacle became clearer during this decade of 1800–1810.[57] Despite the abundance of supernatural effects in several British plays and American adaptations of these plays, American playwrights who wrote original works continued to avoid supernatural elements. Just as Dunlap (and Hodgkinson) hastened to explain away mysterious events, so too did playwrights of this period provide rational explanations for any apparently supernatural events.

One original American play of this decade was White's *The Mysteries of the Castle*, which, unlike Dunlap's *Bluebeard* and Turnbull's *The Wood Daemon*, had no British counterpart; the plot of White's play bore no resemblance to the British play of the same name. White's play incorporated many special effects common to this period — those depicting natural forces (water, fire, etc.) instead of supernatural ones — and so serves as a useful illustration.

The plot centered around two young heroes, Persiles and Lothario, who defended an old Hermit when he was attacked by the villain. The hermit told them of strange occurrences at the nearby decrepit castle. When the three investigated the castle, they discovered two female prisoners, Eleanora and Cornelia, mother and daughter. When Cornelia saw the hermit, she recognized him as her long-lost husband, believed dead. The villain was foiled by an explosion that buried him under the castle.

The spectacle in the play included a "ruined Gothic castle," with a "ruined battlement projecting from a turret," upon which a "mysterious figure" walked, as well as "a Hut, situated in the recesses of a

Forest."⁵⁸ Act II alone presented four distinct settings, including "an apartment in the Palace of Count Reynaldo," "a forest," "a Hermitage, shadowed by trees," and "the interior of a cave."⁵⁹ The final act incorporated "a subterraneous chamber of the Castle" and a dungeon.⁶⁰

Special effects in *The Mysteries of the Castle* included "a violent storm of thunder and lightning," and an off-stage explosion that caused part of the wall to tumble.⁶¹ In addition, the play flirted with the supernatural: Persiles saw a specter and followed it. The specter struck "three times with his lance and they both suddenly [sank] into the floor with a dreadful crash."⁶² The apparent specter, in keeping with American tendencies to eliminate supernatural effects, later proved to be a villain in disguise.

Plays of the third decade, 1811–1820, still used castles (six of the seven plays featured them), and four used abbeys or convents, but several also featured cottages. The plays also seemed to favor exterior over interior settings. For example, five of the seven included scenes in a forest; three featured mountains, and three caverns. *Raymond and Agnes* employed all of these settings, both interior and exterior.⁶³

Outdoor scenes became more elaborate between 1811 and 1820. Many scenes still depended on drops as indicated by the description of the detailed set for the fourth act of *Marmion*:

> the spacious frith [*sic*] of Forth, which, with its bays, is descried [*sic*] in the distance; on its nearest shore to the left, stands the city and castle, their spires and turrets gilt by the sun; behind the city arise lofty hills. The view is closed by mountains, behind the Forth.⁶⁴

Yet several Gothic plays of the period required practicable scenery in addition to drops; in *Bertram*, the tower not only appeared as scenery, but also later held the heroine as she languished in her guilt; the cottage in *The Woodman's Hut* not only served as backdrop but also withstood characters entering and exiting through doors and windows. In *The Mountain Torrent*, the swollen river not only offered breathtaking scenery, but it also posed a threat to characters attempting to cross it, thus increasing the suspense.

Special effects in the period were as varied as the sets. The most popular special effect was still the storm; five of the plays utilized thunder, lighting, wind, or all three. Plays used water more; four plays featured ships that were seen to arrive, depart, or sink. In addition, *Marmion* featured a stream from which the heroine obtained water; *The Bride of the Isles* included a scene in which a character was thrown into the sea. Marches or processions continued to be popular, occurring in four of the seven plays. In the tradition of *A Tale of Mystery, Marmion, Raymond and Agnes*, and *The Bride of the Isles* employed music to heighten emotion. Three of the plays featured collapsing sets; in *The Mountain Torrent*, the bower collapsed; in *The Woodman's Hut*, the bridge and several trees fell, and in *Raymond and Agnes* the back wall of the set collapsed. Fire raged in *The Woodman's Hut*; in the final act both a bridge and a forest blazed, cutting off all escape for the villains. Specters appeared in two plays, *Raymond and Agnes* and *The Vampire; or The Bride of the Isles*; in both plays the specters both ascended into the air and disappeared into the ground. Two of the plays used transparencies to heighten a supernatural effect.

The production of *The Vampire; or The Bride of the Isles* in England offers a glimpse of how supernatural effects were realized on the stage.[65] The effect of moonlight was achieved through the use of patent lamps: "by the side of a tree at the back of which are placed four or five patent lamps with green glasses which, in the first instance, are concealed by a slide — when the Vampire is stretched on the bank this slide is raised gradually by lines worked from the wings, which gives the effect of the moon shining on his face, which is pale and ghastly." The scenes with the sea apparently used rollers: "Caverns and large rocks — platforms behind — shaking sea down to front of stage. Rolling waters to back dark horizon."[66]

Although some supernatural effects occurred in *The Vampire*, most of the plays of this period substituted effects based on natural elements on water, wind, and fire. *The Mountain Torrent*, written by American S.B.H. Judah, is representative.[67] Like the other plays in this decade, *The Mountain Torrent* offered lavish scenery and special effects, and more importantly, depicted natural, outdoor settings in preference to the earlier atmosphere of gloom and decay:

> Scene outside of Marco's cottage; on the left, towards the front, is the outside of the house; on the right, a wooden bridge, old and broken, crosses a rivulet, which flows from the rocks that overhang the stage; at the bottom of the stage, a low wall, hedge, etc., beyond, in the distance, rocks, forest, etc.[68]

As was common by this decade, the bridge was practicable; actors crossed over it.[69] Later in the play, the special effects grew more spectacular as a violent storm and rushing water were combined with the rugged landscape:

Marco's cottage perceptible to the right; at a distance, nearly shaded by trees and overhanging rocks; masses of crags are strewn around; to the right and left a hedge of wood, old and shattered, extending nearly half way and supported by two crags projecting over the precipice makes the crossing; a fall of water rushes over some rocks beneath the bridge, and joins a rapid stream, which is also supplied from several smaller falls, from different parts of the rocks; the whole crowned on the summit by a thick forest, from the top of the first rock to the left is a winding foot-path conducting to the bridge; the scene is nearly dark, and the glare of the lightning at intervals discovers the masses of rocks and gleams on the waters, which are swollen and violently agitated by the wind; the storm becomes more terrible every moment.[70]

At the height of the storm, Trevasi and an assassin struggled on the bridge; the hero entered, stabbed the assassin in the back, and threw him over the bridge. Stage directions dictated, "the lightning glares on the water as he falls in the stream."[71]

Odell provided two pages of description of the scenery and special effects in *The Mountain Torrent*. Although he despised this play, commenting that the language was "nearly the funniest I have ever seen," Odell acknowledged that the spectacle was effective, observing, "however these scenic marvels might appear to our eyes, I have no doubt they were very splendid to the eyes of 1820."[72]

The decade of 1821 to 1830 featured six plays and continued the trend away from castles and abbeys and toward forests and cottages.[73] In this period, only two of the plays featured castles as part of the set and only two abbeys or convents. Four of the plays included cottages in their sets, and two plays each depicted caverns, forests, mountains, or cliffs. The play with the most varied settings was *Warlock of the Glen*, which required an abbey, a chapel, a cottage, a cavern, cliffs, and the sea. Painted drops of distant views of the countryside appeared in all but one of the plays.

Special effects in this period seemed particularly eclectic, representing both supernatural and non-supernatural events. Forces of nature included battering storms (in five of the six plays) and raging waters (Adela fell into the sea in *Warlock of the Glen*, and Agatha into a rivulet in *Presumption*). Explosions were very popular; Rosenfeld noted that the invention of "red fire" encouraged "scenes of conflagration and explosion" and observed that, as a result, melodramas often ended with such scenes.[74] Fire raged in *Presumption*, when the Demon set a cottage burning. Other disasters included collapsing ruins in *Melmoth*, and an avalanche in *Presumption*. Supernatural effects continued as well, with specters in both *One O'Clock* and *Melmoth* and self-lighting candles in *One O'Clock*. Although *Melmoth* made the most use of specific ghastly effects, other plays of the decade, such as *One O'Clock* and *Presumption; or The Fate of Frankenstein,* included them. Such scenes of horror would have been aided by "lurid lighting," which could be effected by "green mediums or green fire burnt at the sides and back of the stage behind standards to give a supernatural tint to spectres as well as by silk shades before the sides and footlights of the stage."[75]

Supernatural effects in this decade differed slightly from earlier ones in that they were more overt, more visually horrifying. Supernatural entities were not ethereal, or good, for that matter; instead, the Demon in *Presumption* and Melmoth in *Melmoth* were forces of evil, and they were very substantial indeed, often grappling with other characters. Processions continued to be popular; four of the six plays included them, and both *The Rose of Arragon* and *One O'Clock* presented two each. Music was used regularly as a means to heighten emotion; in fact, all but one play, *Superstition,* employed music within the scenes.

One play that included many of these diverse special effects was *Melmoth*, Benjamin West's adaptation of the novel by Charles Maturin. This play told the story of the poverty-stricken Walburg and his family in the midst of the Inquisition in Spain. Walburg expected a generous inheritance but was tricked out of it by Melmoth, a demon, who forged a will that left the money to the Church. By reducing the family to direst poverty, Melmoth hoped to force the daughter Immalee to marry him. If he could gain her consent, he would be able to stay on earth; if he could not win her, he would be eternally damned.

Several scenes in *Melmoth* seemed like those in earlier Gothic melodramas with interior scenes set in frightening or oppressive places. For example, the second scene in Act 2 was set in "abbey ruins."[76] The third scene in Act 3 called for a "dungeon of the Inquisition. A lamp suspended from the roof—a grated door on one side—at the back, a small secret panel door."[77]

Exterior scenes in *Melmoth*, instead of displaying bridges, forests, waterfalls, or mountains, used backgrounds of palaces or abbeys. For example, the fourth scene in Act I called for "a view of the Hall of Justice—at the back a large entrance, steps leading to it; on one side the Palace of Guzman—on the other the Monastery—large handsome gates leading to it."[78] The final scene occurred in the "monastic ruins"; the scenic description noted, "Extensive and romantic view of Monastic Ruins by night — an Open space at back — thunder, lightning, wind, etc. — the lightning reveals Tombs and Monuments falling to decay — Tomb and Altar, on one side — on the other, grand Entrance to Monastery."[79]

Special effects in *Melmoth* combined natural and supernatural elements. Thunder, lighting, and wind raged in the final scene; in addition, *Melmoth* employed more overt horrific effects than had been used in earlier plays. Stage directions called for a thunderbolt to descend and strike Melmoth, who then staggered and fell near a ruin, which instantly toppled and crushed him.[80] A particularly ghastly effect occurred when Melmoth was about to marry Immalee in the ruins. Stage directions instructed,

> a large dark cloud descends, gradually opens and exhibits a large dial, with a hand nearly upon the hour of "TWELVE." Lightning, etc. play upon its face.... Melmoth places [Immalee] before the Altar. ... he stamps his foot — the tomb bursts open — the Monk appears, surrounded by Fire — a deep wound is upon his forehead, and his face is pale and ghastly.[81]

Melmoth, then, incorporated the atmosphere of earlier Gothic plays with some more elaborate special effects of later ones. Spectacle in Gothic plays, then, changed in the period between the 1790s and the 1830s, becoming more complex both in scenic design and in the type and number of special effects.

Gothic plays appearing between 1790 and 1800, such as *The Carmelite, The Count of Narbonne*, or *The Sicilian Romance*, used primarily interior scenes set in decrepit castles or abbeys; these settings closely aligned the dramas with Gothic fiction, in which an atmosphere of gloom, mystery, and terror prevailed. Special effects of this period were few, and, as in the fiction of Radcliffe, mysterious events were given rational explanations.

Supernatural effects peaked between 1800 and 1810 with plays adapted from those of Matthew Gregory Lewis.[82] All of these American adaptations included supernatural effects such as ethereal specters, malignant demons, miscellaneous fiends, and martyred humans rising into the air. In this decade, interior scenes became more lavish and began to be advertised at length in newspapers. Plays of the next decade increased the use of outdoor settings, shifting away from interior sets with a gloomy and foreboding atmosphere, to such exterior sets as cottages, forests, seashores, and caverns. These plays eschewed the supernatural in favor of natural catastrophes such as collapsing walls, surging waters, or blazing fires. Indeed, it was during this decade that special effects in Gothic plays moved closer to those of melodramas of the time.

Gothic plays of the final decade, 1820–1830, continued use of many outdoor scenes and natural catastrophes; however, several plays also employed supernatural effects that were more visually horrifying than those of previous Gothic dramas. Audiences viewed the horrors rather than imagining them or hearing them described. Perhaps the publication of *Frankenstein* in 1818 stimulated the further development of the horror scene, one which showed not only apparitions, but also "monsters, skeletons, charnel houses, and other symbols of death and decay."[83]

When American patrons attended Gothic plays between 1794 and 1830, they saw more than an enactment of a story; they also saw spectacular scenery and special effects. Theatrical historians note that plays of this period began to emphasize spectacle more and more. This trend in which playhouses became "theatres for spectators rather than playhouses for hearers" was not perceived as a positive one by many contemporary critics, who complained that the drama was dying because of the public's appetite for spectacle.[84]

As populations boomed in American cities, established theatres faced competition for audiences; new theatres sprang up, as did circuses or amphitheatres, offering novel entertainments.[85] Critics complained that theatres were "prostituted to puppet-shows, rope dancing, pantomimes, and exhibitions of elephants, etc.," in addition to occasional theatrical productions.[86] Established theatres, then, had to fight not only rival theatrical productions but also novel forms of entertainment. These phenomena suggest that audience members increasingly preferred visual entertainment and that established theatres had to emphasize the visual effectiveness of their plays and increase special effects and novelties, or perish.

What then, can we conclude from the presentation of Gothic plays in American theatres between 1790 and 1830? First, changes in overall theatrical practice of American theatres paralleled those of British theatres, probably because they continued to use British designs and designers. For example, the number of scenes and scene changes in American productions of Gothic plays increased significantly between 1794 and 1830, as did those of British productions. Moreover, examination of these scenes reveal a definite shift away from indoor settings to outdoor settings. Another important shift was the change from an almost exclusive use of stock scenery and generic settings to more specific settings created for one particular play. At the same time, American scenery in earlier Gothic plays, such as *The Carmelite* and *The Count of Narbonne*, relied heavily on painted drops, but in later plays, such as *The Woodman's Hut* and *The Mountain Torrent*, it used practicable scenery, such as cottages and bridges.

This change corresponded to scenic changes in Europe, in which "built-up scenery, practicable, free-standing pieces, and ground rows" replaced mere painted scenery, an innovation that Rosenfeld deemed the "most interesting scenic advance of the century." This advance offered yet another benefit, for such set pieces were not only practicable, they also provided a "more asymmetrical variety" to the stage picture and "broke up the formal classical perspectives based on a central vanishing point."[87] Thus the changes in scenery between 1794 and 1830 not only moved the spectacle away from a Neoclassic vision in the types of stage picture presented (ruins instead of formal gardens, for example) but also provided a more Romantic view through the very design (asymmetrical view instead of rigidly symmetrical ones with central vanishing point).[88]

In lighting innovations, too, American theatres followed the lead of theatres in England. Early Gothic plays exhibited little variation in lighting. Later plays, however, frequently showed changes in time of day; many used the effect of moonlight, and some even employed colored lighting to intensify mood. In England such innovations in lighting were credited to DeLoutherbourg and his experiments in his Eidophusikon. For example, as early as 1774, he had created the effect of moonlight by an "Argand lamp in a tin box which shone through an inch aperture"; which, "placed at various distances from the back of scene gave a brilliant or subdued splendour." In his experiments with color, DeLoutherbourg added a "batten of lamps above the proscenium with slips of stained glass before the lamps which threw varying colours on the scenery and tinted the scenes from above and in front."[89] Whether American theatres directly benefited from DeLoutherberg's experiments is uncertain; however, they certainly began using color to enhance special effects.

As in British theatres, American theatres by 1820 had begun to emphasize scenery over actors. As scenery became more important and more practicable, plays became less actor-centered; actors had to work with the scenery, climbing rocks, entering castle doors, crossing bridges, etc., instead of simply standing in front of painted drops. Scenery was now environment rather than merely background, and actors became part of the spectacle. Indeed, processions, in which actors paraded across the stage, were praised for their visual impact and were featured in many Gothic plays of this period in both England and America.[90]

Another American change that paralleled practice in Britain, was the new accessibility of spectacle to the working class. These new patrons flocked to theatres between 1794 and 1830, and new theatres rose up that catered to them. Moreover, older, existing theatres attempted to accommodate this new audience as well. Although much of the spectacular scenery and effects was not new — rising and descending specters, angels, and demons had appeared in Medieval plays and Renaissance masques; the most spectacular effects, however, had hitherto been seen only by the privileged at the court theatres. Now they appeared to audiences in public theatres.

The new prominence of spectacle was obviously a lure for audiences. Indeed it often was advertised more extensively than the story, the playwright, or the actors. For example, in an advertisement in *The Charleston Courier* for the production of *Raymond and Agnes* in 1808, the first sentence, even before the list of cast members, reads: "with additional scenery, (founded chiefly on a principal Episode in the Romance of *The Monk*, got up under the direction of Mr. Placide, with entire new scenery[)]."[91]

The theatrical experience of Americans viewing Gothic plays probably didn't differ much from that of British patrons. Few contemporary accounts compared American productions of Gothic plays unfavorably to British productions in regard to scenery or effects, suggesting that there was "little deviation from English practice in the actual production technique employed in either the Chestnut house or in American theatres." American theatres, like British, used "grooves, divided backscenes or shutters, and drops." In fact, the one deviation in American production techniques from that of the British appears to have been the practice of "flying backscenes rather than lowering them through the stage floor in 'sloats.'"[92]

Second, in Gothic plays, scenery moved away from generic stock settings to more lavish, specialized settings. Settings for earlier Gothic dramas (before 1800) could have been constructed from stock and so would have proved most economical. Later Gothic plays utilized both more lavish scenery and more specific settings — but these plays seemed to have been revived frequently — so that the initial expense in mounting plays like *Bluebeard* and *The Wood Daemon* was recovered through periodic revivals; indeed, these plays were credited with helping the theatres survive lean times. That scenery and special effects became increasingly important to financial success is suggested by the increased amount of advertising space in American newspapers devoted to descriptions of spectacle.

Third, Gothic plays initially offered a visual environment not present in melodramas: an atmosphere of gloom and foreboding.[93] This atmosphere, intended to inspire fear or terror in members of the audience, was created primarily through the spectacle, as realized first through scenery in the earliest Gothic dramas and then through the addition of lavish special effects in later plays. The increasing emphasis on spectacle in the later Gothic plays moved them away from the unique characteristics of "Gothic" literature, with its emphasis on an atmosphere of terror, and more toward pure melodrama. Increasing use of natural rather than supernatural effects reduced what was "Gothic" in the plays.

The use of storms in Gothic plays illustrated this change in emphasis. Storms initially were used in the plays to heighten feeling of gloom and foreboding, in that the scenes were occurring indoors with the storm outdoors; the storm did not physically hamper the characters; it merely affected them mentally. However, because later plays included more scenes out of doors, the storm soon became an active opponent for the characters; they had to battle the storm itself, as in *The Mountain Torrent*.

Fourth, American playwrights generally did not utilize as many supernatural effects as British authors. True, playwrights like Turnbull and Stokes, who adapted works of Matthew Gregory Lewis, utilized the same supernatural effects as he did in his plays. However, when Americans wrote their own plays, they opted for "explained supernaturalism," in which apparent unearthly occurrences were explained rationally, or they avoided supernatural effects and thrilled spectators through displays of pageantry or natural disasters, such as fire or flood.[94] Americans' apparent preference for explainable effects argues for the view that Americans were "children of the eighteenth century," who believed in "the primary value of reason, the absurdity of mythology, and the danger of superstition." Moreover, given the challenges they faced as they attempted to develop the wilderness and expand westward, they necessarily exhibited a "pragmatic rationalism and a concern with material reality."[95]

The period in which Gothic plays flourished on American stages appeared to be a transitional one — moving American scenic practice from Neoclassic stage pictures to Romantic ones, from painted backdrops with actor-centered plays to lavish, practicable scenery with spectacular effects that often eclipsed the actor. Finally, this period, too, saw the composition of audiences changing, with increasing numbers of middle- and working-class patrons demanding ever more novelty and visual stimulation from their plays.

Chapter 8

"What Dreadful Place Is This?"
Women and Dangerous Spaces

Adeline, the young and beautiful heroine, hesitates at the threshold of "a dark and antique apartment" in an abbey owned by the powerful Marquis de Montalt. According to the stage directions in William Dunlap's *Fontainville Abbey*, Adeline has a light in one hand and a "rusty dagger" in the other.[1] Though terrified, the plucky heroine continues her investigation, murmuring aloud, "Why do I wander thus through these abodes of Guilt, these cavern'd hiding holes of blackest horror?"[2] Within a few seconds, Adeline comes upon a chest. She "opens it as with a desperate effort," and "starts from it with horror," crying "Image of death! Phantom of desolation!"[3] The audience, however, sees nothing. Just a few seconds later, Adeline emerges into another chamber, where she meets her foster mother. When Hortensia, Adeline's foster mother, hears of Adeline's terrifying discoveries in the secret chamber, she exclaims, "Alas! Alas! Some deed of dreadful note/Has curs'd these walls with terrors more than fancied!"[4]

Another heroine also encounters terror when she enters a dangerous space owned by a powerful man. Fatima, the heroine in *Bluebeard*, loves the poor but valiant Selim; unfortunately, her father has betrothed her to the rich, mysterious Abomelique, who is rumored to have beheaded several wives. Fatima and her sister Irene are taken to Abomelique's palace. One evening, just before the wedding, Abomelique tells Fatima that he must leave for a few hours and encourages her to explore the palace. He gives her many keys, but tells her not to use one particular key that opens a door within the Blue Apartment. Solemnly Abomelique warns, "That door, and that alone is sacred. Dare to open it, and the most dreadful punishment that tongue can utter will await you." Fatima is more than willing to shun the forbidden chamber, but her sister is wild with curiosity, and persuades Fatima to disobey Abomelique's orders. At last, Fatima stands before the door. But as soon as she puts the key into the lock, "the door instantly sinks, with a tremendous crash and the blue Chamber appears, streaked with vivid streams of blood." More horrors appear, including tombs and "ghastly and supernatural forms," including a skeleton, over whose head appear the words, "The Punishment of Curiosity."[5] The women scream and clutch each other in terror. Fatima drops the key and it breaks. When Abomelique sees the damaged key, he knows that the women have entered the forbidden room, and he cries, "Damnation! Lady this key is charm-fraught, forged in a sulphurous cave, within whose blood be-sprinkled mouth nothing but witchcraft enters to celebrate her frantic revels. This speaks a damning proof against you, and you die!"[6]

Both *Fontainville Abbey* and *Bluebeard* featured a heroine who deliberately ventured into an isolated, enclosed, and threatening space, a space dominated by a villain so powerful that the architecture itself seems to assist him in menacing the heroine. Many of the Gothic plays of the late eighteenth and early nineteenth centuries included some imposing structure that first appeared as a haven for the characters, as did the abbey in *Fountainville Forest* and *Fontainville Abbey*. Sometimes the structure seemed safe because it was a holy space, such as the convent in *Raymond and Agnes* and *Marmion*. In other Gothic plays, the frightening space appeared as a beautiful palace but soon was discovered to harbor a terrible secret, as in *The Wood Daemon* and *Bluebeard*. Regardless of its outward appearance, the building proved a frightening prison for a young heroine. Although the plays differed from the fiction in that their depiction of the architecture changes over the decades, from castles to cottages, from an emphasis on interior scenes to an emphasis on outdoor scenes, the plays still emphasized frightening spaces that threatened the heroine.

In recent decades, many scholars have focused on depictions of female characters in Gothic literature. These studies of "Female Gothic" examined a young woman's "ambivalent relationship to contemporary domestic ideology, especially the joint institutions of marriage and motherhood."[7] Over the years, however, aspects of the approach have been contested and developed.[8]

Many studies have focused on the peculiar architecture often associated with Gothic fiction—and its effect on Gothic heroines. These studies identified the overwhelming presence of a particular type of architecture in Gothic literature that was the "repository and embodiment" of mystery and of the past, and this architecture isolated and incarcerated the heroine.[9] In the novels, the walls of the castle separated the world outside the walls from the world inside the castle, effectively "preventing intrusion from without and escape from within."[10] The heroine sensed the evil within as soon as she entered the space; she immediately experienced an "indefinable feeling of dread."[11]

One of the most important elements examined in Female Gothic studies was the relationship between "Gothic and domestic space."[12] Scholars argued that the "domestic enclosure the gothic novel depicts ... is the inversion of the notion of home celebrated by separate spheres ideology: a place or imprisonment, torture, and threatened rape or death for its female heroines."[13] The message that society promoted, then—that the home was the safest place for women—was subverted in the Gothic, in which these interior spaces were not safe and were in fact, controlled by a all-powerful male.[14] Kate Ellis, in *The Contested Castle*, explored the late eighteenth century and the relationship between "two epiphenomena of middle-class culture: the idealization of the home and the popularity of the Gothic."[15] Ellis argued that any confining space exhibits this contradiction: "the 'safe' sphere of home" was linked "inseparably to its dark opposite, the Gothic castle."[16] Gothic fiction used the castle or other enclosed space "to symbolize both the culture and the heroine"; the space reflected the culture that confined her and the heroine's feelings of "self fear and self disgust."[17]

Along with its capacity to separate a young woman from aid, the frightening space in Gothic literature affected the heroine in other ways. It fired her curiosity and impelled her to wander. Heroines in Ann Radcliffe's castles could "scuttle miles along corridors, descend into dungeons, and explore secret chambers without a chaperone" because the Gothic castle was still an "indoor and therefore freely female space."[18] Although the heroine traversed these spaces, however, she was not safe from the evil housed within its walls.

The "Female Gothic" was subversive in that it revealed a dark side to domesticity that young women of the late eighteenth and early nineteenth centuries were instructed to revere. As such, it identified the very real terror of everyday life for women, who, although not at the mercy of a lascivious villain, may well have endured a tyrant much closer to home. As scholars asserted, the "real tyranny at issue" in Gothic romances was the undisputed power of fathers, who could be "virtual tyrants" in eighteenth and nineteenth century homes.[19] Moreover, just as a Gothic villain could capture a heroine, a husband in the eighteenth century could effectively hide away his wife.[20] Gothic novels, and the plays that were based on them, created for women "a resistance to an ideology that imprison[ed] them even as it posit[ed] a sphere of safety for them."[21]

Studies of the Female Gothic have focused primarily on Gothic novels. Yet Gothic plays, particularly those produced before 1810, featured many of the same characteristics identified in the Female Gothic — particularly those regarding the impact of the architecture on the heroine. As in the novels, Gothic plays suggested that these frightening spaces assisted the villain in pursuing the heroine and effectively separated a woman (or women) from aid. As in the novels, heroines in Gothic plays reacted instinctively to the uneasy atmosphere of the space, vocalizing their dread of their surroundings. In plays, too, the physical structure itself seemed to operate at the will of a powerful male. Heroines in the plays, as in the novels, wandered freely through the frightening dark areas, thus permitting potential Gothic terrors to affect the audience. At some point, however, they transgressed boundaries and discovered a particularly dangerous space, and this act brought them to some climactic situation. Despite their terror, heroines persevered in their adventure and managed to triumph over the villain and claim the space as their own.

Most of the Gothic plays written in the eighteenth and early nineteenth centuries were written or adapted by men and may appear inappropriate to examine through the lens of Female Gothic. Yet, several of these plays, even though written by men, were based on novels of Anne Radcliffe, one of the major writers cited in the Female Gothic tradition. And, although many of the plays were entirely conceived and written by men, they still exhibited a key element identified in the Female Gothic: a frightening interior space that incarcerated the heroine and seemed to symbolize the contradictions present in the lives of real women in the eighteenth and nineteenth centuries.[22] Gothic literature has been perceived as a feminine form, "outside the mainstream of literature";

however it has been written by men as well as women, and "both sexes have been accused of.... Gothic excesses."[23] Some have opted to "complicate the definition" of Female Gothic by including depictions of women in Gothic literature, as well as depictions of "the men who try to marry them or kill them or both."[24]

Early Gothic plays, those produced before 1810, were particularly useful for study because they featured many of the aspects identified in studies of the Female Gothic, particularly the use of a terrifying interior space. Early Gothic plays depicted mostly interior scenes that contained some enclosed space that threatened women. *The Count of Narbonne, The Sicilian Romance, The Mysteries of the Castle, The Castle Spectre, Fountainville Forest, Fontainville Abbey,* and *The Wood Daemon* all included such spaces. In the *Mysteries of the Castle* by John B. White, written in 1808, Ellenora and her daughter Cornelia were incarcerated in a "subterraneous chamber of the castle," and subject to mistreatment from their captors. A young heroine, Rosalva, also ventured into this dangerous space and instantly becomes prey for two henchmen of the villain.[25] In *The Man of Fortitude*, claimed by John Hodgkinson in 1807, Hortensia, a new bride, was captured by banditti just after she left her new husband and "trembling pass'd along the winding stairway," to her chamber.[26] She was carried off and held for three years in a castle. In *The Castle Spectre*, Angela managed to elude the advances of the evil Earl until she entered the dungeon, where she was captured by her pursuer.

Like Gothic fiction, Gothic plays also displayed frightening spaces that simultaneously menaced and drew the heroine to investigate. Ruined castles, decaying abbeys, and dank dungeons provided the settings for most of these early works, and, as in the fiction, Gothic heroines wandered freely through the oppressive darkness and yet vocalized their persistent fears about their actions. In *Fountainville Forest*, Adeline found the "secret Apartment, gloomy and rude," and whispered, "A general horror creeps thro' all my limbs, and almost stifles curiosity."[27] In *One O'Clock; or The Knight and the Wood Daemon*, Una cried "I seek him in vain—My firebrand too is exhausted! Ha! Protect me, heaven! What dreadful place is this?"[28]

Several Gothic plays also exhibited another favorite theme identified in the Female Gothic: the ambivalent feelings inspired by the convent. In Gothic plays, convents appeared as terrible spaces—in *Raymond and Agnes*, the heroine was shut up in one and the hero is shut out. In *Marmion*, one of the heroines was bricked up in the wall when her fickle lover returned her to the convent. Convents represented the "single life," a prospect that was understandably frightening to women of this time who relied upon a husband for economic support.[29]

Although Gothic plays produced before the 1810s depicted many of the same relationships between heroines and space as identified in the novels, plays produced after this time began to shift from stock scenery representations of dank castle interiors to other sorts of settings. Plays began to exhibit more lavish sets, three-dimensional scenery and more outdoor settings such as forests, caves, and cottages. These outdoor settings allowed for impressive spectacles, such as lavish processions and wedding celebrations; *The Rose of Arragon* called for a masque in which children represented the seasons; the *Mountain Torrent* featured a wedding celebration that the villain arranged for his reluctant bride, and *The Bride of the Isles* featured the wedding of a servant girl, who caught the eye of the vampire. As the plays included more exterior scenes, the menacing atmosphere, previously provided by a gloomy castle, was now depicted as a forest or other mysterious outdoor space. In *Superstition*, Mary was accosted by a would-be seducer when she walks through a wood; in *Bertram*, Imogene lost her mind in the forest. Finally, outdoor scenes allowed for more natural disasters: thrilling representations of storms, fires, and floods.

As plays began to require more exterior scenes and began to feature more natural disasters, the role of the heroine changed as well. Heroines in most Gothic plays that appeared after 1810 did not appear as important to overall spectacle as they had when the scenes had occurred inside. There, inside the castle, the heroine's figure, as she hesitantly tiptoed through the murky darkness of a desolate castle, provided an essential component of the spectacle of the play. The audience, both men and women, watched a living woman on the stage portray a young heroine, alone and unaided, unravel a mystery and foil a powerful older male. As the actress crossed in front of the painted scenery, her gestures and her narration certainly embellished the theatrical experience, which did not yet have the advantage of lavish scenery or special effects. Consequently, the actress herself was an important element of the spectacle in Gothic plays that appeared in the plays produced before the 1810s.[30]

In many Gothic plays produced in the 1810s and later, however, the villain was unable to concentrate solely on the heroine; instead he had to contend with storms, fires, floods, and other disasters. Much of the spectacle in these later plays resulted from the villains' confrontations with natural forces: Bertram struggled in a storm at sea; Trevasi in *The Mountain Torrent* fought on a footbridge over raging waters in the midst of a terrible storm; and Ravensworth, in *Superstition*, presided over an execution in the "murky and thick" night "amidst Thunder and Lightning."[31] Consequently, in the midst of this other action, the heroine appeared more passive and less vital to the plot. She often was introduced at the beginning of the play, was carried off to wed the villain, and was fortuitously rescued just before the vows.

The changing spectacle also affected heroines in another way. In early Gothic plays, a heroine found herself in the lair of a Gothic villain who incarcerated her and locked potential rescuers out of the building. In later Gothic plays, however, the heroine encountered danger not only in the villain's space, but also in familiar surroundings. In these plays, the villain no longer was relegated to a particular spot for his evil schemes. Instead, he was free to appropriate spaces that belonged to others. Bertram killed Imogene's husband, Aldobrand, in his own home; he died at Imogene's feet. In *The Bride of the Isles*, the vampire demanded that Lady Margaret marry him in her own family chapel. Melmoth arranged his unholy wedding in the local churchyard. In *The Rose of Arragon*, the Conde Laranda saw Rosaline at a local festival at which friends and relatives were celebrating her approaching marriage to Aurelio, and the Conde abducted her. Thus, unlike villains in earlier Gothic plays who confined their evildoing to their own terrifying spaces in remote locations, villains in later plays freely roamed, mingled in communities, and used holy ground for their own wicked designs. Heroines were no longer safe — even in their own communities and in the midst of their own families.

What then could have been the visual impact of the architecture and its effect on the heroine in Gothic plays on women in audience at the theatre? Scholars of the Female Gothic have claimed that these novels allowed women readers to imagine the dark side of domesticity, that women authors of these works could offer a subversive vision for their readers that critiqued the male-dominated institutions of their day. In the "sinister family dwellings" of Gothic romance, women writers emphasized their own feelings of isolation and confinement due to "patriarchal familial, legal, and class structures."[32] The impressive architecture seemed to stand for more than just the evil of the villain; it also represented larger, social institutions that enveloped women, especially the institution of marriage. These spaces, dominated by men, parodied the domestic ideal of home as haven and revealed the darker side of such supposed sanctuary.

Early Gothic plays, those produced in the 1790s, certainly presented such a view. Heroines found themselves imprisoned in the villain's home and powerless to escape his will. The situation of the heroines seemed to reflect the lives of middle-class women who may have watched these plays: they came from good families; they had been educated, and they were confined. Although the fictional heroines were incarcerated in a remote and frightening space, their real-life counterparts also were confined; in England of the late eighteenth and early nineteenth century, middle-class women were confined to the home as the notion of a "well-regulated home" was idealized. They could use their "newly created leisure" to read books from the circulating library, and their "placement in the home" made them appealing to publishers.[33]

In the early years of the nineteenth century, however, more working-class patrons were flooding into urban centers, both in England and in the United States. Young women, as well as men, were leaving the comparative safety of home and moving to cities "filled with uncertainty and violence," and these young women appeared particularly vulnerable.[34] Though men certainly far outnumbered women in audiences before 1830, some working-class women may have begun to move into the galleries of the theatres, although they may have been described as prostitutes.[35]

During these same years, Gothic plays began to feature fewer heroines of noble pedigree and more of lower-class origins. Moreover, villains in Gothic plays were able to pluck a heroine from the midst of her family and friends. Thus, in Gothic plays of the early nineteenth century, a heroine could be of any class; as long as she was young and attractive, she was in danger. In Gothic plays of the 1810s and 1820s, young heroines of humble origins were just as likely to attract Gothic villains as were women of middle or upper classes.

If women found subversive elements in Gothic fiction, they certainly would have found even more in Gothic plays, because in these plays they could watch a living woman performing actions that flouted conventional "womanly" behavior. Whereas the living females in the audience were restricted in their behavior at theatres, even relegated to particular sections of the theatre, they could watch a living woman on a public stage depicting a plucky and ultimately successful heroine.

Although heroines in Gothic plays ostensibly "reinforc[ed] cultural conditioning," in that they acted "passively before the specter of male authority," they invariably triumphed over the male villain.[36]

In the second and third decades of the nineteenth century, new theatres sprang up, and these theatres often catered to more working-class patrons. Although accounts of theatres before 1830 argue that all respectable women were seated in the boxes, and that unescorted women were prostitutes, more recent studies have argued that some poor but "respectable" working-class women may have been in the galleries and mistaken for prostitutes. During these same years, the depiction of heroines in Gothic plays changed, particularly their placement in dangerous spaces. Although spectators at Gothic plays throughout the period would have watched a young heroine threatened by a powerful male, they would have witnessed a change in the location of the threat. Spectators in the 1790s would have understood this threat to be a danger associated with a specific remote location, removed from everyday life, and thus dangerous only to a select few women. Yet by the 1810s, female spectators saw heroines, often of lowly origin, accosted by villains, often in the supposed sanctuary of their own communities. Female spectators at Gothic plays perhaps recognized that they too, like Gothic heroines, could be controlled and confined by powerful males, whether in a remote, dangerous space or in familiar surroundings.

Despite this message, female spectators undoubtedly enjoyed the transgressions highlighted in Gothic plays. Though the verbal content of the plays appeared to reinforce conventional expectations for female behavior, in that young heroines expressed a desire for the sanctuary of the home and the fulfillment of motherhood, the visual content of the plays did not necessarily depict these sentiments. The visual impact of an actress, who herself was employed out of the home and appearing in a public space, depicting a young heroine who confronted danger and eventually triumphed over a powerful older male certainly contradicted the verbal message. The Gothic heroines, as they traversed dangerous ground, may have subverted the ideology of domesticity for female members of the audience — and done so even more effectively than the Gothic novels.

CHAPTER 9

"A Plain Unvarnish'd Tale"
Adaptations of British Plays for the American Stage

In the play British play *Raymond and Agnes*, by Matthew Gregory Lewis, the hero, Raymond, spies young Agnes emerging from the convent of St. Clair. As she departs with her chaperone, he gazes after her and exclaims, "What a divinity! What a shape! How sweet the expression of her full dark eyes!— Lovely Agnes; never shall I forget this interesting moment"[1] In the American version of the play, written by John Stokes, the hero is not quite so effusive about Agnes' charms, saying merely, "What a divinity! Lovely Agnes, never shall I forget this interesting minute."[2] Such a change was typical of the changes made to British plays by American playwrights.

Because audiences of this time preferred English plays, believing them to be of finer quality, most of the Gothic plays, like other plays of the period, were imported from England and presented, frequently unaltered, on the American stage.[3] At least four American plays, however, did appear during this period. John Stokes, John Turnbull, and William Dunlap each wrote Gothic plays for the American stage: John Stokes wrote *The Forest of Rosenwald*, based on Matthew Lewis' play *Raymond and Agnes*. John Turnbull wrote *The Wood Daemon*, based on Matthew Lewis' play *One O'Clock; or The Knight and the Wood Daemon*, and William Dunlap wrote *Fontainville Abbey*, based on Ann Radcliffe's novel *The Romance of the Forest*. Dunlap also altered George Colman the Younger's *Bluebeard* for the New York stage.[4] Although other American playwrights may have altered British plays for the American stage, they did not claim the new plays as their own. Each of these four plays was published as an American work, and each had a British counterpart that appeared on the London stage at approximately the same time.

James Boaden wrote the British play *Fontainville Forest* in 1794 and American William Dunlap wrote *Fontainville Abbey* in 1795. Both plays were set in the French countryside where Lamotte and his family took shelter in a ruined abbey owned by the evil Marquis of Montalt. Lamotte attempted to rob the Marquis and when the Marquis threatened to press charges, Lamotte reluctantly agreed to help him seduce Lamotte's adopted daughter Adeline. Meanwhile, Adeline discovered a parchment in the abbey which revealed that the Marquis had murdered his own brother; when the Marquis attempted to seduce Adeline, he learned of her discovery and ordered Lamotte to kill her. Lamotte, unable to kill Adeline, prepared to face the Marquis' charges, but an old servant of the Marquis came to the trial and testified that the Marquis indeed had murdered his brother. At this point in the British version, the Marquis committed suicide; in the American version, the Marquis was prevented from taking his life and was instead forced to stand trial.

The British play *Raymond and Agnes; or The Travellers Benighted*, appeared in 1809 and the American *The Forest of Rosenwald* appeared in 1821. Both plays were set in Spain and began with the hero Raymond and his servant leaving home to travel, stopping at an inn in Madrid, and seeing Agnes leaving the convent with her governess. Raymond and his servant then came upon the cottage of Baptista, who headed a band of murderers. Baptista's wife Marguerette, hoped to free herself from her forced marriage by helping Raymond escape. After Agnes and her governess arrived at the cottage also, Baptista gave everyone drugged wine, but Raymond, warned by Marguerette, did not drink and only feigned sleep. As Baptista was about to kill all of them, Marguerette stabbed him and led the others to safety. When Agnes arrived at her new home, however, she was told that she must enter the convent for life. She notified Raymond that she planned to escape that night, disguised as the Bleeding Nun. When Raymond saw the figure of the Bleeding Nun, he assumed it was Agnes, but it was really the specter of Agnes' murdered mother, who begged Raymond to save her daughter. Agnes fell into the hands of the robbers again, and when she rejected their offers of marriage, they prepared to kill her. At this point, Raymond, Theodore and Marguerette arrived, vanquished the robbers, and saved Agnes.

Another play by Matthew Lewis, *One O'Clock; or The Knight and the Wood Daemon*, appeared in London in 1807; *The Wood Daemon*, by American John Turnbull, premiered in Boston in 1808. Both plays were set in Germany. Una, the heroine, was about to marry the mysterious Count Hardyknute, against the advice of her aunt (in the British version) or sister (in the American version) Clothilda. Clothilda told Una that her own adopted child, Leolyn, was the rightful Count, and that Count Hardyknute was an evil villain who usurped the title. Una determined to marry the Count even though she still loved the poor but honest Oswy. When the Count saw Leolyn, he recognized him as the rightful heir and decided to kill him by making him the annual sacrifice for the Wood Daemon. Una tried to rescue the boy but was captured by the Count who informed her that he had made a pact with the Wood Daemon that required him to deliver a human sacrifice each year on the same date before one o'clock in the morning or he himself would be the Wood Daemon's eternal slave. Because Una had rescued Leolyn, she was now to be the sacrifice. As the Count prepared to stab Una, Leolyn pushed forward the hand of the giant clock; it struck one o'clock and the Wood Daemon rose and whisked Count Hardyknute off to hell.

The last play, George Colman the Younger's *Bluebeard*, appeared first in England; William Dunlap then altered the play for the American stage in 1806. These plays were very similar. In each, Fatima loved Selim but was forced by her ambitious father to marry the wealthy Abomolique, even though the approved suitor has had several wives die under mysterious circumstances. Fatima, accompanied by her sister, Irene, and her father, Ibrahim, moved to Abomolique's castle. Abomolique told Fatima that he had to leave on business. He then gave her the keys to the castle but warned her not to open one certain door. Fatima and her sister toured the castle and came upon the mysterious door; as they drew near it, they heard moans. Fatima, fearing that someone was hurt, opened the door and discovered a room streaked with blood. Within the room was a skeleton holding a dart. When Fatima and her sister turned to flee, they dropped the special key and broke it. When Abomolique returned he demanded to see all the keys and quickly learned that Fatima had seen the secret chamber. He then informed her that she must die and dragged her to the secret chamber. As he was about to kill her, Selim broke down the wall and fought the villain. As Abomolique fell near the skeleton, it plunged a dart into his heart.

Although similar in many respects, the American versions of the plays did exhibit some differences from their British models, and, in view of the overall similarities, these relatively minor differences assumed some importance. Playwrights (and theatres) had to please their audiences in order to survive, particularly at this time in American history when anti-theatrical prejudice was only just abating. The fact that playwrights altered the texts at all suggests that they believed the plays as revised would prove more acceptable to American audiences than would the British versions. Thus, a comparison of the American and British plays may offer insights into prevailing attitudes in America between 1794 and 1830.

In general the American and British plays were very similar, though the American plays often differed in language. American plays used more contractions and often simplified spelling; for example, the word "honour" became "honor"; the monster "Hacho" became "Ako" in the American version of *The Wood Daemon*. American playwrights also used less flowery speech as illustrated by the following comparison of the same brief scene from the *Fontainville* plays:

British	**American**
Adel:	*Adel:*
Beseech you, stay, my Lord! Lamotte would speak — my father would explain.	Oh my good lord, my father would explain.
Lamotte: Return! Return! My Lord, vouchsafe one word — in private!	*Marq:* (admiring) Your father! Well, sir, speak.
Marq: You best know whether 'tis prudent to grant this after what has past between us. You can have nought to say, but wha with me your family may share.[6]	*La Motte:* In private, sir. *Marq:* Sure these may hear it.[5]

The idea that Americans preferred plain speech was further supported in the final scene of the American play *Fontainville Abbey* wherein La Motte told the judge, "A plain, unvarnish'd tale, my lord, requires no tutor'ed orator to set it forth."[7]

Although differences in language used in the American and British plays seemed apparent, differences of characterization were more subtle. On the surface the characters in both sets of plays were very similar, usually bearing the same names and often uttering nearly identical speeches. Each play featured a threatened heroine, a murdering villain, and a virtuous hero. However, American characters occasionally exhibited different responses to situations and often expressed different sentiments from their British counterparts.

American plays seemed to attack rigid class structure by deleting references to class differences or by adding references to the equality of all men. For example, in *The Wood Daemon*, American playwright John Turnbull suggested that a monarch must earn his or her subjects' support:

British	American
Not that I conquered forms my glory; but that I conquered in the cause of justice; sceptres are only valuable when extended to bless; and if ever I sighed to possess unbounded power, it was that I might confer unbounded blessings![8]	Twas not to gratify my own ambition that I conquered, but to protect the humble chastise the insolent. Crowns are only worthy of honor when they encircle the brows of virtue, and if ever I sighed for unbounded power, it was only that I might diffuse unbounded happiness![9]

Turnbull also removed the line in which the Count refers to himself as "sovereign." In another example, the evil Marquis in the British *Fontainville Forest* disparaged Lamotte:

British	American
Marquis: Thou wretched fool, who will believe thee? When grac'd with all the eloquence of rank,	*Marquis:* 'Tis not for men like thee to blast superiors; the breaths of thousands, reptiles

British	American
Marquis: (cont.) I stand to answer to the sullied charge made by an outlawed gambler, and a robber. Can you ere hope it will be credited?	*Marquis: (cont.)* like to thee, can never dim a noble's illustrious name....
Lamotte: If I have saved her, I shall die with Transport.[10]	*La Motte:* Thou has uttered truth. Yet know, proud lord, that even where grim Oppression holds his court, still is there some observance paid to justice.[11]

Unlike its British counterpart, the American play added a reference to equality.[12] In addition to emphasizing social equality, the American playwrights made more religious references. In the British *Fountainville Forest*, the heroine's adopted father was supposed to kill her but later reported that he was unable to commit the crime. In the American version, the playwright added an entire scene in which the father, at the bedside of the sleeping heroine, struggled with his conscience. As he aimed the dagger at her heart, he was moved by the heroine's innocent face and dropped to his knees to pray. He then rose, exclaiming, "Yes I'm resolv'd. Demons of hell, ye're [sic] gone!"[13] He exited, saved from mortal sin by prayer.

American plays also emphasized that heaven would protect and reward the virtuous. Although the British plays provided happy endings for the virtuous, American plays belabored the point. For instance, the British *Bluebeard* ended with the struggle between Selim and Abomolique in which the villain was killed. However at the end of the American *Bluebeard*, the characters thanked heaven for their escape, exclaiming, "...Let us away from this rude scene of horror, and bless the providence which nerves the arm of virtue to humble vice and oppression."[14] Another example of religious fervor was revealed in a comparison of the ending lines in the *Wood Daemon* plays; the British play ended with Clothilda's lines, but the American play continued with Una's heartfelt thanks to Heaven:

British	American
Clotilda: My child, my treasure! Kneel, vassals, kneel! Behold your long Lost prince! Behold the count of Holstein![15]	*Clotilda:* My child! And dost thou live? Heroic Una, savior of our infant prince! Instrument of Omnipotent Providence! Accept the tribute of a happy mother's thanks![16] *Una:* To Heaven, our thanks are due! To heaven, then, let us pour forth the gratitude of our souls! Its allseeing eye has pierced the Cavern's gloom — O — Its' unerring hand of justice has snatched the helpless victim of mad ambition from the ponderous dart of death! Rejoice! Virtue and innocence reign triumphant![17]

American plays also stressed that heaven would punish the wicked. In the American version of *The Wood Demon*, one character attributed the villain's horrible demise to heavenly justice, saying "While the shameless wretch, who blasphemingly defied Almighty vengeance, has felt its ireful arm."[18] Even the villains themselves believed that they would be punished; in Turnbull's *The Wood Daemon*, the villain, unlike his British counterpart, stated, "Better had it been, had I still remained in my original crust of deformity, the monster nature made me, than to be transformed at such a price of crime to what I am!"[19] Throughout the American plays the characters continuously commented on virtue, or the lack thereof, and credited Heaven with direct intervention in reward or punishment.

American and British plays also differed in their treatment of sexuality. American playwrights usually omitted sexual references. An example occurred in the British *One O'Clock; or The Knight and the Wood Daemon*, in which Una was under the spell of a love charm from the villain, who declared that it would seduce all female hearts.[20] In the American version of *The Wood Daemon*, however, the playwright eliminated the device of the love charm, so that instead of desiring the Count's person, Una desired only his wealth and position.

The American plays also prevented any extended discussion of virginity, serious or comic. In *Raymond and Agnes*, the British Cunnegonde, presented as old, vain, and unattractive, made repeated references to her virginity. For example, at the convent of St. Clair, she said "Adieu dear mother and when a few more years are passed over my head, I too may leave the temptations of mankind, and take the vows of eternal virginity within the walls of St. Clair!"[21] The American character, named Beatrice, made no such remark. Later in the play Cunnegonde again referred to her virgin state, crying, "Oh that I had dedicated myself to a life of perpetual virginity in the holy convent of St. Clair! Then should I have escaped the dangers with which my innocence is surrounded!"[22] Once again, the American character omitted this speech. Overall, American characters did not exhibit any interest in the physical charms of other characters, nor did they make any humorous references to virginity.

Another topic treated differently by American and the British playwrights was the social behavior of female characters. The American versions of the plays presented the female character as less self-sufficient than her British counterpart — unless she was directly aided by heaven. For example, in both *The Forest of Rosenwald* and in *Raymond and Agnes*, the character of Agnes was described as "innocent" and "delicate." However, in the British play, delicate Agnes managed to gun down a villain, whereas in the American play, Agnes ran upstage during the climactic fight scene and waited for the men to save her.[23]

If an American heroine was assertive and self-reliant in a play, she attributed her unconventional actions to Divine Guidance. In *Fontainville Abbey*, the American Adeline stood up and accused the villain in a public trial, whereas the British Adeline was represented by males. However the American Adeline hastened to explain that her unconventional behavior was inspired by Heaven: "Heav'n hath preserved me from his baneful arts, that I might meet him, face to face, and blast him."[24] Similarly in the American play *The Wood Daemon*, Una refused to accept praise for her daring rescue of a child; instead she credited Heaven: "To heaven our thanks are due; its unerring hand of justice has snatched the helpless victim of mad ambition from the ponderous dart of death! Virtue and innocence reign triumphant!"[25] Overall, the American female characters appeared more passive, exhibiting less assertiveness and self-sufficiency than the British characters.

If a female character in an American play did act in an unconventional manner, and if she failed to attribute her deed to heavenly guidance, she was characterized as morally flawed. In both the *Forest of Rosenwald* and in *Raymond and Agnes*, Marguerette, reluctant wife of the bandit Baptista, stabbed her husband in order to free herself and the captives. However, the playwrights differed in their justification of Marguerette's actions. In the British play, Marguerette stabbed Baptista as he was about to murder the innocent, sleeping heroine. In the American play, however, Marguerette stabbed Baptista as he was descending the stairs, making her deed seem cold-blooded.

The British playwright also allowed Marguerette to justify her life with Baptista; she explained, "necessity, not choice, has made me what I am."[26] The American playwright omitted this line, permitting Marguerette no excuses for her questionable life.

Finally, in both plays, Marguerette had an infant son; in the British version, she automatically took him along when she leads the captives to safety; in the American version she forgot him. Although Marguerette eventually returned for the baby, her momentary forgetfulness suggested that she was an unfit mother.[27] The British playwright made Marguerette a more sympathetic character; the American playwright portrayed her as morally flawed and unwomanly. Thus in the American play, Marguerette's aggressive, unconventional behavior was aligned with undesirable qualities.

In addition to demonstrating that American female characters behaved in conventional ways or offer appropriate excuses, American playwrights, more than British, emphasized the desirability of matrimony. In fact, in one American play, the playwright took pains to ensure that the audience realized that a female character was the villain's battered wife rather than his battered mistress. In *The Forest of Rosenwald*, Marguerette had a child by the bandit leader Baptista; in the

American play, Marguerette painstakingly explained the legality of her marriage:

British	American
Marguerette: By brutal force he made me his; by force detains me here, to witness deeds of horror that harrow up my soul.[28]	*Marguerette:* In a wretched hour he dragged me to the unfrequented village church; in whose unpeopled chancel none but the officials of the ceremony witnessed my vows of duty uttered in terror of a bandit's threats. Hither he bore me back as his wife and prisoner.[29]

Another reference to matrimony appeared in the American version of *The Wood Daemon;* Una asked the Count, "What greater proof of love can you exact, than what I have already given — my voluntary consent to your bride, whene'er 'twill please you to conduct me to the altar?"[30] This particular reference was not present in the British play.

In addition to extolling matrimony as the most desirable state for a woman, females in both the American and the British plays glorified motherhood; all of the heroines confided that they grew up without a mother's influence, and most sought surrogate mothers in other female characters.[31] The heroines not only venerated their mothers, they themselves wished to become mothers; if they did not express the wish directly, they implied it through their antipathy toward a life of enforced celibacy in the convent.[32] Once again, the American plays made even more references to motherhood than did the British. For example, in the American version *of The Wood Daemon*, Una, the childless heroine, exclaimed, "Ah moment of a mother's joy — how I envy and applaud thy transports!" Clotilda responded, "Ah, who could mistake the transports of a doating [sic] mother, when bounteous Providence restores to her arms a lost son!"[33] Neither of these speeches appeared in the British play. The American *Fontainville Abbey* also made more references to motherhood than did the British play.[34]

Although heroines in both the American and the British plays were encouraged to contemplate matrimony and motherhood, they were *not* permitted to contemplate physical love with the hero, even within marriage. However, the British heroines frequently speculated about the horrors of forced sexual relations with the villain, usually outside of marriage, whereas the American heroine was not permitted to do even that. In the American plays, the villain did not overtly threaten the heroine sexually; therefore she was prevented from musing aloud about a fate worse than death. In the British *Fountainville Forest*, the lascivious Marquis directly propositioned Adeline, saying, "This lonely place will rather fix a gloom forever on your youth, that should be led to happier scenes of gay, voluptuous love." Adeline understood only too well and retorted, "I thank you, Sir, for thus at once displaying the glaring infamy design'd for me!" The Marquis then declared that Adeline must be his "by kindness, or by force!"[35] By contrast, in the American version, William Dunlap removed entirely the scene in which the evil Marquis attempted to seduce Adeline; not only did the action occur offstage, but the Marquis only managed to hold Adeline's hand before he was stopped.[36] This alteration ensured that American audiences would be spared overt suggestions of illicit sex. In another example, Una in the American version of *The Wood Daemon* never mused on the physical attractiveness of the villainous Count Hardyknute, but her British counterpart did. Although both British and American female characters desired matrimony and motherhood, American characters expressed these sentiments more often, yet were less likely to discuss any aspect of sexuality.

In summary, an examination of these American alterations for American audiences revealed some obvious changes in the language of the American versions of the plays and more significant changes in sentiments expressed by American characters. The American versions included speeches not present in the British works, speeches that attacked class structure and extolled equality of man. In addition, the American plays made many more religious references than did the British plays and credited heaven with direct intervention in saving the virtuous and punishing the wicked, and the American plays eliminated nearly all references to sexuality. Finally, American female characters exhibited less assertive behaviors than did their British counterparts, and they expressed more positive attitudes toward matrimony and motherhood. Perhaps the changes made to the British plays reflected prevailing

American social attitudes towards language, equality, religion, sex, and the expected social behavior of women.

The changes to the language of the plays as well as the repeated references to equality suggested that the playwrights believed the audience held strong views about these matters. Many Americans had argued for an American language, urging that the new nation "purify" its language from British corruption and adopt simple spelling and plain speech.[37] References to equality also echoed sentiments of the period, for the colonies had only recently fought the Revolutionary War and would soon fight the War of 1812. The nation had sought to forge an identity apart from Britain, and changes in language, eliminating references to monarchy, as well as an emphasis on social equality helped to accomplish this objective.[38]

The increased religious references as well as the decreased sexual ones in American plays may have been responses to the religious revivals throughout New England. American playwrights may have believed that frequent references to God would make their plays more acceptable to those members of the audience who retained doubts about the morality of the theatre. Clergymen continued to oppose theatres on the grounds that they promoted immorality and idleness, and because they housed various unsavory patrons, particularly prostitutes.[39] Playwrights may have attempted to forestall censure by ensuring that the plays overtly promoted virtue; they then went one step further by suggesting that the theatre could foster virtue, as did William Dunlap: "What engine is more powerful than the theatre? No arts can be made more effectual for the promotion of good than the dramatic and the histrionic."[40]

That American Gothic plays depicted a narrow interpretation of morally acceptable behavior for females, emphasizing the desirability of matrimony and motherhood and avoiding references to their sexuality, perhaps reflected America's views of women's place.[41] In the late eighteenth and early nineteenth centuries in the United States, marriage was particularly important for women. De Tocqueville observed that in America, "the independence of woman [was] irrecoverably lost in the bonds of matrimony" and that a wife abided "in her husband's home" "as if it were a cloister."[42] However, De Tocqueville added that young American women understood what was expected of them and that they entered into matrimony "voluntarily and freely."[43] Indeed society made little provision for a single woman; she often ended up in the home a male relative, serving as a helper. Therefore, many women sought matrimony.[44]

Following the Revolutionary War, the American concept of motherhood was "significantly transformed" in response to a rapidly changing world.[45] During these years, the new nation was in "social disequilibrium" because of urban growth, westward expansion, and the rise of industrialization. This disequilibrium and the ensuing concern over the nation's morals and its stability caused Americans to stress maternal responsibilities.[46] After the Revolution, motherhood was perceived as the major source of women's power; women assumed responsibilities for fostering the proper morals as well as Republican virtues, so that their sons would become the leaders of the future.[47]

Perhaps the repressive prudery associated with American society after 1830 was already applied to public entertainments of the 1810s and 1820s. *The Boston Weekly Magazine* damned one production because of indecent references, and even before citing the innuendoes, the periodical noted,

> but before we continue our intended remarks on this subject, we beg our female readers, if we should be honoured with any, to proceed no farther in the perusal of our essay. ... it is now our painful duty to assure them, that it would derogate from their character even to *peruse* any just and searching criticism on performances, which they could not *attend* with an unblenched innocence.[48]

One month later, the same periodical featured a lengthy article on "Indecency in Conversation," in which the author asserted,

> it is distressing to a heart warmed and enlightened by moral feeling, to hear that low and disgusting language of the bagnio and brothel brought into general use and approbation. Yet, that that is at present the case, shamefully the case, with those young men from whom society is entitled to hope better things, is undeniable. There are indeed some exceptions to this assertion in the characters of those who, treading in the steps and emulating the virtues of their fathers, promise to become ornaments to society and to stand unweakened amid the torrent of corruption.[49]

American versions of Gothic dramas ensured that such potentially offensive references were omitted.

At the same time, women especially were forbidden to discuss sexual matters. Historian Nancy Cott asserts that the ideal women of this time (between 1790 and 1830) were "passionless" sexually, a perception probably influenced by Calvinism and literature. In the early eighteenth century, writers such as Jeremy Collier and Samuel Richardson began to attack "aristocratic libertarianism" and portrayed "sexual promiscuity as an aristocratic excesses that threatened middle class virtue and domestic security."[50]

The ideology of passionlessness seemed associated with the rise of evangelical religion. Women represented the majority in the Protestant churches in America by the mid–1700s and continued to increase their numbers into the nineteenth century. By the mid–1700s, ministers had discarded similes to Eve and instead portrayed women as more attuned to religion than men. The evangelical view of women emphasized their spiritual natures rather than their physical qualities.[51] American playwrights of this period may have tried to adapt their heroines to the expectations of the audiences, to reinforce the existing views about appropriate female behavior.

In summary, these alterations made by American playwrights suggest that American audiences were opposed to rigid class systems and welcomed mention of the inherent equality of all men, that they also apparently welcomed public declarations of the importance of virtuous living, and that they appreciated frequent references to the power of heaven. Conversely, audiences evidently did not welcome any public references to sex and did not tolerate comic treatment of virginity. Finally, American audiences, even more than the British, seemed to view the ideal woman as a sexually passive and unassertive being who considered matrimony and motherhood as her greatest achievement. The fact that these plays succeeded on the American stage suggests that audience members approved of the sentiments expressed; therefore, these plays, "made in America" between 1794 and 1830, probably reflected uniquely American views of important issues.

CHAPTER 10

"This Sort of Thing"
Reception of Gothic Plays in America

> This tragedy in our humble opinion, has no equal for the diabolical turpitude of its characters, the shocking depravity of its scenes, or the execrable tendency of its moral. As a performance, it neither can nor should be beheld without disgust.[1]

This contemporary review of a popular Gothic play may appear harsh; however it was fairly representative of the usual critical response to these plays. Later critics simply dismissed them as "this sort of thing" and lumped them together with melodramas.[2]

As Gothic dramas reached the height of their popularity in the United States between 1794 and 1830, theatrical criticism, which had been sporadic during the eighteenth century, began to appear regularly in periodicals.[3] Most of the critics writing for these periodicals were professional men: lawyers, journalists, legislators, ministers, and "men of letters," members of the "highly-educated minority" who wrote criticism in their spare time. This group, then, represented a "practically homogeneous upper class" who resolved to refine the stage and "legislate culturally for other classes."[4] They viewed themselves as watchdogs of society and assumed a paternal attitude toward audiences in their criticism.[5]

Theatrical criticism by these men took various forms: some addressed the plays as produced, commenting on the players and their talents, particularly stars, and occasionally discussing scenery and special effects. Another form, addressed in an earlier chapter, concentrated on "attacking or defending the utility and morality of the theatre"; criticism of this type noted objectionable behavior on the part of managers, actors, or patrons.[6] In addition to these forms of criticism, a third form appeared between 1794 and 1830 that addressed the dramas themselves as literary works.

Theatrical critics found little to admire in Gothic dramas, and they missed no opportunity to belittle the talent of the playwrights who wrote them, the ethics of the managers who produced them, or the taste of the public who supported them. The gap between the critical evaluation of Gothic dramas and the public's enthusiastic patronage of them may provide insight into the forces affecting theatre of this time.

At the end of the eighteenth century, many American dramatic critics, disgusted with the contemporary dramatic literature, returned to Shakespeare and touted his works as "desirable models for drama."[7] Thus, between 1794 and 1830, new works were regularly compared—unfavorably—with Shakespeare's. Critics protested that the public was not as appreciative of Shakespearean productions as they should have been. Complaining about the number of empty boxes at a 1825 performance of *As You Like It*, one critic grumbled:

> Now in the name of all the gods at once, why is this? Have our citizens lost all relish for pure drama? This state of things, however cannot last—taste and refinement will be in fashion by and by, and when the manager discovers that the public are ready to partake of good and wholesome food, he will, undoubtedly, supply them, and at no board can it be furnished up in better style than at the Park theatre.[8]

Critics often complained about the dearth of Shakespearean plays offered by theatrical managers:

> We are contented to admit at the dramatic feast—(for children must sometimes be pleased as well as men)—the occasional sugar plumbs [sic] of show ... and are these kickshaws to supersede the soul-reviving viands so profusely supplied us by the illustrious Caterer of Avon?[9]

Some even expressed appreciation when managers dared to present Shakespearean productions when they knew such plays would not fill the house:

> We feel much gratified, when the managers hazard the loss of a few dollars, to indulge us with Shakespeare, and duly appreciate their motives. They have too much taste, and too high a regard for the goodly customs of our ancestors, to applaud the blasphemous modern philosophy, and the flat, uninteresting dialogue of Kotzebue, and of Holcroft.[10]

These same critics regularly condemned the "improbable romances" present in the contemporary drama—"the melodramas, operas, fairy plays, spectacle extravaganzas, and the like."[11] One protested,

> It is with feelings of regret, that we find the legitimate drama is almost entirely thrown aside, and in its place substituted such trash as *Tom and Jerry*, slack-rope swinging, tight-rope dancing, etc.[12]

Critics seldom lost an opportunity to condemn such fare through references to Shakespeare:

> But who that looks upon Shakespeare, as the "god of his idolatry" can avoid viewing with mingled contempt, abhorrence, and indignation, those managerial iconoclasts, who erect upon the degraded altar of Thespis, the monster of MELO DRAME![13]

Critics particularly detested those productions that emphasized spectacle, which they described as "trash," and which included "the whole canon of melodramas, burlettas, pantomimes, and light entertainments that depended for their merit upon extravaganza and spectacle, upon fantastic settings and fanciful costumes."[14] Gothic dramas, particularly those produced in the 1820s, certainly fit these descriptions, and were criticized accordingly.

Although chastising managers for producing these seemingly inferior plays, the critics acknowledged that managers had to please the public and that "the publick in the final resort, govern the stage."[15] They recognized that, despite their best attempts to elevate the taste of the public, the public clearly preferred those plays that featured spectacle. In 1800, a disgruntled patron addressed the manager of the Chestnut Street.

Theatre the *Philadelphia Gazette*: "Several of the minority have deserted the Theatre since the appearance of *The Castle Spectre*. ... have mercy on us Mr. Wignell!"[16] As one Bostonian observed gloomily in 1807, "the present dramatical taste is rather for the sentimental and marvellous [sic] than for nature and truth."[17] Clearly such attacks had little effect. Audiences continued to patronize productions of Gothic dramas, along with melodramas, burlettas, and extravanganzas. Indeed, between 1794 and 1830, productions of Gothic dramas were so popular that they rivaled those of Shakespeare in all the theatrical centers.

Between 1800 and 1816, the Shakespearean plays produced most often in Philadelphia and Charleston were *Hamlet, Macbeth, Richard III,* and *Romeo and Juliet*. In Philadelphia, Shakespearean productions

CHARLESTON THEATRE.

This Evening, Monday, February 25,

Will be presented, the celebrated *COMEDY*, of the

School for Scandal.

SIR PETER TEAZLE,	Mr. TURNBULL,	CARELESS,	Mr. WEST,
SIR OLIVER SURFACE,	Mr. WHITLOCK,	TRIP,	Mr. PLACIDE,
JOSEPH SURFACE,	Mr. STORY,	SNAKE,	Mr. CHARNOCK.
CHARLES SURFACE,	Mr. HODGKINSON,		
CRABTREE,	Mr. BARRYMORE,	LADY TEAZLE,	Mrs. WHITLOCK,
SIR BENJAMIN BACKBITE,	Mr. SULLY,	MARIA,	Mrs. PLACIDE,
ROWLEY,	Mr. DYKES,	LADY SNEERWELL,	Miss FIELD,
MOSES,	Mr. WILMOT,	MRS. CANDOUR,	Mrs. SIMPSON.

Between the PLAY and FARCE,

Ground and Lofty Tumbling,

By MR. SULLY.----CLOWN, MR. BERRY.

To which will be added, HOLCROFT's celebrated *MELO DRAME*, of the

Tale of Mistery.

The different passages accompanied with Music, expressive to the passages and situations of the Scene.

BONAMO,	Mr. TURNBULL,	MALVOGLIO,	Mr. CHARNOCK,
ROMALDI,	Mr. HODGKINSON,	PIERO,	Mr. WILMOT,
FRANCISCO, (a dumb man)	Mr. PLACIDE,	EXEMPT,	Mr. BARRYMORE,
STEPHANO,	Mr. STORY,	SPEARMEN, ARCHERS, &c. &c.	
MONTANO,	Mr. DYKES,	SELINA,	Mrs. VILLIERS,
MICHELLI, (a miller)	Mr. SULLY,	FIAMETTA,	Mrs. SIMPSON.

In ACT SECOND,

A GARDEN prepared for HYMENIAL FESTIVITY,
With GARLANDS, FLOWERS, &c.

In ACT THIRD,

The Rock of Arpennaz,

With a MILL, RUSTIC BRIDGE, &c. &c.

Charleston: Printed by W. P. Young, No. 41, Broad-Street.

were significantly more popular than those of Gothic plays. However, in Charleston during these years, Gothic plays far outnumbered those of Shakespeare.

This ratio changed in these cities between 1816 and 1830. Productions of *Othello* were particularly popular at this time along with *Romeo and Juliet* and *Richard III*. Productions of Shakespeare's plays increased significantly in Charleston during these years; simultaneously, productions of Gothic plays decreased sharply. However, in Philadelphia, productions of Shakespeare declined, but productions of Gothic plays remained constant.

Critics, dismayed by the public's enthusiastic reception of Gothic dramas, sought to explain their popularity. They concluded that the appeal of the Gothics, like that of melodramas and extravaganzas, lay in "the pomp of these spectacles," which "generally [destroyed] all interest in the dialogue." and caused "pleasure [to pass] from the ear to the eye."[18]

Yet, the appeal of Gothic dramas was not so easily explained because several of the most popular did not feature innovative scenery or special effects.[19] Unquestionably, their production values, both musical and visual, accounted for much of their popularity, but unlike melodramas, which most often did rely heavily on spectacle for their allure, many Gothic plays must have appealed to patrons for other reasons.

One reason for the popularity of many Gothic plays may have been that they featured the talents of a major male star.[20] For example, the role of the Earl of Osmond in *The Castle Spectre* proved a popular acting vehicle for John Hodgkinson, Thomas Cooper, William Wood, and James Fennell, among others. One critic noted, "We have seen Cooper, Hodgkinson, Rutley, and some other celebrated actors do that part, who gave a description of the vision with an effect which might be said to 'freeze the chil'd [sic] blood.'"[21]

The role of Sir Edward Mortimer in *The Iron Chest* likewise attracted many major male stars of the day, including Thomas Cooper, Robert Maywood of Drury Lane (whom Wood called the "novelty of the season"), James Fennell, Edmund Kean, Edwin Forrest, and Junius Brutus Booth, Sr.[22] Junius Brutus Booth, in particular, was noted for his

Opposite: Playbill for the Charleston Theatre's 1805 production of *A Tale of Mistery* [sic] featuring John Hodgkinson as the villain Romaldi. The Harvard Theatre Collection, Houghton Library.

performance of Sir Edward Mortimer. In his memoir, *The Stage*, James Murdoch recounted his experience of playing Wilford, the young secretary in *The Iron Chest*, opposite Booth's Sir Edward Mortimer. In the climactic scene, Wilford secretly opens Sir Edward's mysterious chest to learn his horrible secret; however, the young man is discovered by an enraged Sir Edward who becomes violent. In his first performance as Wilford, Murdoch found himself literally stunned by Booth's power. He recounts:

> I had proceeded so far as to open the chest, and, stooping over the papers, awaited trembling, on my knee the appointed signal for action. The time seemed an eternity, but it came at last. The heavy hand fell on my shoulder. I turned, and there, with the pistol held to my head, stood Booth, glaring like an infuriated demon. Then for the first time I comprehended the reality of acting. The fury of that passion-flamed face and the magnetism of the rigid clutch upon my arm paralyzed my muscles, while the scintillating gleam of the terrible eyes, like the green and red flashed of an enraged serpent, fascinated and fixed me spellbound to the spot. A sudden revulsion of feeling caused me to spring from the knees, but, bewildered with fright and a choking sensation of undefined dread, I fell heavily to the stage, tripping Mr. Booth, who still clutched my shoulder. I brought him down with me, and for a moment we lay prostrate. But suddenly recovering himself, he sprang to his feet with almost superhuman strength dragging me up, as I clung to his arm in terror.... I sank down again stunned and helpless. I was aroused to consciousness, however by a voice calling on me, in suppressed accents, to rise, and then became aware the Mr. Booth was kneeling at my side. He helped me to my feet whispering in my ear a few encouraging words, and then dexterously managed, in spite of the accident and my total inability to speak, to continue the scene to its close.[23]

The character of Sir Edward continued to attract famous actors well into the 1830s.

Several stars found the title role in *Bertram* attractive; apparently the role was written for "the purpose of allowing Mr. Kean, an English actor of considerable celebrity to display some tragic powers that are peculiar to himself."[24] Kean performed the role in 1821 and 1826, but the *Boston Weekly Magazine* compared the performance of Cooper favorably to that of Kean, noting that Cooper "was in *Bertram* equally remarkable for the judgment with which he conceived the part, and the unequalled vigour with which it was executed."[25] Junius Brutus Booth, Sr. performed the role in 1824 and Edwin Forrest in 1827.

Famous actresses, too, found in Gothic plays effective vehicles for their talent. Earlier Gothic plays, such as *The Count of Narbonne, The Carmelite, The Sicilian Romance, Fontainville Forest,* and *Fountainville Abbey,* offered serious leading roles for older females.

The appearance of famous actresses in Gothic plays, then, also may have contributed to the popularity of these plays between 1794 and 1830.The role of Angela in *The Castle Spectre* and Matilda in *The Carmelite* were popular roles for leading actresses, as were Fatima in *Bluebeard*, Una in *The Wood Demon*, Adelaide in *Adelmorn*, and Imogene in *Bertram*.[26]

The idea that productions of Gothic plays would have benefited from stars, particularly British ones, was not an unfavorable reflection on the plays themselves. In these years, theatres repeatedly performed the same plays in repertory, and, as a result, patrons frequently knew the plays very well. Consequently, patrons may have attended the theatre not so much to watch the plot as to view a favorite actor performing a particular role. And, because they often saw many different stars perform the same roles, they were able to compare performances. For example, audiences in New York in 1826 had the opportunity to see four major stars interpret the role of Sir Edward Mortimer in *The Iron Chest*: Kean performed the role in May at the Park; J.B. Booth, Sr., at the Chatham in October, Mr. Wilson at the Lafayette in November, and Edwin Forrest at the Bowery in December.

Actors themselves often were responsible for increasing the number of productions of Gothic plays. Visiting stars often selected favorite plays from their repertoire for their stay at a theatre, and even lesser known company actors were permitted to choose a favorite play for their benefit night. Naturally, actors chose plays that best showcased their talents, and Gothic plays, with their juicy roles, were popular choices. For example, Edmund Kean often revived the role of Sir Edward; in 1830 in New York, Kean performed the role at the Park in September, November, and December. Similarly, Thomas Cooper performed the role of *Bertram* at the Park each year, sometimes several times a year, from 1826 until 1830. Despite frequent revivals of the same play, patrons evidently continued to enjoy watching their favorite actor perform a favorite role; in 1821 Edmund Kean performed the role Sir Edward Mortimer in Philadelphia, and the receipts for that performance were $727.25, comparing well with the other offerings of the week, which included Kean's performances in *Macbeth* and *The Merchant of Venice*.[27]

A second possible reason for the popularity of some Gothic dramas, particularly those written before 1800, was their resemblance to tragedy as opposed to melodrama. Gothic plays appeared to be a mixture of the two forms, offering more spectacle than that provided by tragedies and more complexity of character than that provided by melodramas.

Most critics of the period considered the difference between serious drama and melodrama to be one of degree: the plots in melodramas were simply "more intricate and horrible, the characters more virtuous or villainous, and the settings even more spectacular and fanciful." Also, melodramas insisted that "poetic justice" would overcome wickedness so that virtue would be rewarded and evil punished. In contrast, serious drama, or the "bastardized tragic form" presented virtuous heroes and heroines who "always seemed to die, nobly but conveniently, as the curtain fell."[28]

Gothic dramas often appeared more like "serious drama" than melodrama. For example, although several Gothic dramas did include demons or specters, most included no supernatural elements. Moreover, whereas action certainly became more emphasized in Gothic plays of the 1820s, it was not so prevalent in earlier ones, where language was emphasized instead. Finally, although poetic justice usually prevailed in Gothic dramas, occasionally the virtuous did die (the guiltless ingenue in *The Count of Narbonne* or the ill-used heroines in *Bertram* and *Marmion*). In addition, several Gothic melodramas featured the death or destruction of a main character who served as a villain-hero (*Bertram*, *Marmion*, or Sir Edward in *The Iron Chest*).

The fact that Gothic plays possessed characteristics of both forms enabled them to appeal to a wider range of patrons. Like tragedies, Gothic plays often provided complex characters (particularly in the characters of villains), and, occasionally, unhappy conclusions. Such distinctions may have made Gothic dramas more appealing to upper class audiences who particularly favored tragedies. This idea was further supported by an analysis of the productions of five Gothic plays in New York between 1824 and 1830, a time of intense competition among theatres. The analysis revealed that of the five most popular Gothic plays in New York, the ones that retained their popularity at the Park theatre were *Bertram* and *The Iron Chest*, plays that featured more complex characters and emphasized language over spectacle.

However, Gothic plays also were able to compete for lower class audiences, for, like melodramas, they sometimes provided visual or aural special effects. This emphasis on scenery and special effects over language undoubtedly appealed especially to immigrants, who were moving into the cities in ever-increasing numbers.

In summary, Gothic plays reached the height of popularity at the time when theatrical criticism was just beginning in America. These critics were of the upper class, and in their constant attempts to reform the taste of the ordinary public, they frequently employed the strategy of belittling Gothic plays (and melodramas) by comparing them unfavorably to those of Shakespeare. Yet Gothic plays competed well with productions of Shakespeare in at least two of the theatrical centers.

The critics, despite their energetic efforts, were unable to quash attendance at Gothic plays, perhaps because they never quite pinpointed their unique appeal. Although they had concluded that spectacle was the major lure in melodramas, they never distinguished between melodramas and Gothic plays, nor considered those aspects that were unique to Gothic dramas. Yet, because several of the most popular Gothic plays did not offer particularly impressive visual effects, they probably appealed to audiences for other reasons: the presence of a major star in the leading role, the innovative use of music in the play, or the unique blend of tragic elements and melodramatic ones.

The disparity between the reception of Gothic dramas by critics and that of the audience is particularly interesting in that the critics, members of the upper classes professed great disdain of Gothic dramas, and it was true that by the 1820s, most Gothic plays appeared primarily at those theatres associated with lower classes, which suggests that they were no longer considered appropriate fare for the elite. However, a few Gothic plays, those resembling tragedies, retained their popularity at these theatres for more elite patrons, even though the very same plays were appearing simultaneously at theatres for lower classes.

As long as Gothic plays resembled serious drama, offering more complex characters and tragic form, they proved popular with upper-class audiences. Many of the Gothic dramas produced before 1810 adhered to this structure, and it was at this time that these plays appeared frequently at the Park and the Chestnut. Moreover, *Bertram*, although written later, also featured a complex villain-hero and a tragic ending, and it too retained its popularity at these theatres associated with upper-class patrons.

Although Gothic dramas never won critical acclaim, they won popular acclamation from audiences at all theatres in the major theatrical centers of the United States. The unique blend of tragedy and melodrama in Gothic plays enabled them to appeal to a wide range of patrons.

CHAPTER 11

A Gothic View of America

Gothic plays enjoyed their greatest popularity at a time of tremendous change in American society. Between 1794 and 1830, populations in the theatrical centers doubled or even tripled. Much of the increase was from immigration and from workers crowding into the cities. That these new arrivals attended the theatres is suggested by the regular expansion of theatres in every city. Moreover, the average worker could have afforded a ticket to the theatre, for a gallery seat cost roughly the equivalent of a quarter of a day's earnings. The years between 1795 and 1830 also were a time of cultural change; systems of deference were breaking down, and Americans were seeking to establish their own culture apart from Britain.

During this period, the theatrical experience in America reflected a resurgence of concern with morality, and many attacked the stage. Critics accused the dramas themselves of promoting immorality; in addition they attacked the actors, the managers, and the patrons in the theatre. Gothic plays provided excellent vehicles for theatrical managers hoping to stem such accusations of immorality, in that usually in these plays, virtue triumphed and evil was vanquished. Moreover, Gothic plays provided actors and actresses with characters who were absolutely chaste and virtuous, thus aiding their personal reputations off the stage. Although audience behavior at Gothic plays was just as unruly as that at any other type of play in the period—patrons in the boxes chattered; those in the pit occasionally shoved and pushed; men in the gallery smoked, drank, and swore, and those in the upper boxes did even more objectionable things—theatrical managers could defend Gothic plays and the audiences who attended them by proclaiming that these particular plays vividly reminded patrons about the dire consequences of sin.

An analysis of the patterns of productions of Gothic plays reflects the changing composition of audiences. Gothic dramas appeared first in the 1790s at the major (often only) theatre in each city that served all classes. With the erection of new theatres that catered to lower classes, these established theatres increased productions of Gothic plays, presumably to compete. However, in the 1820s, as more new theatres emerged that targeted working class patrons particularly, older established theatres performed fewer Gothic plays, usually only the ones that featured a major tragedian in the leading role. The newer theatres, however, produced these same plays with stars as well as Gothic plays more dependent upon visual stimulation. This was particularly true in New York theatres in the 1820s, the time of greatest competition among theatres there.

The most popular Gothic plays between 1794 and 1830 were *Bluebeard*, *The Castle Spectre*, *A Tale of Mystery*, *Bertram*, and *The Iron Chest*; although all of these plays received productions in all the theatrical centers, Philadelphia seemed more receptive to those Gothic plays more like tragedy, perhaps because they were able to procure the finest tragedians for their theatres, and thus, because of the actors' choice as well as that of theatrical managers wishing to display the special talents of these actors, they preferred this type of Gothic play. Conversely, critics in Boston frequently moaned about the inferior quality of their actors, and they produced significantly more Gothic plays that relied on spectacle. Thus, theatrical managers could use Gothic plays to display or compensate for their acting companies.

The major characters in Gothic plays possessed some particular traits not shared by characters in melodramas. Young heroes were unique in their deference to older males. Older heroes were portrayed as wiser and more masterful than younger men; these older characters and often drove the action of the play. Young heroines in Gothic plays were usually motherless and showed extreme, unquestioning obedience to their fathers. They expressed their desire for matrimony and motherhood even more often than heroines in melodramas. Gothic heroines appeared more assertive than heroines in melodramas, but only when they acted on behalf of others. They had to fight off a lascivious villain more often than heroines in melodramas. These young, virginal heroines sometimes were contrasted with older female characters who had not remained chaste and who, as a consequence, had been punished. The young heroine's fearful musings about the illicit intentions of the villain allowed the audience to contemplate sexual activity without ever condoning it. Gothic plays also presented another type of heroine: the older woman, who was devoted wife and loving mother. These women never were depicted as physically attractive; instead they were admired for their good deeds and saintly behavior. Gothic plays were most noted for their portrayal of the villain; this character, unique to these plays, suffered terrible guilt from the crime he had once committed, yet was unable to fully repent his deed. He was always an older man who exercised complete control over all with whom he came in contact.

Gothic plays achieved popularity at a time of scenic innovation in theatre; however, most of American scenic practices paralleled those of Britain, probably because American theatres continued to use British designs and designers. During these years in America, as in Britain, scenery reveals a shift from indoor to outdoor settings; scenery became more specific for individual productions, often built for a particular play, and three-dimensional, practicable scenery began to replace painted flats. Also, as plays became more scenically interesting, they became less actor-centered. Even the advertising began to publicize the scenery more than the actors, and theatrical managers commented that these spectacular plays helped to keep the theatres financially solvent.

Innovations in lighting too, followed those first instituted in Britain. Technicians gained greater control over light between 1794 and 1830; in the early years, plays demanded little variation; however, later plays required changes in time of day, and special effects such as colored lights and the effect of moonlight. Gothic plays offered a unique atmosphere of gloom and foreboding, first through scenery and later through special effects; however, their increasing emphasis on spectacle moved them away from the Gothic gloom and more toward melodrama. American Gothic plays did not rely so much on supernatural effects; instead American playwrights and adapters offered explainable effects.

When American playwrights wrote their own Gothic plays or adapted British ones, they exhibited notable changes from British playwrights. The American versions included speeches that railed against subjugation to a monarchy and also against class distinctions. Also, American playwrights included more religious references and eliminated sexual ones. Finally, American playwrights made more speeches advocating matrimony and motherhood than did their British counterparts.

Although Gothic plays were undeniably popular with audiences, they did not win over the critics, who lumped Gothic plays with melodramas, burlettas, extravaganzas, and other more visual entertainments and pronounced them all inferior dramatic works. The critics, usually members of the upper classes, attempted to elevate the taste of the public by comparing Gothic plays unfavorably with works by Shakespeare. Yet several Gothic plays were as popular with upper class patrons, probably because they, like Shakespeare's plays, promoted the art of oratory, featured a renowned tragedian, offered a complex character who was master of his universe, and provided a moral lesson. Gothic plays, however, managed to appeal to a cross-section of American society, perhaps because they often were a blend of tragedy and melodrama and thus appealed to a wide audience. As more patrons arrived who were less comfortable with the English language, Gothic plays moved more from the tragic form to one closer to the pure visual stimulation of melodrama.

Because Gothic plays flourished on the American stage between 1794 and 1830, a time of enormous change both in theatrical practice as well as in American society itself, these plays, and the manner of their production on the American stage, provide some insight into changing theatrical practices. Moreover, because many people at this time considered theatre to be an extremely powerful means of persuasion, their commendations and complaints about Gothic plays and their production, as gleaned through written criticism, attendance figures, production histories, or other sources, reveal more than mere trends in theatrical practice; they provide insight into the values of society itself. Although most of these sources confirm that trends in American drama and theatrical practice paralleled those of Britain, several uncover aspects of American society that were decidedly unique.

Gothic dramas appear to have been a special form of melodrama, the earliest form, that blended some of the complexities of character in tragedy with the visual stimulation and excitement of melodrama. The earliest Gothic dramas were more similar to tragedy; later ones, those written after the success of *A Tale of Mystery*, tended more toward melodrama. In Gothic plays, virtue always triumphed over evil, and, as an added fillip, evil-doers suffered excruciating torment. However, Gothic plays proved unique in their blend of melodrama and tragedy, thus attracting a wide audience; upper-class patrons could appreciate a famous tragedian's skill at oratory and lower-class audiences, perhaps less comfortable with the English language, could appreciate the lavish scenery and breath-taking effects.

One of the greatest changes in theatrical practice in both countries during these years was the increased emphasis on spectacle — to the extent that critics complained that patrons attended the theatre to see a play rather than to hear one. The changes made in the scenery of Gothic plays reflected overall changes in production techniques: between 1794 and 1830, scenery increasingly depicted outdoor vistas. Scenery in Gothic plays also became more specific, often built for a particular production; also it became increasingly three-dimensional and practicable. These new sets, constructed as they were for individual productions, undoubtedly cost the management more to produce and thus may have hastened the institution of the long run.

Production of Gothic plays also reflected the increasing manipulation of lighting in the theatre; in the 1790s, lighting in Gothic plays was only able to provide general illumination and to indicate, simplistically, time of day; by the 1820s, however, manipulation of light had advanced to the extent that lighting, through control of intensity and color, could enhance mood.

The major characters in Gothic plays reflected trends in dramatic literature and theatrical practice in the late eighteenth and early nineteenth centuries. The most dramatically complex roles were those of villains; in the tradition of the Byronic hero, this character suffered such pangs of guilt and remorse that he became increasingly sympathetic. Most importantly, in Gothic dramas, all the major villains were older males. No comparable roles existed for young men or older women. Gothic plays also reflected the growing trend of using only young, attractive actresses in leading roles. Early Gothic plays offered several roles for older woman; however, after 1800, as the plays became more visual and relied less on oratory, most of the leading female roles required younger actresses, and even those smaller roles available for older actresses were those of comic old women or servants. Thus, in theatre, at the time of the star system, the best roles, those that best displayed an actor's range and versatility, appear to have been for older male actors.

In addition to reflecting theatrical practice, Gothic plays and their productions also reflected societal practices. The texts of Gothic plays prescribed expectations for social behavior for Britons and Americans. In Gothic plays, older elite males, heroes or villains, exerted absolute control over their environment. They dominated younger men, who deferred to their judgment, and they demanded unquestioning obedience from all women, regardless of age.

In this age of preoccupation with morality, Gothic plays neatly countered most objections to the theatre, providing a moral message in the drama, particularly in regard to the sanctity of female virtue. In addition, Gothic melodramas enabled actors and actresses to present moral behavior to audiences, which seemed to directly affect the public's opinion of their personal reputations. Finally, Gothic dramas were thought to affect members of the audience, which, although not credited directly with eliminating profane behavior in the theatres, at least afforded the hope of improving the behavior of individuals who were affected by the plays. Moreover, Gothic dramas also offered a unique bonus: patrons could freely mull over possible sexual situations without ever condoning such behavior. These plays, then, provided the public not only a thrilling theatrical experience, but, at the same time, an improving one. The ability of Gothic plays to satisfy both the public's desire for entertaining theatricals as well as the critics' demand for moral theatricals made them particularly appropriate fare for the theatre.

Although audiences at productions of Gothic dramas in both England and the United States undoubtedly shared much the same theatrical experience, they may have received slightly different messages about cultural expectations and values. American productions of Gothic plays revealed our dependence upon the culture of Britain; however, they also pointed up ways in which American culture had already deviated.

During the late eighteenth and early nineteenth centuries, Americans certainly appeared ambivalent in their efforts at cultural independence, demanding recognition for American cultural efforts and simultaneously lionizing British playwrights, actors, and scene designers, but they had succeeded in forging some distinctive national characteristics. These characteristics manifested themselves in the revisions of British Gothic dramas made by American adaptors before these plays appeared on American stages. Surface revisions—simplifying language and spelling, eliminating any references to monarchy and class division—reflected the militantly democratic values present in the new nation that had only recently fought the Revolutionary War and the War of 1812. In addition, American playwrights' preference for explainable special effects, rather than supernatural ones, reinforced the argument that Americans preferred to think of themselves as rational, practical children of the Enlightenment.

Other revisions to British plays, however, suggested another way in which Americans viewed themselves as different from Britons; many American apparently considered themselves as more moral and virtuous than their European counterparts. The plays made more references to Heaven and divine intervention and consistently credited Heaven with their triumph over evil. Americans particularly wished to be perceived as moral in sexual matters, as suggested by the systematic elimination of references to sexual activity, especially humorous ones. This eradication affirmed the power of the Puritan influence in this country and suggested that American playwrights attempted to make their plays more moral, more virtuous, than those of the British.

Gothic plays, as adapted for the American stage, provided an opportunity to explore American society's standards for personal behavior. Roles were more clearly prescribed in American plays than in those of British playwrights. In America, young men were to exhibit respect for older males and allow those men to control the environment. Even more apparent, Gothic plays for the American stage depicted all women, young and old, as obedient to older men. Young women were to remain sexually passive or passionless and yet desire matrimony and motherhood. Older women, as depicted in the American Gothic plays, and, by extension, in society, were to view themselves solely as devoted wives and mothers. They were not encouraged to pursue any other occupation or role, and under no circumstances were they to exhibit any signs of sexuality. Instead they were to define their lives and their worth by their piety and good works.

American revisions of Gothic plays, then, hint that this country, despite its emphasis on personal freedom, actually was more repressive for females than was Britain. Although American women, according to the accounts of foreign visitors, lost much of their freedom when they married, they were encouraged — urged, cajoled, and even threatened — into seeking matrimony and motherhood, by American Gothic plays. In addition, they were instructed by these plays to remain passionless, both before and after marriage.

Thus, an examination of Gothic plays adapted for the American stage between 1794 and 1830 reveals that the new country had indeed managed to form its own cultural identity apart from Britain and that this identity consisted of at least three aspects: Americans wished to be known for their fierce defense of personal freedom, their staunch support of marriage and family, and their strict requirements for virtuous living. However, American versions of the plays also revealed that those who most benefited from these conditions were older males, and those whose lives were more restricted by the observance of these conditions were primarily women. The picture of America, then, as reflected in productions of American Gothic plays, depicted a land of freedom and opportunity — but only for some.

Although certain characteristics of the Gothic reappeared in plays and films of the twentieth and twenty-first centuries, most Gothic melodramas, so popular in the early 1800s, did not enjoy many revivals after the 1830s.[1] When *The Castle Spectre* was revived at the Gaiety Theatre in 1880, critics commented that the revival was "at once a proof and a warning of the depraved taste of our ancestors."[2] Yet, clearly, Gothic plays, with their contradictory mix of transgression and moral righteousness, staunchly "American" sentiments and reverence for European tradition, decorous speeches and indecorous actions were particularly compelling fare for the patrons of this critical period in the young United States.

Appendix 1

Plays in sample listed by date of first noted performance in the United States

Cumberland, Richard. *The Carmelite*, 1794.
Dunlap, William. *Fontainville Abbey*, 1795.*
Boaden, James. *Fountainville Forest*. 1794.
Siddons, Henry. *The Sicilia Romance*, 1795.
Jephson, Robert. *The Count of Narbonne*, 1795.
Andrews, Miles. *The Mysteries of the Castle*, 1796.
Colman, George. *The Iron Chest*, 1797.
Lewis, Matthew G. *The Castle Spectre*, 1798.
Hodgkinson, John. *The Man of Fortitude*, 1800.*
Dunlap, William. *Bluebeard*, 1801.*
Lewis, Matthew G. *Adelmorn*, 1802.
Dunlap, William. *Ribbemont*, 1803.*
Holcroft, Thomas. *A Tale of Mystery*, 1803.
White, John Blake. *Mysteries of the Castle*, 1806.*
White, John Blake. *Foscari*, 1806.*
Turnbull, J.D. *The Wood Daemon*, 1808.*

Stokes, John. *The Forest of Rosenwald*, 1808.*
Colman, George. *Bluebeard*, 1811.
Lewis, Matthew Gregory. *Raymond and Agnes; or The Travelers Benighted*, 1811.
Baillie, Joanna. *De Monfort*, 1811.
Barker, James Nelson. *Marmion*, 1812.*
Arnold, Samuel. *The Woodman's Hut*, 1816.
Maturin, Charles. *Bertram*, 1816.
Judah, Samuel. *The Mountain Torrent*, 1820.*
Planche, J. *The Vampire; or Bride of the Isles*, 1820.
Walker, C.E. *The Warlock of the Glen*, 1821.
Judah, Samuel. *The Rose of Arragon*, 1822.*
Peake, Richard. *Presumption; or The Fate of Frankenstein*, 1823.
West, Benjamin. *Melmoth the Wanderer*, 1823.
Lewis, Matthew G. *One O'Clock; or The Knight and the Wood Daemon*, 1823.
Barker, James Nelson. *Superstition*, 1824.*

*Indicates an American playwright or adaptor.

Appendix 2

*Immigration by Country, 1820 to 1830**

	Brit.	Ire.	Other NW	Italy	Germ.	Scan.
1820	2410	3614	452	30	968	23
1821	3210	1518	521	63	383	24
1822	1221	2267	522	35	48	8
1823	1100	1908	528	33	183	7
1824	1264	2345	671	45	230	20
1825	2095	4888	719	75	450	18
1826	2319	5408	968	57	511	26
1827	4186	9766	1829	35	432	28
1828	5352	12,488	4700	34	1851	60
1829	3179	7415	1065	23	597	30
1830	1153	2721	1305	9	1976	19

*Source: John Andriot, Population Abstract of the United States, Vol. 1 (McClean, VA: Andriot Associatates, 1983), 106. NW is an abbreviation for Northwestern countries which combined into one total for immigration: Netherlands, Belgium, Luxembourg, Switzerland, and France.

Appendix 3

*Average Daily Wage of Laborers in the Philadelphia Area Between 1785 and 1830**

1795	1.00	1807	1.00	1819	1.00
1796	1.00	1808	.75	1820	—
1797	1.00	1809	1.00	1821	.75
1798	1.00	1810	1.00	1822	.75
1799	1.00	1811	1.00	1823	1.00
1800	1.00	1812	1.00	1824	1.00
1801	1.00	1813	1.00	1825	1.00
1802	.75	1814	1.00	1826	1.00
1803	.75	1815	1.00	1827	1.00
1804	1.00	1816	1.00	1828	1.00
1805	1.00	1817	1.00	1829	1.00
1806	1.00	1818	1.00	1830	1.00

*Source: John, Andriot, ed. Historical Statistics of the United States, Part I (McClean, VA: Andriot Associates, 1983), 163.

Appendix 4

Daily Wage for Common Labor on the Erie Canal, 1828 to 1830*

1828	.71
1829	.75
1830	.75

**Source: Andriot, Historical Statistics of the United States, Part I, 163.*

Appendix 5

*Prices in Massachusetts from 1780 to 1830 with Dollar Equivalents from 1780 to 1800**

Item	1780–1800	1801–1820	1821–1830
Butter (pound)	8 pence (11 cents)	11 pence	9 pence
Candles (pound)	11 pence (15 cents)	11 pence	8 pence
Cheese	5 pence (7 cents)	6 pence	4 pence
Cider (gallon)	3 pence (4 cents)	9 pence	10 pence
Coffee	11 pence (15 cents)	13 pence	10 pence
Eggs (dozen)	4 pence (6 cents)	11 pence	8 pence
Flannel (yard)	21 pence (29 cents)	33 pence	29 pence
Flour	2 pence (3 cents)	3 pence	2 pence
Gin	62 pence (86 cents)	58 pence	60 pence
Gloves	27 pence (37 cents)	26 pence	26 pence
Milk	2 pence (3 cents)	2 pence	2 pence

*Source: Michael G. Mulhall, The Dictionary of Statistics *(London: George Routledge and Sons, Ltd., 1899), 188.*

Appendix 6

*Equivalencies of One Pound to One Dollar, 1782 — 1796**

	Equivalent worth of One Pound to 18th Century Dollar	Equivalent worth of One Pound to 1991 Dollar
Massachusetts	$3.33	$43.97
New York	$2.50	$32.98
Pennsylvania	$2.66	$35.17
South Carolina	$4.28	$56.53

*Source: John J. McCusker, How Much Is That in Real Money? (Worcester, MA: American Antiquarian Society, 1992), 333.

Appendix 7

Equivalencies of One Pence to 18th Century Dollars and Cents (1782–1796) and 1991 Dollars and Cents*

City	Worth of One Pence to 18th Century Dollar and Cents	Worth of One Pence to 1991 Dollar and Cents
Massachusetts	1.38 cents	18.32 cents
New York	1.04 cents	13.74 cents
Pennsylvania	1.10 cents	14.65 cents
South Carolina	1.78 cents	23.55 cents

**Source: McCusker, How Much Is That in Real Money?, 333.*

Notes

Introduction

1. Matthew Gregory Lewis, *The Castle Spectre* (London: J. Bell, 1798), in *Seven Gothic Dramas*, 149–224, ed. Jeffrey N. Cox (Athens: Ohio University Press, 1992), 212.
2. Lewis, The *Castle Spectre*, 214.
3. Lewis, *The Castle Spectre*, 219.
4. Alfred Longueil, in his article, "The Word Gothic in Eighteenth Century Criticism," *Modern Language Notes* 38 (1923), observed that the problem of definition is complicated, because the term "Gothic" changed its meaning over the centuries, first from "barbarous" to "medieval." The term first was a name for Germanic tribes; then in the early Renaissance it took on the meaning of "barbarous." Then Horace Walpole, promoting the connotation of "medieval," subtitled his novel *The Castle of Otranto*, "A Gothic Story." Although Walpole's novel was initially termed "Gothic" because of its medieval aspects, the supernatural elements that the author included soon became so closely associated with the term that with the publication of *The Castle of Otranto* the third meaning of "Gothic," that of "supernatural," emerged as an outgrowth of the other two, 453–460.
5. Botting, 3.
6. Ibid.
7. Frederick Frank's *Guide to the Gothic* (Metuchen, NJ, and London: The Scarecrow Press, Inc.,1984) and *Through the Pale Door* (New York: Greenwood Press, 1990) provided annotated bibliographies of Gothic literature through the twentieth century.
8. David Stevens in *The Gothic Tradition* (Cambridge: Cambridge University Press, 2000) observed that "gothic" sites on the web often are dedicated to selling products and that the label has been used to describe nearly "every aspect of human creativity," 5.
9. Punter, in *The Literature of Terror* (London: Longman, 1980), identified several important early studies of Gothic literature, including Edith Birkhead's *The Tale of Terror*, Eino Railo's *The Haunted Castle*, J.M.S. Tompkin's *The Popular Novel in England*, Montague Summers' *The Gothic Quest*, and Davendra Varma's *The Gothic Flame*, 13–15.
10. David Punter, *The Literature of Terror*, 16–18. Studies that examined Gothic literature include (among others) Judith Wilt's *Ghosts of the Gothic: Austen, Eliot, and Lawrence*; Elizabeth R. Napier's *The Failure of Gothic: Problems of Disjunction in an Eighteenth-Century Literary Form*; and George E. Hagerty's *Gothic Fiction/Gothic Form*. Some notable studies include Donald Ringe's *American Gothic: Imagination and Reason in Nineteenth Century Fiction*; William Patrick Day's *In the Circles of Fear and Desire*; and Victor Sage's *Horror Fiction in the Protestant Tradition*. A study that investigates deconstruction and Gothic works is Eve Kosofsky Sedgwick's *The Coherence of Gothic Conventions*.
11. Diane Hoeveler, "The Female Gothic: An Introduction"; online at www.virginia.edu.
12. Juliann Fleenor, ed., *The Female Gothic* (Montreal: Eden Press, 1983), 8.
13. Ellen Moers, *Literary Women* (London, 1977), 138.
14. Fleenor, 14.
15. Fleenor, 8.
16. Fleenor, 14.
17. Fleenor, 15.
18. Paula Backscheider, *Spectacular Politics*

(Baltimore: Johns Hopkins University Press, 1993), 149.

19. Martin Tropp, *Images of Fear: How Horror Stories Helped Shape Modern Culture (1818–1918)* (Jefferson, NC: McFarland & Company, Inc., 1990), 15.

20. Tropp, *Images of Fear*, 15.

21. Botting, 6.

22. Botting, 7; Moers, 139.

23. Eugenia Delamotte, *Perils of the Night* (New York: Oxford University Press, 1990), 22.

24. Botting, 6–7.

25. Matthews, 52.

26. Matthews, 52.

27. Matthews, 52.

28. Eric Savoy, "The Rise of American Gothic," in *The Cambridge Companion to Gothic Fiction*, 167–188, ed. Jerrold E. Hogle (Cambridge: Cambridge University Press, 2002), 167.

29. Leslie Fiedler, *Love and Death in the American Novel* (New York: Doubleday, 1966), 144.

30. Fiedler asserted that Americans soon began to write their own Gothic works, finding "American equivalents of the moors, hills, and forests," and adapting the symbols of "attitudes toward the past" for the American experience. Because America "had no history of aristocratic privilege," the aristocratic impulse of the seduction theme translated into feminism and anti-intellectualism," 144–145.

31. Savoy, 167. Fiedler claimed that Charles Brockden Brown adapted the Gothic for America and influenced later writers such as Poe and Hawthorne and determined "the future of the gothic novel in America," 145. Fiedler claims that Brown "substitutes the haunted forest" for the castle and dungeon and that "the change of myth involves a profound change of meaning." In American Gothic, "the heathen, unredeemed wilderness and not the decaying monuments of a dying class, nature and not society becomes the symbol of evil," and the Indian and the "savage colored man" become the villains, 160. Recent studies that have considered issues of race in "American Gothic" of the nineteenth and twentieth centuries include Justin D. Edward's *Gothic Passages*, (Iowa City: University of Iowa Press, 2003); Teresa A. Goddu's *Gothic America* (New York: Columbia University Press, 1997); Leslie Ginsberg's "Slavery and the Gothic Horror of Poe's 'The Black Cat,'" in *American Gothic: New Interventions in a National Narrative*, ed. Robert K. Martin and Eric Savoy (Iowa City: University of Iowa Press, 1998), 99–128; Robert Martin's "Haunted by Jim Crow," in *American Gothic: New Interventions in a National Narrative*, 129–142 ; and George Piggford's "Looking into Black Skulls," in *American Gothic: New Interventions in a National Narrative*, 143–160. In a related study, Kari J. Winter examined Gothic novels and slave narratives in *Subjects of Slavery, Agents of Change: Women and Power in Gothic Novels and Slave Narratives, 1790–1865* (Athens, GA: The University of Georgia Press, 1992).

32. Allan Lloyd-Smith, "Nineteenth Century American Gothic," in *A Companion to the Gothic*, 109–121, ed. David Punter (Oxford: Blackwell, 2001), 109.

33. Backscheider, 57.

34. Landmark studies of Gothic literature include Edith Birkhead's *The Tale of Terror* (London: Constable, 1921; reprint, New York: Russell and Russell, 1963); Eino Railo's *The Haunted Castle* (London: E.P. Dutton, 1927; reprint, New York: Humanities Press, 1964); and Montague Summers' *The Gothic Quest* (London: Fortune Press, 1938; reprint, New York: Russell and Russell, 1964); all of which sought to provide a historical background for Gothic literature. After these early historical works, Devendra Varma published his influential and widely cited work, *The Gothic Flame* (London: A. Barker, 1957; reprint, New York: Russell and Russell, 1966), in which he traced the evolution of the term "Gothic" and discussed how the term came to be applied to specific works. After these early scholars investigated the history of Gothic literature, others critically examined the form. Robert Hume's essay "Gothic versus Romantic: A Revaluation of the Gothic Novel," *PMLA* 84 (March 1969), published in 1969, argued that Gothic novels were more than just a "collection of ghost-story devices" and that they could be distinguished from romantic literature of the same period by their distinctive characteristics. first, their concern for interior mental processes; second, their attempts to induce a "powerful emotional response" in the reader (as opposed to an intellectual one); third, their frequent use of supernatural elements, and finally, their most distinguishing feature, their use of atmosphere.

35. The following historians did not use the term "Gothic," either in text or index to refer to plays: John Bernard, *Retrospections of the Stage* (London: Henry Colburn and Richard Bentley, 1830); Maurice Willson Disher, *Blood and Thunder* (London: Frederick Muller, 1949); William Dunlap, *History of the American Theatre* (New York: J. & J. Harper, 1832); Barnard Hewitt, *Theatre*

U.S.A. (New York: McGraw Hill, 1959); Arthur Hornblow, *A History of the Theatre in America* (New York: J.B. Lippincott, 1919; reprint, New York: Benjamin Blom, 1965); James Ireland, *Records of the New York Stage*, Vol. 1 (New York: 1866; reprint, New York: Benjamin Blom, 1966); Richard Moody, *America Takes the Stage* (Bloomington: Indiana University Press, 1955); George O. Seilhamer, *History of the American Theatre* (Philadelphia: Globe Printing House, 1888–1891; reprint, New York: Greenwood Press, 1968).

36. *The Charleston Courier*, 6 May 1803.

37. Marybeth Inverso, *The Gothic Impulse in Contemporary Drama* (Ann Arbor: UMI Research Press 1990), 8, argued that the Gothic and melodramatic were "deeply antithetical modes, so much so that the appellation 'Gothic Melodrama' was in effect a self-contradiction." Peter Brooks, *The Melodramatic Imagination: Balzac, Henry James, Melodrama and the Mode of Excess* (New Haven: Yale University Press, 1976), 20, contended that the melodrama "tends to diverge from the Gothic in its optimism, its claim that the moral imagination can open up the angelic spheres as well as the demonic depths and can allay the threat of moral chaos."

38. Evans, 8.

39. The population for this study consists of plays identified by two or more critics or historians as "Gothic." For a list of plays, see Appendix 1.

40. Booth, 69.

41. Brooks, 20.

42. C. Dallett Hemphill, *Bowing to Necessities* (New York: Oxford University Press, 1999), 125.

Chapter 1

1. William Dunlap, *Fontainville Abbey*, 207.

2. Jeffrey H. Richards, in *Theatre Enough: American Culture and the Metaphor of the World Stage* (Durham, NC: Duke University Press, 1991), suggested that early settlers in America would "use theatre not simply as a rhetorical nicety but often as a trope deeply reflective of America's place," xvii. Richards also claimed that though "in history, Americans share with British writers a common language of stage, actor, play and mask," but that "by the late eighteenth century, that language often separates British and American interests," xvii.

3. Shane White, *Stories of Freedom in Black New York* (Cambridge, MA: Harvard University Press, 2002) pointed out that though the New York State legislature officially ended slavery in New York in 1799, the pace of abolition was "glacial"; many were not free until 1827, 13.

4. For a detailed account of early theatres and their founders in Philadelphia, New York, and Boston, see Heather Nathan's *Early American Theatre from the Revolution to Thomas Jefferson* (Cambridge: Cambridge University Press, 2004).

5. Weldon Durham, ed. *American Theatre Companies 1749–1887* (New York: Greenwood Press, 1986), 548.

6. John Andriot, *Population Abstract of the United States*, Vol. 1 (McLean, VA: Andriot Associates, 1983), 362, 548, 673, 712.

7. U.S. Bureau of the Census, *Historical Statistics of the United States, Colonial Times to 1970* (Washington, DC: 1975), 106.

8. Joseph F. Kett, *Rites of Passage* (New York: Basic Books, 1977), 38.

9. Jean Matthews, *Towards a New Society* (Boston: Twayne Publishers, 1990), 3.

10. Raymond Mohl, ed., *The Making of Urban America* (Wilmington, DE: Scholarly Resources, 1988), 32

11. Matthews, 4. Some studies have argued that the "distribution of urban wealth" changed less rapidly from the Revolution to the early nineteenth century.

12. Mohl, 33

13. For an account of the "economic and political crises" of the late eighteenth century and resulting competing entertainments of the late eighteenth affected established theatres, see Heather Nathans' *Early American Theatre from the Revolution to Thomas Jefferson* (Cambridge: Cambridge University Press, 2004).

14. Mohl, 31.

15. Matthews, 8.

16. Shane White, 13.

17. Richard L. Bushman, *The Refinement of America* (New York: Alfred A. Knopf, 1992), xv.

18. Bushman, xv.

19. Bushman, xvi.

20. Claudia Johnson, *American Actress* (Chicago: Nelson Hall, 1984), 5.

21. Johnson, 13.

22. Johnson observed that prostitutes frequently received free passes for the theatre to encourage their attendance, 14.

23. Johnson asserted that even as late as 1842, New York's Park Theatre had to abandon the experiment of banning prostitutes

from the theatre when business suffered too greatly, 15

24. Philadelphia produced *The Carmelite* in 1794 and *The Sicilian Romance* in 1795; New York produced *The Carmelite* in 1794 and *Fontainville Abbey* in 1795; Boston produced *The Sicilian Romance* and *The Mysteries of the Castle* in 1796; Charleston produced *The Carmelite* in 1796 and *The Sicilian Romance* in 1797.

25. Matthews, 47.

26. *The Edinburgh Review*, as quoted in Matthews, 56.

27. *The Port-Folio*, 21 November 1807.

28. *Boston Spectator*, 1 January 1814.

29. *The Minerva*, 20 April 1822.

30. *The Port-Folio*, 23 May 1807.

31. *The NewYork Mirror and Ladies' Literary Gazette*, 7 May 1825.

32. Dunlap, *History of the American Theatre*, 264.

33. *The Polyanthos*, September 1813.

34. *The Critic*, 22 November 1828.

35. *American Quarterly Review*, June 1827; *The Critic*, 22 November 1828.

36. *American Quarterly Review*, June 1827.

37. *Thespian Mirror*, 1 March 1806.

38. *The Minerva*, 6 December 1823.

39. *The Boston Gazette*, 24 February 1794.

40. *The Boston Gazette*, 24 February 1794.

41. This preface preceded a review of Colman the Younger's play *Who Wants a Guinea* as performed at Covent Garden's Theatre Royal. *Port-Folio*, 14 September 1805.

42. In Philadelphia, the Chestnut Street faced competition from the Olympic, which opened in 1812 and the Walnut, which opened in 1823. In New York, the Chatham Garden opened in 1824 and the Bowery in 1826, competing with the Park Theatre. In Charleston, the City Theatre opened in 1794, just one year after the Charleston Theatre. In Boston, the Federal Street Theatre encountered competition from the Haymarket, which opened in 1797.

43. Durham, 387.

44. Charles Pritner, "William Warren's Management of the Chestnut Street Theatre Company," Ph.D. diss. (University of Illinois, 1961), observed that the Chestnut kept to their established prices of one dollar for boxes, seventy-five cents for the pit, and fifty cents for the gallery until 1823, 31. The Park Theatre still advertised these prices as of 1823 as indicated by a notice in *The Minerva*, 14 June 1823.

45. *Ladies' Literary Gazette, The New York Mirror*, 16 July 1825.

46. Because so much confusion exists about what plays were correctly deemed "Gothic," I have compiled a list of thirty plays identified as Gothic by two or more of the following historians: Bertrand Evans in *Gothic Drama From Walpole to Shelley*, Michael Booth in *English Melodrama*, George C.D. Odell in *Annals of the New York Stage*, and David Grimsted in *Melodrama Unveiled*. Because most of these historians addressed British plays primarily, I also include those plays identified as "Gothic" by Oral Coad in "The Gothic Element in American Literature before 1830," *The Journal of English and Germanic Philology* 24 (1925): 72–93. Finally, although Bertrand Evans was the only historian who noted *Fountainville Forest* by James Boaden as "Gothic," I included it in the population because its American counterpart, *Fontainville Abbey* by William Dunlap, which was included in the sample, uses the same characters and plot. To determine dates of productions, I used daybooks for each city; these include Thomas Pollock's *The Philadelphia Theatre in the XVIII Century* (Philadelphia: University of Pennsylvania Press, 1933); Reese James' *The Old Drury of Philadelphia* (Philadelphia: University of Pennsylvania Press, 1932); Eola Willis' *The Charleston Stage in the XVIII Century* (Columbia, SC: The State Company, 1924); W. Stanley Hoole's *The Antebellum Charleston Theatre* (Tuscaloosa: University of Alabama, 1946); George C.D. Odell's *Annals of the New York Stage*, Vols. 1–3 (New York: Columbia University, 1927); Mary Ruth Michael's "History of the Professional Theatre in Boston" (Ph.D. diss., Radcliffe, 1941). Unfortunately, two of these daybooks are not complete from 1790 to 1830.

Chapter 2

1. George Colman, *The Iron Chest* (London: Hurst, Rees, and Orme, 1808), in *The British Theatre; or A Collection of Plays* (New York: Georg Olms Verlag, 1970), 21.

2. Letter from Edmund Simpson in Harvard Theatre Collection, quoted in Odell, II: 588.

3. Wood, *Old Drury*, 322. Although a comprehensive daybook of performances does not exist for the years 1800 to 1810, summaries of seasons indicate that Gothic plays appeared in nearly every season.

4. Weldon Durham, ed., *American Theatre Companies 1749–1887* (New York: Greenwood Press, 1986), 181.

5. Bernard, *Retrospections of America*, 264.

6. *The Theatrical Censor and Musical Review*, 1828, as quoted in Calvin Pritner's "William Warren's Management of the Chestnut Street Theatre Company" (Ph.D. diss., University of Illinois, 1961), 24.

7. Bureau of the Census, *Historical Statistics of the United States*, 163.

8. Bureau of the Census, *Historical Statistics of the United States*, 163.

9. John J. McCusker, *How Much Is That in Real Money*? (Worcester, MA: American Antiquarian Society, 1992), 333. Figure 8 is based on 240 pence to the pound, 333.

10. Durham, 181.

11. John Andriot, ed. *Population Abstracts of the United States* (McLean, VA: Andriot Assoc., 1983), 548.

12. *The Port Folio*, 31 January 1807.

13. *The New York Mirror, and Ladies' Literary Gazette*, 12 February 1825. Despite the view that the Park was losing desirable patrons, Henneke suggested that perhaps the less desirable, rowdier patrons were the ones defecting to the newer houses, thus, in fact, increasing the respectability of the Park. Henneke quoted Frances Trollope, 339, who remarked that, in New York of 1829, the Park theatre was "the only one licensed by fashion." The Bowery, according to Frances Trollope in *Domestic Manners of the Americans*, ed. Donald Smalley (New York: Alfred A. Knopf, 1949), was not considered fashionable, and the Chatham was "utterly condemned by the bon ton," 89.

14. *Columbian Centinel*, 10 January 1807, as quoted in Henneke, 57.

15. *The New York Mirror, and Ladies' Literary Gazette*, 22 May 1824.

16. Billy J. Harbin, "Hodgkinson's Last Years: At the Charleston Theatre, 1803–1805" *Theatre Survey*, 13 November 1972, 27.

17. Bernard 159.

18. The Tremont Theatre opened on September 24, 1827. For an account of the investors, company and opening bill, see Clapp's *Record of the Boston Stage*, 248–258.

19. *Boston Weekly Magazine*, 25 January 1817.

20. Lest the managers get complacent, a notice in *The Emerald* in 1807 warned, "One word however to the managers. What are in fact the novelties of the season? If, as has been intimated, they consist of occasional recruits, picked up by chance for 'three evenings' at a time, let us tell you that it will not be sufficient to satisfy the expectations, or command the patronage of the public. The Theatre in Boston, is universally allowed to be better supported than any other on the continent. This liberality requires a corresponding exertion."

The writer concluded by noting that if the managers did not comply, they could expect "a beggarly account of empty boxes," 19 September 1807.

21. Wood, 208.

22. William Dunlap in *History of the American Theatre* (New York: J. & J. Harper, 1832; reprint, New York: Burt Franklin, 1963). *The Castle Spectre* opened the winter season at the Park in September of 1809, with Mrs. Poe as Angela, Mr. Young as Osmond, and Mr. Poe as Hassan, 265.

23. *New York Mirror*, 15 January 1825.

24. *New York Mirror*, 15 January 1825.

25. Durham, 78.

26. *The Boston Weekly Magazine*, 11 February 1804, critiqued a production of *The Castle Spectre*, referring to the piece as a stock play. The article praised Mr. Barrett's Osmond, noting that his voice "possesses uncommon strength and his performance is always marked with spirit and energy." The article added that Mrs. Powell's Angela was played "with her usual excellence," but that the part of Percy [was] better suited to the powers of Mr. Jones than of Mr. Darley; it was however mediocre." The critique concludes with this observation: "Mrs. Baker acquitted herself handsomely in Alice. In her performance of the parts of old women this season, Mrs. B. has received much deserved applause. The entertainments of the evening drew a crowded audience."

27. *The Massachusetts Mercury*, 22 October, 1799.

28. *Boston Weekly Magazine*, 9 November 1816.

Chapter 3

1. Maturin, 348.

2. Reese James, 210.

3. *The New York Mirror, and Ladies' Literary Gazette*, 12 March 1825.

4. *Mirror of Taste and Dramatic Censor* (Philadelphia), January 1810.

5. Calvin Pritner, "William Warren's Management of the Chestnut Street Theatre" (Ph.D. diss., University of Illinois, 1961), 23.

6. Henneke asserted that when theatres in New York, Philadelphia, and Boston increased the number of tiers of boxes, prostitutes took over the third tier, 84.

7. Ben Graf Henneke, "The Play-goer in

America, 1752–1800" (Ph.D. diss., University of Illinois, 1956), 83.

8. *Mirror of Taste and Dramatic Censor*, May 1810.

9. "The Moralist," *Charleston Courier*, 1 February, 1806.

10. *Mirror of Taste and Dramatic Censor*, January 1810.

11. *Philadelphia Magazine*, 7 March 1818.

12. *The Cynick*, 19 October 1811. However, the same periodical noted that even box seats were no longer safe for respectable ladies.

13. *The Cynick*, 19 October 1811.

14. Shane White, 81.

15. Shane White maintained that blacks in New York seemed to have attended the theatre frequently but were not permitted to sit anywhere other than the gallery. White also related that black Americans in the gallery at the theatre in Boston grew very vocal on behalf of Kean; he quoted an 1825 newspaper account of black patrons in Boston loudly supporting Kean from the gallery as more prosperous patrons heckled that actor, 81.

16. William Wood, *Personal Recollections of the Stage*, 323.

17. The *Boston Weekly Magazine* was especially harsh on the production noting that "this tragedy ... has no equal for the diabolical turpitude of its characters, the shocking depravity of its scenes, or the execrable tendency of its moral," 9 November 1816.

18. The review in the *Boston Weekly Magazine* ranted that though Imogene, though "blest with every personal accomplishment, the adored wife, the believed mother, is described as descending, with the facility of a harlot, from the nuptial couch of matrimony, to grovel in the adulterous embraces—not of a gallant, gay Lothario, but of an outlawed rebel, a cut-throat robber," 9 November 1816.

19. The actress was the wife of William Wood, and he notes her experience in his *Recollections of the Stage* (Philadelphia: H.C. Baird, 1855), 208.

20. *Mirror of Taste and Dramatic Censor*, January 1810.

21. *Mirror of Taste and Dramatic Censor*, May 1810.

22. *Mirror of Taste and Dramatic Censor*, May 1810.

23. *Mirror of Taste and Dramatic Censor*, May 1810.

24. *Mirror of Taste and Dramatic Censor*, 1811.

25. *The Port-Folio*, 31 January 1807.

26. *The New-York Mirror and Ladies' Literary Gazette*, 24 January 1824.

27. *Boston Spectator and Ladies' Album*, 8 September, 1827.

28. *Boston Weekly Magazine*, 12 October 1816.

29. *The Cynick*, 19 October 1811.

30. *The Cynick*, 19 October 1811.

31. *Othello* was advertised as "a moral dialogue depicting the evil effects of jealousy and other Bad Passions and Proving that Happiness can only Spring from the Pursuit of Virtue," as quoted in Hewitt, 26.

32. Periodicals were *The Port-Folio*, *The Polyanthos*, and *The Theatrical Censor*.

33. *The Port-Folio*, 21 December 1805.

34. *The Polyanthos*, March 1806; *The Port-Folio*, 21 December 1805.

35. *The Port-Folio*, October 1818.

36. *The New York Mirror, and Ladies' Literary Gazette*, 18 September 1824.

37. *The New York Mirror, and Ladies' Literary Gazette*, 18 September 1824.

38. *The Polyanthos*, 3 January 1801.

39. *The New York Mirror, and Ladies' Literary Gazette*, 29 May 1824.

40. *The New York Mirror, and Ladies' Literary Gazette*, 13 November 1824.

41. Dunlap, *History of the American Theatre*, New York: J. & J. Harper. 1832, 405.

42. *Mirror of Taste and Dramatic Censor*, October 1810.

43. *Mirror of Taste and Dramatic Censor*, October 1810. Claudia Johnson discussed the reputation of the upper boxes in her article "That Guilty Third Tier:" Prostitution in Nineteenth Century Theatres," in *Victorian America*, ed. Daniel Walker Howe (Pittsburg: University of Pennsylvania, 1976). However, Rosemarie Bank argued in "Physics and the New Historiography," *Journal of Dramatic Theory and Criticism* 5 (Spring 1991), that perhaps evidence is not conclusive about the presence of prostitutes in the third tier. Sentiments expressed in newspaper articles and editorials of the day, as well as comments by Francis Wemyss and William Wood, supported Johnson's claim. One cryptic remark in the *Philadelphia Magazine*, 28 March 1818, stated, "We were placed in a very critical situation, during the representation of this piece, being exiled to the second row; and it being *pairing* time in that part of the house, we were scarcely able to hear a word of the afterpiece."

44. Timothy J. Gilfoyle in *City of Eros* (New York: W.W. Norton & Co., 1992) commented that leading theatres in New York permitted prostitutes in the uppermost tier of

seats and that "for over three decades, prostitutes claimed the third their as their own social space," 67.

45. Dunlap, *History of the American Theatre*, 211.

46. Dunlap, *History of the American Theatre*, 211.

47 "An Old Philadelphian," *Mirror of Taste and Dramatic Censor*, 30 November 1810.

48. *The Charleston Courier*, 15 November 1815.

49. Dunlap, in *History of the American Theatre*, suggested that "if a regulation was enforced, that no female should come to a theatre unattended by a protector of the other sex, except such whose standing in society is a passport to every place, the evil would be effectively remedied," 211.

50. Dunlap, *History of the American Theatre*, 210.

51. *Mirror of Taste and Dramatic Censor*, October 1810.

52. *Mirror of Taste and Dramatic Censor*, October 1810.

53. *Mirror of Taste and Dramatic Censor*, May 1810.

54. *Mirror of Taste and Dramatic Censor*, January 1810.

55. *The Philadelphia Magazine*, 7 March 1818.

56. *Mirror of Taste and Dramatic Censor*, January 1810.

57. *The Charleston Courier*, 14 November 1808.

58. Patrons were not expected to remain quietly passive throughout the performance especially when that performance was not good. An article in *The American Monthly Magazine and Critical Review,* April 23, 1817, commented that "the glorious privilege of hissing should never be resigned by an enlightened auditory, and this testimony of disapprobation should be extended to the scene and sentiment where they deserve it as well as to the acting. We wish we could hear it oftener exercised in the New York Theatre."

59. Charles Durang, "The Philadelphia Stage from the Year 1749 to the Year 1855," *Philadelphia Sunday Dispatch* as quoted in Pritner, 23. A periodical criticized the Philadelphia audience for being "indulgent to a blameable excess," in their discrimination of acting, for if a performer was "possessed of a very moderate share of June 1806. talents," his entrance was "always cheered by their applause, although, in the part he may that evening have undertaken, he deserve every manifestation of disgust," *The Theatrical Censor*, 2.

60. "The Drama," *Something,* 18 November 1809, 7–8, as quoted in Henneke, 77.

61. *The Cynick.* 19 October, 1811.

62. *The Cynick.* 19 October, 1811.

63. *Mirror of Taste and Dramatic Censor,* October 1810.

64. *The Philadelphia Magazine,* 16 May 1818.

65. Pritner quoted the *Mirror of Taste and Dramatic Censor,* January 1810, which stated that for a lady to visit the theatre on that night was "a violation of the laws of fashion," 76.

66. Respectable ladies who did manage to obtain a seat in the boxes might now be "confounded with a class of females too gross to be mentioned, who, under the patronage of the manager or their own impudence, venture with their cullies so near the spectators as to destroy by their conversation or their managers, all the pleasure that might be derived from the orchestra or the stage," *The Cynick,* 19 October 1811.

Chapter 4

1. Lewis, *The Castle Spectre*, 175.
2. Hemphill, 69.
3. Ibid.
4. Chesterfield, Philip Dormer Stanhope, 4th Earl of, *Letters to His Son by the Earl of Chesterfield,* Introduction by Oliver H.G. Leigh (Washington, DC: M. Walter Dunne, 1901), ix.
5. Hemphill, 71.
6. Hemphill, 71.
7. Chesterfield, I: 107.
8. Ibid.
9. Edmund M. Hayes, "Mercy Otis Warren versus Lord Chesterfield," *William and Mary Quarterly,* 40 (October 1983): 618.
10. Hayes, 618.
11. John Trusler, *Principles of Politeness and of Knowing the World; by the Late Lord Chesterfield* (Philadelphia: Robert Bell, 1778), 5.
12. Chesterfield, I: 8.
13. In *The Sicilian Romance,* the force consists of the uncle of the wronged wife and his soldiers; in *Fontainville Forest* and *Fontainville Abbey,* a representative of the courts is on hand to condemn the Marquis. Groups of soldiers led by a minor character resolve the action in White's *The Mysteries of the Castle* and in *The Woodman's Hut.*
14. John Hodgkinson, *The Man of Fortitude* (New York: David Longworth, 1807), 26. Heroes sometimes continue their fidelity

after their sweetheart dies. In Miles Andrew's *The Mysteries of the Castle* (London: T.N. Longman, 1795), in *English and American Drama of the Nineteenth Century* (New Caanan, CT: Readex, 1963), microfiche, Carlos has been notified that his beloved Julia, who was forced to marry another, has died. He tells his companion, "Never will I quit this gloomy edifice, till I discover my poor Julia's sad remains, dreadful idea! the mangled relicks [sic] of her beauteous form," 38.

15. Andrews, 31. Similarly Wilford in George Colman the Younger's *The Iron Chest* (London: W. Simpkin and R. Marshall, 1823), in *Plays by George Colman the Younger and Thomas Morton* (Cambridge: Cambridge University Press, 1983), states, "I respect virtue and misfortune too much to shock the one or insult the other, 11. Bertrand in *The Man of Fortitude* declares, "Be innocence my armor, God my trust," 9.

16. Hodgkinson, 7.

17. Matthew Gregory Lewis, *The Castle Spectre* (London: J. Bell, 1798), in *Seven Gothic Dramas*, ed. Jeffrey N. Cox (Athens: Ohio University Press, 1992), 154.

18. Richard Cumberland, *The Carmelite*, in *The London Stage*, Vol. 3 (London: Sherwood and Co., n.d.), 5.

19. John Blake White, *The Mysteries of the Castle* (Charleston, SC: John B. White, 1807), 50.

20. Hodgkinson, 22.

21. Lindor in *The Sicilian Romance*, Theodore in *The Count of Narbonne*, Carlos in Andrew's *The Mysteries of the Castle*, Selim in *Bluebeard*, Stephano in *A Tale of Mystery*, Lothario and Persiles in White's *The Mysteries of the Castle*, Raymond in *Raymond and Agnes* and *The Forest of Rosenwald*, Ferdinand in *The Woodman's Hut*, Alonzo in *The Mountain Torrent*, Aurelio in *The Rose of Arragon*, Lorenzo in *Melmoth*, Oswy in *One O'Clock; or The Knight and the Wood Daemon*.

22. Samuel Judah, *The Rose of Arragon; or The Vigil of St. Mark* (New York: S. King, 1822), in *Three Centuries of Drama* (New Canaan, CT: Readex, 1963), microfiche, 5. Other young heroes who disguised their true rank include Raymond in *Raymond and Agnes*, Raymond in *The Forest of Rosenwald*, and Percy in *The Castle Spectre*.

23. Judah, 1.

24. Judah, 7. Other heroes also sought parental blessings; in Thomas Holcroft's *A Tale of Mystery*, in *The Hour of One*, ed. Stephen Wischhusen (London: Gordon Fraser, 1975), Stephano said to his father, "We will return to claim your blessing," 23.

25. Protectors of the heroine in fact preferred to see her dead than dishonored, as illustrated by Persiles, in *The Mysteries of the Castle*, who, upon viewing his sister's apparently lifeless body, rejoiced, saying, "Heaven be praised! she is safe, [dead] safe beyond the reach of such inhuman villains!" 49.

26. Judah, 31.

27. This same situation occurred in *The Castle Spectre* when Angela saved the life of her father by of stabbing the Earl.

28. Similarly in *Presumption; or The Fate of Frankenstein*, the protagonist Frankenstein succeeded in animating lifeless tissue but almost instantly regretted his experiment, tortured by the conviction that his presumption and pride in his work had brought destruction upon those he loved.

29. This scenario also appeared in *The Mysteries of the Castle* by John Blake White.

30. William Dunlap, *Ribbemont; or The Feudal Baron* (New York: D. Longworth, 1803), in *Three Centuries of Drama*, (New Canaan, CT: Readex, 1963), microfiche, 28.

31. Dunlap, *Ribbemont*, 46.

32. Ibid, 61.

33. Dunlap, 72. Similarly, in *The Carmelite*, St. Valori also mistakenly assessed a situation; he returned home after a twenty-year absence and found his wife in the company of a young man. Enraged, St. Valori at first decided to kill himself and then he tried to kill the young man, only to learn that he was his own son. Upon realizing his folly he cried, "Bind up his wounds! Oh if I've slain my son, perdition will not own me," 13.

34. Grimsted, 178.

35. In the twenty-seven plays in which villains appeared, twenty-two were titled.

36. Colman, 19.

37. Colman, 49.

38. Colman, 52.

39. Lewis, *The Castle Spectre*, 9.

40. Lewis, *The Castle Spectre*, 48.

41. Lewis, *The Castle Spectre*, 66.

42. Lewis, *The Castle Spectre*, 23.

43. Boaden, 20.

44. Boaden, 33.

45. Boaden, 50.

46. Boaden, 66.

47. Joseph Kett, *Rites of Passage* (New York: Basic Books, 1977), 94.

48. Kett, *Rites of Passage*, 95.

49. Chesterfield, I: 34.

50. However, mothers of heroes, like those of heroines, generally did not appear in the plays.

51. Sally Allen McNall, *Who Is in the House* (New York: Elsevier, 1981), 3.

52. *The Kaleidoscope*, Boston, 12 December, 1818.
53. Chesterfield, I: 281.
54. Bruce McConachie, in *Melodramatic Formations* (Iowa City: University of Iowa, 1992), contended that elite males enjoyed "fairy-tale melodramas produced by paternalistic stock companies between 1820 and 1835," xii. He explained that such melodramas addressed fears of the upper class males about their loss of control over their children, their cities, and their nation in a time of rapid social change, 2.
55. McConachie reported that the Arch Street Theatre in Philadelphia, built in 1828, was erected by some of the wealthy men of that city; the Lafayette Theatre, built in 1825 in New York City was financed largely by General Charles W. Sandford, a prominent lawyer; in Boston, the Tremont Street Theatre, built in 1827 was financed by "gentlemen of wealth and influence," 7.
56. Tyrone Power, *Impressions of America* (London: Richard Bentley, 1836), I: 164, quoted in McConachie, 9.
57. McConachie, 9.

Chapter 5

1. Miles Andrews, *The Mysteries of the Castle*, 47.
2. Barbara Welter's essay, "The Cult of True Womanhood: 1820–1860," *American Quarterly* 18 (Summer 1966): 151–176, was credited as having a huge impact on fields of American women's studies, and American women's literature. In her essay, Welter identified four behaviors that women were expected to exhibit: piety, purity, submissiveness, and domesticity. Mary Kelley, in "Beyond the Boundaries," *Journal of the Early Republic* 21 (spring 2001): 73–78, reported that later studies by Lori Ginzburg and Barbara Lerslie Epstein have challenged Welter's findings and argued that some of these "behavioral tents" actually empowered women. For example, white women could use their "gendered quality of piety" to take leadership roles in reform movements and purity could be used as a "formidable weapon of righteousness" against the sexual double standard, 75. Kelley contended that the quality of "submissiveness" as identified by Welter should be changed to "deference" because the fiction of the antebellum age is "shot though with ambivalence, tension, and contradiction," and the heroines engage in "acts of subversion" instead of "docile compliance," 76. I find that heroines in Gothic plays also exhibited these "acts of subversion," more so in their actions than in their words. For an opposing view, see Laura McCall, "'Shall I Fetter Her Will': Literary Americans Confront Feminine Submission, 1820–1860," *Journal of the Early Republic* 21 (Spring 2001), who argued that a dependent woman was considered ideal in fiction of this period.
3. Gerda Lerner, "The Lady and the Mill Girl: Changes in the Status of Women in the Age of Jackson, 1800–1840," in *A Heritage of Her Own*, 182–196, ed. Nancy F. Cott and Elizabeth H. Pleck (New York: Simon and Schuster, 1979), asserted that for "almost a hundred years sympathetic historians have told the story of women in America by deriving from the position of middle class women a generalization concerning all American women," and argued that "to avoid distortion, any valid generalization concerning American women after the 1830s should reflect a recognition of class stratification," 192. Yet few women were admitted to American theatres between 1794 and 1825, and those who were occupied the boxes and arrived with an escort.
4. Fleenor, 18.
5. Frances Trollope, 74.
6. Richard Butsch in "Bowery B'hoys and Matinee Ladies: The Re-Gendering of Nineteenth-Century American Theater Audiences," *American Quarterly* 46 (September 1994), commented that "respectability was at its core a gendered concept" and noted that middle class women, "particularly wives and mothers" carried designations of respectability," 375.
7. For example, when patrons at the Chestnut Street Theatre in Philadelphia rioted against Edmund Kean in 1825, William Wood observed that "the greatest portion of the female auditors retired in disgust from the disgraceful scene." Moreover, the manager of the Chestnut commented that the "worst result" of that unhappy occurrence was "an apprehension on the part of the female audience of future difficulties which deterred many from ever visiting the theatre for a long time again," 322.
8. Fleenor, 15.
9. Subsequent studies by Lori Ginzburg, Barbara Leslie Epstein, and Carrol Smith-Rosenberg challenged Welter's tenets, contending that they actually empowered women by helping them enter charitable and reform movements.
10. See Rosemarie K. Bank's "Hustlers in the House: The Bowery Theatre as a Mode of

Historical Information," in *The American Stage*, 47–64, ed. Ron Engle and Tice L. Miller (Cambridge: Cambridge University Press, 1993).

11. *Mirror of Taste and Dramatic Censor*, November 1810.

12. *Mirror of Taste and Dramatic Censor*, November 1810.

13. Holcroft, 26; Robert Jephson, *The Count of Narbonne* (London: Longman, Hurst, Rees, and Ormer, n.d.), in *The British Theatre*, Vol. 19 (Frankfurt: Minerva GMBH, 1969), 9; Dunlap, 3; White, 23; Hodgkinson, 21; Matthew Gregory Lewis, *Raymond and Agnes; or The Travellers Benighted* (New York: Samuel French, n.d.), *English and American Drama of the Nineteenth Century* (New Canaan, CT: Readex, 1963), microfiche, 16; John Stokes, *The Forest of Rosenwald* (New York: Dramatic Repository, 1821), *Three Centuries of Drama* (New Canaan, CT: Readex, 1963), (microfiche) 20.

14. Andrews, *The Mysteries of the Castle*.

15. Andrews, 8; Jephson, 4; Lewis, *The Castle Spectre*, 16; White, 48; J.D. Turnbull, *The Wood Daemon; or The Clock Has Struck* (Boston: B. True, 1808), *Three Centuries of Drama* (New Canaan, CT: Readex, 1963), (microfiche) 6; James Nelson Barker, *Superstition* (Philadelphia: A.R. Poole, n.d.), 412.

16. James Boaden, *Fountainville Forest*, in *The Plays of James Boaden*, ed. Steven Cohan (New York: Garland Publishing, Inc. 1980), 23. Out of the sample of thirty-one plays, at least twenty young heroines were motherless.

17. Barker, *Superstition*, 9.

18. Juliann Fleenor maintained that Gothic fiction "reflects a patriarchal paradigm that women are motherless yet fathered and that women are defective because they are not males," 15.

19. Reginald in *The Castle Spectre*, De Manfreis in White's *The Mysteries of the Castle*, Benorio in *The Rose of Arragon*, and D'Arenza in *The Mountain Torrent* all fall into the clutches of the villains, thus endangering their daughters.

20. Jephson, 4. Also, in *The Mysteries of the Castle*, Julia, forced into an miserable marriage with a villain, excused her father, saying, "Unhappy parent!, who, misled by treachery, and lured by gain, hath doom'd his child to misery and death," 42.

21. Jephson, 12.

22. Lewis, *The Castle Spectre*, 171.

23. Andrews, 42.

24. Jephson, 2.

25. Hodgkinson, 20.

26. Rosemarie Bank, in her article "The Second Face of the Idol: Women in Melodrama," in *Women in American Theatre*, ed. Helen Krich Chinoy and Linda Walsh Jenkins (New York: Theatre Communications Group, 1987), asserted that heroines of early melodramas (before 1850) were generally believed to be passive and helpless. She observes that further research may show them to be more self-sufficient than previously believed, 243.

27. Angela in *The Castle Spectre* stabs Osmond; Fatima in both versions of *Bluebeard* snatched the magic charm protecting the villain resulting in his death; Marguerette in *Raymond and Agnes* and in *The Forest of Rosenwald* killed her husband; the young heroine Agnes in *Raymond and Agnes* shot one of the villains. Finally, in *The Rose of Arragon* the young heroine stabbed the villain as he attempts to kill her father.

28. Ribbemont, 55.

29. Before 1810, such heroines appeared in *The Carmelite* (1794), *The Sicilian Romance* (1795), *The Count of Narbonne* (1796), *The Man of Fortitude* (1800), and *Ribbemont* (1803). After 1810, such a heroine was featured only in *The Warlock of the Glen* (1821).

30. Cumberland, 3.

31. C.E. Walker, *The Warlock of the Glen* (London: John Lowndes, 1820), in *English and American Drama of the Nineteenth Century* (New Canaan, CT: Readex, 1963), microfiche, 2.

32. Dunlap, *Ribbemont*, 60.

33. William Dunlap, *Fontainville Abbey*, in *Adaptations of European Plays* (New York: Scholars' Facsimiles & Reprints, 1988), 199.

34. Henry Siddons, *The Sicilian Romance* (n.p., 1794), in *Three Centuries of Drama* (New Canaan, CT: Readex, 1963), microprint, 21.

35. Siddons, 4.

36. Cumberland, 4.

37. White, 53.

38. Siddons, 52.

39. Maturin, 350.

40. Charles Maturin, *Bertram* (London: John Murray, 1816), in *Seven Gothic Dramas*, ed. Jeffrey N. Cox (Athens: Ohio University Press, 1992), 348.

41. James Nelson Barker, *Marmion* (New York: D. Longworth, 1816), 14.

42. James Fordyce, *Sermons for Young Women* in *Female Education in the Age of Enlightenment*, Vol. 2, Introduction by Janet Todd (London: William Pickering, 1996), 224.

43. Fordyce, I.:104.

44. Margaret Nash, "Rethinking Repub-

lican Motherhood: Benjamin Rush and the Young Ladies' Academy of Philadelphia." *Journal of the Early Republic* 17 (Summer 1997): 171–191, asserted that studies have shown that more formal educational opportunities increased for both girls and boys as early as 1750.

45. *The Polyanthos*, November 1813. The author, "Pauciloquens," summed up his argument: "their beauty I admire; their frailties I can forgive. But I cannot submit to be taught by them. Everlasting ignorance is better than this."

46 "Woman: Sketches of the History, Genius, Disposition, Accomplishments, Employments, Customs and Importance of the Fair Sex in All Parts of the World" (London: G. Kearsley, 1790), micropublished in *History of Women* (New Haven, CT: Research Publications, Inc., 1975).

47. James Fordyce, I: 273.
48. Hemphill, 107.
49. John Gregory, *A Father's Legacy to His Daughters* (Dublin: John Colles, 1774), in *Female Education in the Age of Enlightenment*, Introduction by Janet Todd (London: William Pickering, 1996), 15.
50. Rosemarie Zagarri, "The Rights of Man and Woman in Post-Revolutionary America," *The William and Mary Quarterly* 55 (April 1998): 207.
51. William Dunlap, *Diary of William Dunlap (1766–1839)*, Vol. 1 (New York: New York Historical Society, 1930).
52. *Mirror of Dramatic Taste and Censor*, July 1811.
53. *Mirror of Dramatic Taste and Censor*, July 1811.
54. Gregory, 15.
55. Daniel Scott Smith, "Family Limitation, Sexual Control, and Domestic Feminism in Victorian America," in *A Heritage of Her Own*, ed. Nancy F. Cott and Elizabeth H. Pleck (New York: Simon and Schuster, 1979), 226.
56. *Mirror of Dramatic Taste and Censo*, October 1810.
57. *The Emerald*, 10 July 1806.
58. Janet Wilson James, *Changing Ideas about Women in the United States, 1776–1825* (New York: Garland Publishing, 1981), 127.
59. *Boston Weekly Magazine*, 7 December 1816.
60. *Charleston Courier*, 9 February 1803.
61. Smith, 226.
62. *Advice from a Lady of Quality to Her Children in the Last Stage of a Lingering Illness* (Boston: S. Hall, 1796), 76; micropublished in *History of Women* (New Haven, CT: Research Publications, Inc., 1975).
63. Fordyce, I: 17.
64. Hemphill, 108.
65. Hemphill maintained that although most of the authors of advice books for women in this period were "primarily middle class Englishmen," Americans continued their "loyalty to British tutelage," and these works remained popular in this country into the 1800s, 107.
66. Fordyce, I: 21.
67. Fordyce, I: 19–20.
68. Fordyce, I: 109–110.
69. Gregory, 5.
70. Hemphill, 112.
71. Hemphill, 112.
72. Hemphill, 112. Hemphill conceded however, that "all of that lay in the future, if it happened at all."
73. Fordyce, I: 155–156.
74. Fordyce, I: 278.
75. *Mirror of Taste and Dramatic Censor*, July 1811.
76. *New York Mirror, and Ladies' Literary Gazette*, 2 August 1823.
77. *Boston Spectator*. 7 January, 1815.
78. Nancy F. Cott, in *A Heritage of Her Own*, suggested that wives "clung to married status longer than men did, even when aware of their spouses' wrongs"; in fact, wives waited almost five years after the onset of the first offence (adultery, desertion, etc.) before suing for divorce, whereas aggrieved husbands waited for only two and one-half years.. Although Cott's figures are for the eighteenth century, several of her examples were drawn from the latter decades and thus are applicable to this study, 121.
79. Samuel K. Jennings, *The Married Lady's Companion, or Poor Man's Friend*, in *Root of Bitterness*, ed. Nancy F. Cott (Boston: Northeastern University Press, 1986), 113. Mary Kelley, in *Private Woman, Public Stage* (New York: Oxford University Press, 1984), observed that divorce could not be automatically accepted as a solution. Even though legislation regarding divorce in the United States was less restrictive by the end of the eighteenth century, many continued to oppose the idea. In addition to those voicing pragmatic concerns about the fate of a divorced woman, others expressed disapproval on spiritual grounds. As late as 1869, a novel presented a mistreated wife who states, "I could not recognize the validity of divorces, for human hands could not unlike God's fetters," 237.
80. McNall, 13.

81. Margaret Nash in "Rethinking Republican Motherhood: Benjamin Rush and the Young Ladies' Academy of Philadelphia," *Journal of the Early Republic* 17 (Summer 1997), suggested that Kerber and other historians have "overstated the importance of Republican Motherhood" and that other factors must be considered, such as Enlightenment beliefs, "practical needs" for knowledge and "rational approaches to religion," 171–172. Nash argued that it was not just women's roles as mothers that gave justification for their education — instead she claimed that Rush emphasized women's power over grown men. Nash states that Rush's position suggested that "republican womanhood, as much or more than republican motherhood, motivated his belief in female education," 178.

82. Fordyce, 34–35.

83. See Nancy F. Cott, "Passionlessness: An Interpretation of Victorian Sexual Ideology, 1790–1850," in *A Heritage of Her Own*, 162–181, ed. Nancy F. Cott and Elizabeth Pleck (New York: Simon and Schuster, 1979). Cott used the term passionlessness "to convey the view that women lacked sexual aggressiveness, that their sexual appetites contributed a very minor part (if any at all) to their motivations," 163. Cott asserted that this idea may have appealed to women; "the ideology of passionlessness favored women's power and self-respect," 168.

84. Fordyce, I: 128.

85. Fordyce, I: 129.

Chapter 6

1. Claudia Johnson, *American Actress* (Chicago: Nelson-Hall, 1984), 54.

2. William Dunlap, *The Diary of William Dunlap*, 267.

3. Bernard, *Retrospections of America*, 263. In 1792, the Coinage Act set up the first U.S. official money system and used the dollar as the basic unit. However, people in the United States continued to use foreign coins as well. See also http//library.thinkquest.org.

4. William Dunlap, *The Diary of William Dunlap*, 267.

5. *The Polyanthos*, September 1813.

6. *The Polyanthos*, September 1813, remarked that "the performances of Payne, Morse, Cleary, and Robertson, fully convince, that when they do thus come forward, want of talent is not an obstacle in the way of success; and American actors have perhaps little reason to complain of public neglect."

7. *The Cynick*, 19 October, 1811.

8. *The New York Mirror, and Ladies' Literary Gazette*, 20 November, 1824.

9. *The New York Mirror, and Ladies' Literary Gazette*, 20 November, 1824.

10. Wood, 137–138.

11. *The New York Mirror, and Ladies' Literary Gazette*, 30 July, 1825.

12. Dunlap, *History*, 365–366.

13. *Mirror of Taste and Dramatic Censor*, January 1810.

14. *The New York Mirror, and Ladies' Literary Gazette*, 20 November 1824.

15. Bernard, *Retrospections of America*, 263.

16. *The Polyanthos*, April 1806. *The Portfolio*, October 1810, commented that a number of less talented actors tended to imitate Cooke, but "without the talents to extenuate the offense."

17. Davis, Tracy. *Actresses as Working Women: Their Social Identity in Victorian London* (London: Routledge, 1991), 19.

18. *Philadelphia Repository*, 31 October, 1801.

19. Joseph Ireland, *Records of the New York Stage* (New York: 1866; reprint, New York: Benjamin Blom, 1966), 105.

20. Dunlap, *History*, 203.

21. Ireland, 105.

22. *Charleston City Gazette*, 6 June 1803.

23. Dunlap, *History*, 203.

24. Dunlap, *History*, 203.

25. Wood, 111.

26. Ireland, 105.

27. Bernard, *Retrospections of America*, 266.

28. *Theatrical Censor*, 4 December 1805.

29. *Charleston Courier*, 2 May, 1803.

30. *Charleston Courier*, 6 May 1803.

31. Philip Highfill, Jr., and Kalman A. Burmin, *A Biographical Dictionary of Actors, Actresses, Musicians, Dancers, Managers and Other Stage Personnel in London, 1660–1800* (Carbondale: Southern Illinois University Press, 1978), 187.

32. Dunlap, *Diary*, 260–261.

33. Dunlap, *Diary*, 303.

34. *Boston Gazette*, 28 May 1812.

35. *Poulson's Daily Advertiser*, 28 May 1812.

36. Dunlap, *History*, 202.

37. Ireland, 106.

38. Ireland, 106.

39. Clapp, 40.

40. Clapp, 39.

41. Bernard, *Retrospections of America*, 264.

42. Clapp, 40.

43. Roscius," *The Philadelphia Minerva*, 13 February 1796.
44. "Theatricus," *Philadelphia Gazette*, 7 April 1795.
45. "Mercutio," *Philadelphia Repository*, 31 October 1801.
46. Dunlap, *History*, 239.
47. Bernard, *Retrospections of America*, 264.
48. *Philadelphia Repository*, 31 October 1801.
49. *Philadelphia Repository*, 31 October 1801.
50. *Philadelphia Repository*, 31 October 1801.
51. Clapp, 40.
52. Ireland, 151.
53. Clapp, 21, asserts that Mrs. Powell was renowned in London and even performed with Mrs. Siddons and presented a command performance before the king; however, Donald A. Sears, in his article "The Biographical Muddle of Mrs. Snelling Powell," *New England Quarterly* 33 (September 1960): 368–371, claims that Clapp (and subsequent historians) confused Mrs. Snelling (Harrison) Powell with another Mrs. Powell (formerly Mrs. Farmer), a famous British actress.
54. Dunlap, *History*, 134.
55. Clapp, 152.
56. Clapp, 84.
57. Bernard, *Retrospections of America*, 318.
58. Quoted in Clapp, 152.
59. *Boston Daily Advertiser*, 7 May, 1813.
60. Quoted in Clapp, 184.
61. Bernard, *Retrospections of America*, 317; Clapp, 21.
62. Philip Highfill, Jr., and Kalman A. Burnim related that contemporary notices give her last names as Sidus; however, in the Bodleian Library is a statement from her father that listed his name as Tobias George, 134.
63. Dunlap *History*, 225–226.
64. Dunlap, *History*, 226.
65. Bernard, *Retrospections of America*, 69.
66. Dunlap, *History*, 228. Highfill and Burnim reported that a manuscript presently in the Folger Library maintained that Mrs. Oldmixon was pregnant when she came to the United States and "was oblig'd to assume" the name of Oldmixon because "she was in the way that Women wish to be who Love their Lords & because the Trans-Atlantics [Americans] have more regard to Appear[ance]s than People on this side of the Water," 158.
67. Dunlap, *Diary*, 239.
68. Dunlap, *Diary*, 242.
69. Dunlap, *History*, 228.
70. Dunlap, *Diary*, 267.
71. Dunlap, *Diary*, 243.
72. Dunlap, *Diary*, 355.
73. *City Gazette*, 29 October 1805. The paper reported that Mrs. Oldmixon sang "the beautiful music of Giardini, the height to which she ascended, making a double octave from G, can only be credited by those who have the delight of listening to the necromancy of her notes."
74. *City Gazette*, 29 October, 1805.
75. *Charleston Courier*, 1 November, 1805.
76. Dunlap *History* 225.
77. Wood, 139.

Chapter 7

1. Lewis, *One O'Clock; or The Knight and the Wood Daemon*, 49.
2. John Wolcott, "A Case Study of American Production: English Source and American Practice," *The Ohio State University Theatre Collection Bulletin* 15 (1968): 11.
3. Wolcott, 10.
4. Clifford E. Hamar, "Scenery on the Early American Stage," *The Theatre Annual* 7 (1948–1949): 88.
5. William Burke Wood, *Personal Recollections of the Stage* (Philadelphia: H.C. Baird, 1855), 237. Wood identified those who presented the scenery as Richards, Hodges, and Rooker, artists of the first reputation of their day.
6. The nine plays were Richard Cumberland's *The Carmelite*, Henry Siddon's *The Sicilian Romance*, William Dunlap's *Fontainville Abbey*, James Boaden's *Fontainville Forest*, Robert Jephson's *The Count of Narbonne*, Miles Andrew's *The Mysteries of the Castle*, George Colman the Younger's *The Iron Chest*, John Hodgkinson's *The Man of Fortitude*, and Matthew G. Lewis's *The Castle Spectre*.
7. Paul Ranger, "Terror and Pity Reign in Every Breast," in *Gothic Drama in the London Patent Theatres, 1750–1820* (London: Society for Theatre Research, 1991), 42.
8. Michael Booth in *English Melodrama* remarked on the popularity of castle and abbey settings in early Gothic plays, 68.
9. Cynthia Griffin Wolff, "The Radcliffean Gothic Model: A Form for Feminine Sexuality," in *The Female Gothic*, ed. Juliann Fleenore (Montreal: Eden Press, 1983), 209. Wolff argued that "the overtly sexual impli-

cations of this recurrent situation are inescapable, even in eighteenth century Gothic fiction," 209.

10. Richard Cumberland, *The Carmelite*, in *The London Stage*, Vol. 3 (London: Sherwood and Co., n.d.), 10. For example, in *The Carmelite*, Acts II, III, and IV all occurred in "An apartment in the Castle," and Act V unfolded in "a chapel with an altar decorated with the funeral trophies of Saint Valori."

11. *The Dramatic Censor*, 4 December 1805.

12. Hodgkinson's list was published in Richard Stoddard's "Stock Scenery in 1798," *Theatre Survey* 13 (November 1972): 102.

13. Scenes that occurred in a hall were included in *The Iron Chest*, *Fontainville Abbey* and *Fontainville Forest*, *The Mysteries of the Castle*, *The Sicilian Romance*, *The Castle Spectre*, *The Count of Narbonne*, and *The Man of Fortitude*.

14. Miles Andrews, *The Mysteries of the Castle* (London: T.N. Longman, 1795), in *English and American Drama of the Nineteenth Century* (New Canaan, CT: Readex, 1963), microfiche, 5.

15. Matthew Gregory Lewis, *The Castle Spectre* in *Seven Gothic Dramas*, ed. Jeffrey N. Cox (Athens: Ohio University Press, 1992), 181, 207.

16. Cumberland.

17. Such a scene came to be known as a "carpenter's scene." Interview, Alan S. Jackson, State University of New York at Binghamton, October 21, 2003.

18. Another special effect that was not supernatural was Percy's jump from the tower window. *The Thespian Mirror*, 1 March 1806, criticized the effect because the tables and chair in the scene were "placed in a situation which seemed to invite Percy's flight," 77.

19. Andrews, 60. The boat probably was a cutout on wheels that rolled behind the ground row of the shore, Interview, Alan S. Jackson.

20. Sybil Rosenfeld, *Georgian Scene Painters and Scene Painting* (Cambridge: Cambridge University Press, 1981), 61.

21. Rosenfeld, 62.

22. James Boaden, *Fontainville Forest*, in *The Plays of James Boaden*, ed. Steven Cohan (New York: Garland Publishing, Inc., 1980), 25; Matthew Gregory Lewis, *The Castle Spectre* (London: J. Bell, 1798), in *Seven Gothic Dramas*, ed. Jeffrey N. Cox (Athens: Ohio University Press, 1992), 210.

23. *The Oxford English Dictionary*, s.v. "lanthorn," lists the word as a form of "lantern."

24. The lanthorrn probably was lit, but shuttered so that the light would not be seen by the audience. Interview, Alan S. Jackson.

25. Andrews, 32, 35.

26. Henry Siddons, *The Sicilian Romance* (n.p., 1794), *Three Centuries of Drama* (New Canaan, CT: Readex, 1963), microprint, 19.

27. Although Hodgkinson claimed authorship of *The Man of Fortitude* (New York: David Longworth, 1807), William Dunlap, in *History of the American Theatre*, (New York: J & J Harper, 1832; reprint, New York: Burt Franklin, 1963), stated that he had written the original play under the title of *The Knight's Adventure*. Dunlap contended that Hodgkinson changed some of the verse to prose, added "a comic buffoon and a lady," retitled the work, and claimed ownership, 330. In this play, as in *Fontainville Abbey*, any apparent supernatural effects were explained away; the specters were discovered to be banditti in disguise.

28. Willard Thorp, "The Stage Adventures of Some Gothic Novels," *PMLA* 43 (1928): 482. Rosenfeld commented that the vision of specters on stage was enhanced by the use of a gauze cloth which hung between audience and specter and speculated that this technique had been developed by DeLoutherburg, 63.

29. Boaden, *Fontainville Forest*, 69.

30. Dunlap, *Fontainville Abbey*, 9.

31. Plays first performed in the U.S. in this period were *Bluebeard*, *Adelmorn, A Tale of Mystery*, *Ribbemont*, *Foscari*, White's *The Mysteries of the Castle*, *The Forest of Rosenwald*, and *The Wood Daemon*.

32. Barnard Hewitt, "Pure Repertory, New York Theatre, 1809," *The Theatre Annual* 10 (1952): 38.

33. John Blake White, *Foscari* (Charleston: John B. White, 1807), 14.

34. These figures probably were cutouts rather than actors. Actors were "too heavy and floppy." Interview, Alan S. Jackson.

35. Ranger, 75.

36. As quoted in George C.D. Odell, *Annals of the New York Stage* (New York: Columbia University Press, 1927), II:133.

37. *The Philadelphia Magazine*, 28 February 1818.

38. Odell, II: 380.

39. *Bluebeard* also benefited from the use of live elephants. Wood commented in 1813 that "a learned elephant contributed in Philadelphia this season to the attraction of "Blue Beard" now revived," 186.

40. George Colman the Younger, *Bluebeard* (London: W. Simpkin and R. Marshall,

1823), in *Plays by George Colman the Younger and Thomas Morton* (Cambridge: Cambridge University Press, 1983), 22.
41. Dunlap, *Bluebeard*, 36.
42. Quoted in Odell, II: 133.
43. Odell, II:133.
44. Odell, II:133.
45. As quoted in Odell, II:134.
46. Turnbull's play, acted and performed in 1808, actually appeared earlier than Lewis' original, but the plays were nearly identical because Turnbull based his version on the printed prospectus of Lewis' play. Oral Coad, in "The Gothic Element in American Literature Before 1835," *The Journal of English and Germanic Philology* 24 (1925), called Turnbull's version "a hodge-podge even worse than the original," 77. Because of the scenic similarity in the two plays, and because daybooks and advertisements sometimes did not note whose version was presented, I have not distinguished between the two versions when discussing the scenery.
47. Odell, III: 298.
48. Odell, III: 298.
49. Turnbull, 5.
50. The Chestnut Theatre File, Historical Society of Pennsylvania, Philadelphia, PA.
51. Quoted in Odell, II: 298–299.
52. Matthew Gregory Lewis, *One O'-Clock; or The Knight and the Wood Daemon* (London: Simpkin and R. Marshall, 1824), in *English and American Drama of the Nineteenth Century*, (New Canaan, CT: Readex, 1963), microfiche, 49.
53. J.D. Turnbull, *The Wood Daemon; or The Clock Has Struck* (Boston: B. True, 1808), in *Three Centuries of Drama* (New Canaan, CT: Readex, 1963), microfiche, 24.
54. Plates from scripts for toy theatres suggested the visual impact of specific scenes. This script, published by G. Skelt, apparently was based on an 1811 production of *The Wood Daemon; or The Hour of One*, performed at the Lyceum in London.
55. Collapsing walls would have used "flap changes." Interview, Alan S. Jackson.
56. Thomas Holcroft, *A Tale of Mystery*, in *The Hour of One*, ed. Stephen Wischhusen (London: Gordon Fraser, 1975), 11, 14, 15.
57. Plays written or adapted by American playwrights in this decade included *Ribbemont* and *Bluebeard* by William Dunlap, *Foscari* and *The Mysteries of the Castle* by John Blake White, *The Forest of Rosenwald* by John Stokes, and *The Wood Daemon* by John Turnbull. Three of these plays were only slightly changed from the British originals; however Dunlap's *Ribbemont; or The Feudal Baron*, White's *Foscari*, and White's other play, *The Mysteries of the Castle*, did not have British counterparts.
58. John Blake White, *The Mysteries of the Castle* (Charleston, SC: John B. White, 1807), 43, 5.
59. White, *The Mysteries of the Castle*, 29.
60. White, *The Mysteries of the Castle*, 49, 54.
61. White, *The Mysteries of the Castle*, 5, 64.
62. White, *The Mysteries of the Castle*, 45.
63. Odell quoted a review in the *Chronicle* of January 18, 1804, that praised Lewis' *Raymond and Agnes*: "we have seldom witnessed a pantomime that conveyed a story more interesting, or that was furnished with incidents more striking ... received by a crowded house with deepest attention, and honored at its conclusion with loud applause." Odell, however, dismissed the play as "showy and unpleasant," II: 192.
64. James Nelson Barker. *Marmion* (New York: D. Longworth, 1816, 39.
65. Promptbook quoted in Rosenfeld, 179.
66. Rosenfeld, 179.
67. Odell noted that *The Mountain Torrent* was one of the last plays presented at the Park Theatre before it was destroyed by fire in 1820, III: 558. He disliked the play, saying that it was "but an attempt to pour sour European wine into American bottles ... one of the stalest of melodramas," III: 557.
68. Samuel Judah, *The Mountain Torrent* (New York: T. Longworth, 1820), in *Three Centuries of Drama* (New Canaan, CT: Readex, 1963), microfiche, 2.
69. Odell, III: 558.
70. Judah, *The Mountain Torrent*, 26.
71. Judah, *The Mountain Torrent*, 29.
72. Odell, III: 559.
73. Representatiave plays were *The Warlock of the Glen, The Rose of Arragon, Melmoth, One O'Clock; or The Knight and the Wood Daemon, Frankenstein,* and *Superstition.*
74. Rosenfeld, 177.
75. Rosenfeld, 178.
76. Benjamin West, *Melmoth the Wanderer* (London: J. Lowndes, n.d.), in *English and American Drama of the Nineteenth Century* (New Canaan, CT: Readex, 1963), microfiche, 20.
77. West, *Melmoth the Wanderer*, 30.
78. West, *Melmoth the Wanderer*, 11.
79. West, *Melmoth the Wanderer*, 34.
80. West, *Melmoth the Wanderer*, 36.
81. West, *Melmoth the Wanderer*, 35.
82. Lewis' plays were *Adelmorn, One*

O'Clock; or The Knight and The Wood Daemon, and *Raymond and Agnes.*
83. Rosenfeld, 178.
84. Richard Cumberland, as quoted in Paul Ranger's *Terror and Pity Reign in Every Breast,* 86. Also, David Grimsted, *Melodrama Unveiled* (Chicago: University of Chicago Press, 1968) quoted several critics who complained about theatres that specialized in "pasteboard pageantry," and "conflagrations," 79.
85. Oscar Brockett, *History of the Theatre* (Boston: Allyn and Bacon, 1991), stated that The Walnut, built in 1812, challenged The Chestnut in Philadelphia; in New York City, the Olympic Theatre, built in 1812, competed with the Park; in Boston, the Tremont Street Theatre, built in 1827, vied with the Federal Street Theatre, 416.
86. *The Mirror of Taste and Dramatic Censor,* April 1810.
87. Rosenfeld, 42.
88. Rosenfeld credited DeLoutherbourg with "carrying the use of broken perspective further than any of his predecessors," 44.
89. Rosenfeld, 61.
90. Paul Ranger commented that processions were popular at Drury Lane but admitted that he found it "difficult to account for the popularity of processions in gothic drama," because the processions "reflected nothing of life outside the theatre," 75.
91. *The Charleston Courier,* 18 May 1808.
92. John F. Wolcott, 19.
93. Robert Hume, in "Gothic Versus Romantic: A Revaluation of the Gothic Novel," *PMLA* (March 1969), argues that the "key characteristic" of the Gothic novel is not any device, but its atmosphere of "evil and brooding terror," 236.
94. Coad concluded that the "explained supernaturalism" as popularized by Mrs. Radcliffe was the "dominant influence in American Gothic drama." Coad argues that four-fifths of plays written in this period (around 1794 to 1835) that might be termed Gothic do not exhibit actual supernaturalism, but instead "gain their effect through setting and mysterious occurrences that arise from natural causes," 79.
95. Donald Ringe, *American Gothic* (Lexington: University Press of Kentucky, 1982), 2–3.

Chapter 8

1. Dunlap, *Fontainville Abbey,* 175.
2. Dunlap, *Fontainville Abbey,* 175.
3. Dunlap, *Fontainville Abbey,* 176.
4. Dunlap, *Fontainville Abbey,* 179.
5. George Colman the Younger, 21.
6. George Colman the Younger, 21.
7. Carol Margaret Davison, "Haunted House/Haunted Heroine: Female Gothic Closets in 'The Yellow Wallpaper.'" *Women's Studies* 33 (2004): 48.
8. Davison, 50.
9. Davison, 50.
10. DeLamotte, 19.
11. DeLamotte, 20. DeLamotte cited Maurice Levy's concept of the "anxiety of the threshold," 20.
12. Punter, *The Literature of Terror,* 212.
13. Mary Chapman, "The Masochistic Pleasures of the Gothic," in *American Gothic: New Interventions in a National Narrative,* 183–201, ed. Robert K. Martin and Eric Savoy (Iowa City: University of Iowa Press,1998), 190.
14. Chapman, "The Masochistic Pleasures of the Gothic," 190.
15. Ellis, ix–x.
16. Ellis, x.
17. Fleenor,12.
18. Moers, 191.
19. DeLamotte, 156.
20. DeLammotte observed that as femmes couvertes, married women were secreted away, 157.
21. Ellis, x.
22. Eugenia DeLamotte commented that the "men's and women's Gothic shared many common concerns—most notably an obsession with the problem of the boundaries of the self" and she conceded not all women writers approach this issue in the same way. However, DeLamotte maintained that "the boundary of the self was a crucial issue for women in some special ways," 25.
23. Fleenor, 8.
24. Diane Hoeveler, "The Female Gothic."
25. White, 52.
26. Hodgkinson, 21..
27. Boaden, *Fountainville Forest,* 38.
28. Lewis, *One O'Clock; or The Knight and the Wood Daemon,* 60.
29. DeLamotte, 161.
30. For a description of British actresses in Gothic plays, see Paula R. Backscheider, *Spectacular Politics* (Baltimore: The Johns Hopkins University Press, 1993).
31. Barker, 68.
32. DeLamotte, 161.
33. Ellis, x.
34. Ellis, x.
35. See Rosemarie Bank, "The Bowery

Theatre as a Mode of Historical Information," in *The American Stage*, ed. Ron Engle and Tice L. Miller (Cambridge: Cambridge University Press, 1993) Bank also quoted statistics from Christine Stansell about numbers of women in theatres by the 1850s in *Theatre Culture in America, 1825–1830* (Cambridge: Cambridge University Press, 1997), 92.

36. Jill Dolan, *The Feminist Spectator as Critic* (Ann Arbor: The University of Michigan Press, 1988), 2.

Chapter 9

1. Matthew Gregory Lewis, *Raymond and Agnes*, 7.
2. John Stokes, 9.
3. So great was the feeling against native plays that Dunlap did not claim *Fontainville Abbey* as his own play at its premiere in 1795. *History of the American Theatre* (New York: J. & J. Harper, 1832; reprint, New York: Burt Franklin, 1963), 264.
4. Each of these plays received at least three productions at a major theatre in either New York, Philadelphia, Charleston, or Boston.
5. William Dunlap, *Fontainville Abbey*, in his *Adaptations of European Plays* (New York: Scholars' Facsimiles & Reprints, 1988), 171.
6. James Boaden, *Fountainville Forest*, in *The Plays of James Boaden*, ed. Steven Cohan (New York: Garland Publishing, Inc., 1980), 17.
7. Dunlap, 201.
8. Matthew Gregory Lewis, *One O'Clock; or The Knight and the Wood Daemon*, English and American Drama of the Nineteenth Century (New Canaan, CT: Readex, 1963), microprint, 28.
9. J.D. Turnbull, *The Wood Daemon; or The Clock Has Struck* (Boston: B. True, 1808), in *Three Centuries of Drama* (New Canaan, CT: Readex, 1963), (microprint,) 15.
10. Boaden, 62.
11. Dunlap, 194.
12. The American version of *Bluebeard* also included a reference to equality; this play followed the British version almost verbatim until the final scene, in which the American playwright inserted a section wherein Selim freed the slaves of Abomolique, and the slaves responded "Thanks to our deliverer!" William Dunlap, *Bluebeard* (New York: D. Longworth, 1806), in *Three Centuries of Drama* (New Canaan, CT: Readex, 1963), microprint, 51.
13. Dunlap, *Fontainville Abbey*, 190.
14. William Dunlap, *Bluebeard*, 51.

15. Lewis, *One O'Clock; or The Knight and the Wood Daemon*, 66.
16. Turnbull, 33.
17. Turnbull, 33.
18. Turnbull, 33.
19. Turnbull, 28.
20. Lewis, *One O'Clock*, 32.
21. Lewis, *Raymond and Agnes*, 7.
22. Lewis, *Raymond and Agnes*, 14.
23. In the British play, the stage directions noted that the villain Jacques "is shot by Agnes."
24. Dunlap, *Fontainville Abbey*, 23.
25. Turnbull, 33.
26. Lewis, *Raymond and Agnes*, 14.
27. Barbara Welter, "The Cult of True Womanhood," *American Quarterly* 18 (Summer 1966), observed that a "true woman naturally loved her children; to suggest otherwise was monstrous," 171.
28. Lewis, 10.
29. Stokes, 14.
30. Turnbull, 18.
31. In the *Fontainville* plays, Adeline found a mother figure in Madame La Motte. In the *Raymond and Agnes* plays, Agnes stated that the abbess of St. Clair was like a mother to her. In *The Wood Daemon* plays, Una turned to Clotilda (depicted as her sister or her aunt) for guidance.
32. In *Fontainville Abbey*, the heroine describes the convent as "a dreary, sickly, endless, hopeless void!" 165.
33. Turnbull, 13.
34. Adeline, in the American *Fontainville Abbey*, opened her first lengthy speech with "O my kind mother — so I'm taught to call thee." Dunlap had the characters refer to each other as "mother" and "daughter" more frequently than did Boaden in the British play, 163.
35. Boaden, 34.
36. La Motte, watching from a window exclaimed, "See how the blushes clothe her beauteous cheek while now with rank familiarity he seizes her hand," Dunlap, 184.
37. Noah Webster was responsible for promoting a more phonetic system of spelling. In his article, "Words as Social Control: Noah Webster and the Creation of the American Dictionary," *American Quarterly* 28 (Fall 1976), 424, Richard Rollins argued that in Webster's earlier works, he attempted to forge "An American tongue," to encourage America's independence from "a vile and corrupt England." Rollins adds that as early as 1788 he believed that the use of language could "purify society."
38. See Mary Diana Neufeld, "The Adap-

tation of the Gothic Novel to the English Stage, 1765–1826" (PhD diss., Cornell University, 1978), in which she compared several American plays to British versions and notes that references to monarchy are often eliminated.

39. The clergy not only blamed the theatres for promoting idleness; they also blamed them for causing various disasters: some attributed the 1793 Yellow Fever Epidemic on the opening of the Chestnut Street theatre in Philadelphia. Other religious groups stated that the fatal fire at the Richmond theatre in 1812 was an "act of God" against theatres. See Harrold Shiffler's "Religious Opposition to the Eighteenth Century Philadelphia Stage," *Educational Theatre Journal* 14 (October 1962): 223.

40. William Dunlap, *History of the American Theatre* (New York: J. & J. Harper, 1832; reprint, New York: Burt Franklin, 1963), 130.

41. Welter identified the "four cardinal virtues" of True Womanhood as "piety, purity, submissiveness, and domesticity," 152.

42. Alexis de Tocqueville, *Democracy in America* (New York: Modern Library, 1981), 88.

43. Alexis de Tocqueville, 89.

44. Janet Wilson James, *Changing Ideas about Women in the United States, 1776–1825* (New York: Garland Publishing, 1981), 127.

45. Sally Ann McNall, *Who Is in the House* (New York: Elsevier, 1981), 3.

46. McNall, 13.

47. Linda Kerber, *Women of the Republic* (Chapel Hill: University of North Carolina Press, 1980), 170.

48. *Boston Weekly Magazine*, 19 July 1817.

49. *Boston Weekly Magazine*, August 1817.

50. Cott and Pleck, 165.

51. Cott and Pleck, 164.

Chapter 10

1. *Boston Weekly Magazine*, 9 November 1816.

2. Oral Coad, "The Gothic Element in American Literature before 1835," *The Journal of English and Germanic Philology* 24 (1925): 79.

3. Vincent Angotti, "American Dramatic Criticism 1800–1840" (Ph.D. diss., University of Kansas, 1967), reported that some historians had designated 1802–1803 as "the Birth of Criticism" in America, 8.

4. William Charvat, *The Origins of American Critical Thought, 1800–1835* (Philadelphia: University of Pennsylvania Press, 1936), maintained that at no other point in American history was the culture so "completely and directly dominated by the professional classes." Charvat added that these critics achieved a kind of "homogeneity of outlook" because of the rise of the Federalist party and the "fear of popular outbreaks." These critics, then, saw the need for control in American society, 5.

5. Charvat, 7.

6. Angotti contended that most of these attacks on the theatre appeared in Philadelphia and Boston, "strongholds" of Quaker and Puritan religious thought, 101.

7. Charvat, 120.

8. *The New York Mirror, and Ladies' Literary Gazette*, 28 May 1825.

9. *Boston Weekly Magazine*, 19 October 1816. Although critics complained about the limited number of Shakespearean plays on the stage, Lawrence Levine, in *Highbrow/Lowbrow* (Cambridge, MA: Harvard University Press, 1988), observed that productions of Shakespeare were done much more often in the early years of the nineteenth century than in the latter part, because by then, Shakespeare was no longer part of the theatrical mainstream, but instead was considered part of "polite society." Levine suggested that Shakespeare's plays were probably performed often in the early nineteenth century for several reasons. First, these plays, like the culture, enshrined the art of oratory. Next, Shakespeare was considered a "moral" playwright, and his plays were good bets for theatres that often still had to defend themselves against charges of immorality. Third, Shakespearean plays were good vehicles for stars, and, finally, Shakespearean plays appealed particularly to American culture because they put individuals at the center of the universe and allowed each man to be master of his fate. These same features seemed to be the most attractive features of Gothic plays.

10. *The Port Folio*, 23 January 1802.

11. Angotti, 168. Charvat commented that generally, criticism in magazines "either ignored or condemned the drama which the public was enjoying on the stage," particularly the "German sentimental domestic tragedy and then French melodrama," 124.

12. *The New York Mirror, and Ladies' Literary Gazette*, 13 December 1823.

13. *Boston Weekly Magazine*, 19 October 1816.

14. Angotti, 185, 168.

15. *The Polyanthos*, March 1806.

16. *Philadelphia Gazette*, 12 April 1800.

17. *The Emerald*, 10 January 1807.

18. *The Emerald*, 17 January 1807.

19. Of these five plays, only *Bluebeard* was noted for lavish scenery and special effects. Although *A Tale of Mystery* became famous as the first melodrama, it was not noted particularly for its spectacle.

20. Stars appeared in Gothic plays from the start; *The Mysteries of the Castle* in New York, credited by Odell as starting "this sort of thing," boasted a host of famous actors: Thomas Cooper as the romantic lead, John Hodgkinson as the comic second lead, Louis Hallam, Junior, as the villain Montoni, and Mrs. Johnson as the ingenue.

21. *The Thespian Mirror*, 1 March 1806.

22. Of one production, Dunlap wrote "I rec [sic] much pleasure from *The Iron Chest* notwithstanding the disgusting circumstance of M Morris playing Lady Hellen [sic]. Fennel's Rawbold was exquisite and Cooper's Mortimer, in general good," *Diary of William Dunlap, 1766–1839* (New York: Benjamin Blom, 1969), 146.

23. James Murdoch, *The Stage* (New York: Benjamin Blom, 1880; reissued 1969), 184.

24. *Boston Weekly Magazine*, 30 November 1816.

25. *Boston Weekly Magazine*, 30 November 1816.

26. Other actresses who routinely appeared in ingenue roles were Mrs. Snelling, Mrs. Powell, Mrs. Johnson, Mrs. Barrett, Mrs. Duff, Miss Darley, Mrs. Poe, and Miss Holman.

27. Receipt amount in Reese James, *The Old Drury* (Philadelhpia: University of Pennsylvania Press, 1957), 322.

28. Angotti, 185.

Chapter 11

1. The play of *Dracula*, popular in the United States during the 1920s and again in the 1970s, featured many elements popular in Gothic melodramas: ominous atmosphere, threatening spaces, and the triumph of virtue. Like the heroine in Gothic melodramas, the heroine in *Dracula* was pursued by a powerful, mesmeric older male. She was not safe from the villain, even in her own home, surrounded by her family. Moreover, like heroines in Gothic plays, the heroine in *Dracula* was considered corrupted or impure when she falls victim to the villain, even though such an encounter was not her choice.

2. *The Times*, 21 February 1952.

Works Cited

Adelsperger, Walter. "Aspects of Staging of Plays of the Gothic Revival in England." Ph.D. diss., The Ohio State University, 1959.

"Advice From a Lady of Quality to Her Children in the Last Stage of a Lingering Illness." Boston: S. Hall, 1796. Micropublished in *History of Women*. New Haven, CT: Research Publications, Inc. 1975.

Alden, John. "A Season in Federal Street." *American Antiquarian Society Proceedings*, n.s. 65–66 (April 1955): 9–24.

Andriot, John, ed. *Population Abstracts of the United States*. McLean, VA: Andriot Associates, 1983.

Angotti, Vincent. "American Dramatic Criticism 1800–1840." Ph.D. diss., University of Kansas, 1967.

Backscheider, Paula. *Spectacular Politics*. Baltimore: The Johns Hopkins University Press, 1993.

Bank, Rosemarie K. "Hustlers in the House: The Bowery Theatre as a Mode of Historical Information." In *The American Stage*, 47–64. Ed. Ron Engle and Tice L. Miller. Cambridge: Cambridge University Press, 1993.

———. "Physics and the New Theatre Historiography." *Journal of Dramatic Theory and Criticism* (Spring 1991): 65–84.

———. "The Second Face of the Idol." In *Women in American Theatre*, 240–245. Ed. Helen Krich and Linda Walsh Jenkins. New York: Theatre Communications Group, 1987.

Bernard, John. *Retrospections of America, 1707–1811*. New York: Harper & Brothers, 1887.

———. *Retrospections of the Stage*. London: Henry Colburn and Richard Bentley, 1830.

Birkhead, Edith. *The Tale of Terror: A Study of the Gothic Romance*. London: Constable, 1921. Reprint, New York: Russell and Russell, 1963.

Booth, Michael. *English Melodrama*. London: Herbert Jenkins, 1965.

Botting, Fred. *Gothic*. London: Routledge, 1996.

Brockett, Oscar. *History of the Theatre*. Boston: Allyn and Bacon, 1991.

Brooks, Peter. *The Melodramatic Imagination*. New Haven: Yale University Press, 1976.

Bureau of the Census. *Historical Statistics of the United States*, Vol. 1. Washington, DC, 1975.

Bushman, Richard L. *The Refinement of America*. New York: Alfred A. Knopf, 1992.

Butsch, Richard. "Bowery B'hys and Matinee Ladies: The Re-Gendering of Nineteenth Century Theater Audiences." *American Quarterly* 46 (September 1994): 374–405.

Charvat, William. *The Origins of American Critical Thought*. Philadelphia: University of Pennsylvania Press, 1936.

Chesterfield, Philip Dormer Stanhope, Earl of. *Letters to His Son by the Earl of Chesterfield*. Introduction by Oliver H.G. Leigh. Washington, DC: M. Walter Dunne, 1901, ix.

Chinoy, Helen Krich, and Linda Walsh Jenkins. *Women in American Theatre*. New York: Theatre Communications Group, 1987.

Clapp, William. *A Record of the Boston Stage*. New York: 1853. Reprint, New York: Benjamin Blom, 1968.

Coad, Oral. "The Gothic Element in American Literature before 1835." *The Journal of English and Germanic Philology* 24 (1925): 72–93.

Cott, Nancy F. "Passionlessness: An Interpretation of Victorian Sexual Ideology, 1790–1850." In *A Heritage of Her Own*, 162–181. Ed. Nancy F. Cott and Elizabeth Pleck. New York: Simon and Schuster, 1979.

Cott, Nancy F., ed. *Root of Bitterness*. Boston: Northeastern University Press, 1986.

Cott, Nancy F., and Elizabeth H. Pleck. *A Heritage of Her Own*. New York: Simon and Schuster, 1979.

Davis, Tracy. *Actresses as Working Women: Their Social Identity in Victorian London*. London: Routledge, 1991.

Davison, Carol Margaret. "Haunted House/ Haunted Heroine: Female Gothic Closets in 'The Yellow Wallpaper.'" *Women's Studies* 33 (2004): 47–75.

DeLamotte, Eugenia C. *Perils of the Night*. New York: Oxford University Press, 1990.

Disher, Maurice Willson. *Blood and Thunder*. London: Frederick Muller, 1949.

Dolan, Jill. *The Feminist Spectator as Critic*. Ann Arbor: The University of Michigan Press, 1988.

Dudden, Faye E. *Women in the American Theatre*. New Haven: Yale University Press, 1994.

Dunlap, William. *Diary of William Dunlap, 1766–1839*, Vol. 1. New York: New York Historical Society, 1930.

_____. *History of the American Theatre*. New York: J. & J. Harper, 1832. Reprint, New York: Burt Franklin, 1963.

Durham, Weldon, ed. *American Theatre Companies 1749–1887*. New York: Greenwood Press, 1986.

Edwards, Justin D. *Gothic Passages*. Iowa City: University of Iowa Press, 2003.

Ellis, Kate Ferguson. *The Contested Castle*. Urbana: University of Illinois Press, 1989.

Evans, Bertrand. *Gothic Drama From Walpole to Shelley*. Berkeley: University of California Press. Reprint, Millwood, NY: Kraus Reprint, 1977.

Fiedler, Leslie. *Love and Death in the American Novel*. New York: Stein and Day, 1966. Rev. ed., New York: Doubleday, 1992.

Fleenor, Juliann. *The Female Gothic*. Montreal: Eden Press, 1983.

Fordyce, James. *Sermons for Young Women*. In *Female Education in the Age of Enlightenment*, Vol. 2. Introduction by Janet Todd. London: William Pickering, 1996.

Frank, Frederick. *Guide to the Gothic*. Metuchen, NJ, and London: The Scarecrow Press, Inc., 1984.

_____. *Through the Pale Door*. New York: Greenwood Press, 1990.

Genest, John. *Some Account of the English Stage*. 10 vols. Bath, 1832.

Gilfoyle, Timothy J. *City of Eros*. New York: W. W. Norton, 1994.

Gregory, John. *A Father's Legacy to His Daughters*. Dublin: John Colles, 1774. In *Female Education in the Age of Enlightenment*. Introduction by Janet Todd. London: William Pickering, 1996, 15.

Goddu, Teresa A. *Gothic America*. New York: Columbia University Press, 997.

Grimsted, David. *Melodrama Unveiled*. Chicago: University of Chicago Press, 1968.

Hamar, Clifford. "Scenery on the Early American Stage. *The Theatre Annual* 7 (1948–949): 84–02.

Hanawalt, Leslie. "The Rise of Gothic Drama 1765–1800." Ph.D. diss., University of Michigan, 1929.

Harbin, Billy J. "Hodgkinson's Last Years: At the Charleston Theatre, 1803–1805." *Theatre Survey* 13 (November 1972): 20–43.

Hemphill, C. Dallett. *Bowing to Necessities*. New York: Oxford University Press, 1999.

Henneke, Ben Graf. "The Play-goer in America, 1752–1800." Ph.D. diss., University of Illinois, 1956.

Hewitt, Barnard. "Pure Repertory, New York Theatre, 1809." *The Theatre Annual* 10 (1952): 28–39.

_____. *Theatre U.S.A*. New York: McGraw Hill, 1959.

Highfill, Philip H., and Kalman A. Burmin. *Biographical Dictionary of Actors, Actresses, Musicians, Dancers, Managers and Other Stage Personnel in London, 1660–1800*, A. Carbondale: Southern Illinois University Press, 1978.

Hill, Lyn Stiefel. "There Was an American Toy Theatre!" *Theatre Survey* 16 (Nov. 1975): 165–184.

Hoeveler, Diane. "The Female Gothic: An Introduction." www.virginia.edu.

Hogan, Charles Hogan, ed. *The London Stage*. Vol. 3. Carbondale: Southern Illinois University Press, 1968.

Hoole, W. Stanley. *The Antebellum Charleston Theatre*. Tuscaloosa: University of Alabama, 1946.

Hornblow, Arthur. *A History of the Theatre in America*. New York: J.B. Lippincott, 1919. Reprint, New York: Benjamin Blom, 1965.

Hume, Robert D. "Gothic versus Romantic: A Revaluation of the Gothic Novel." *PMLA* 84 (March 1969): 282–290.

Inverso, Marybeth. *The Gothic Impulse in*

Contemporary Drama. Ann Arbor: UMI Research, 1990.
Ireland, Joseph. *Mrs. Duff.* Boston: James R. Osgood and Company, 1882.
_____. *Records of the New York Stage.* New York: 1866. Reprint, New York: Benjamin Blom, 1966.
Irving, Washington. *Letters of Jonathan Oldstyle.* New York: Columbia University Press, 1941.
Jackson, Alan S. Interview. Vestal, NY, 21 October 2003.
James, Janet Wilson. *Changing Ideas about Women in the United States, 1776–1825.* New York: Garland Publishing, 1981.
James, Reese Davis. *The Old Drury of Philadelphia.* Philadelphia: University of Pennsylvania, 1957.
Jennings, Samuel K. *The Married Lady's Companion, or Poor Man's Friend.* In *Root of Bitterness,* 113–116. Ed. Nancy F. Cott. Boston: Northeastern University Press, 1986.
Johnson, Claudia. *American Actress: Perspective on the Nineteenth Century.* Chicago: Nelson Hall, 1984.
_____. "That Guilty Third Tier: Prostitution in Nineteenth Century Theatres." In *Victorian America,* ed. Daniel Walker Howe. Pittsburgh: University of Pennsylvania, 1976.
Kaufman, Pamela. "Oedipus and the Gothic Drama: A Psychologic Study of the Gothic Drama in Eighteenth Century England." Ph.D. diss., University of California at Los Angeles, 1970.
Kelley, Mary. "Beyond the Boundaries." *Journal of the Early Republic* 21 (spring 2001): 73–78.
_____. *Private Woman, Public Stage.* New York: Oxford University Press, 1984.
Kerber, Linda. *Women of the Republic.* Chapel Hill: University of North Carolina, 1980.
Kerr, John H. "The Bankruptcy of the Chesnut [sic] Theatre, Philadelphia, 1799." *Theatre Research* 11 (1971): 154–172.
Kett, Joseph F. *Rites of Passage.* New York: Basic Books, 1977.
Lerner, Gerda. "The Lady and the Mill Girl: Changes in the Status of Women in the Age of Jackson, 1800–1840." In *A Heritage of Her Own,* 192–196. Ed. Nancy F. Cott and Elizabeth H. Pleck. New York: Simon and Schuster, 1979.
Levine, Lawrence. *Highbrow/Lowbrow.* Cambridge, MA: Harvard University Press, 1988.
Lloyd-Smith, Allan. "Nineteenth Century American Gothic." In *A Companion to the Gothic,* 109–121. Ed. David Punter. Oxford: Blackwell, 2001.
Longuiel, Alfred. "The Word 'Gothic' in Eighteenth Century Criticism." *Modern Language Notes* 38 (1923): 453–460.
Loomis, Emerson. "Gothic Drama as Source for Gothic Fiction in the Magazines." *Notes and Queries* 15 (1968): 28–29.
Lovejoy. Arthur O. "On the Discrimination of Romanticism." In *Essays in the History of Ideas.* Baltimore: Johns Hopkins University Press, 1948.
Martin, Robert K., and Eric Savoy. *American Gothic: New Interventions in a National Narrative.* Iowa City: University of Iowa Press, 1998.
Mathews, Brander, and Laurence Hutton, eds. *Kean and Booth and Their Contemporaries.* Boston: L.C. Page & Company, 1900.
Matthews, Jean. *Toward a New Society.* Boston: Twayne Publishing, 1990.
McCall, Laura. "'Shall I Fetter Her Will': Literary Americans Confront Feminine Submission, 1820–1860." *Journal of the Early Republic* 21 (spring 2001) 95–113.
McConachie, Bruce. *Melodramatic Formations.* Iowa City: University of Iowa Press, 1992.
McCusker, John J. *How Much Is That in Real Money?* Worcester, MA: American Antiquarian Society, 1992.
McNall, Sally Allen. *Who Is in the House.* New York: Elsevier, 1981.
McNamara, Brooks. *The American Playhouse in the Eighteenth Century.* Cambridge, MA: Harvard University Press, 1969.
Meyers, Helene. *Femicidal Fears.* Albany: State University of New York Press, 2001.
Michael, Mary Ruth. "History of the Professional Theatre in Boston to 1815." Ph.D. diss., Radcliffe, 1941.
Modleski, Tania. *Loving with a Vengeance.* New York: Routledge, 1990.
Moers, Ellen. *Literary Women.* Garden City, NY: Doubleday & Co., Inc., 1977.
Mohl, Raymond, ed. *The Making of Urban America.* Wilmington, DE: Scholarly Resources, 1988.
Moody, Richard. *America Takes the Stage.* Bloomington: Indiana University Press, 1955.
Murdoch, James. *The Stage.* New York: Benjamin Blom, 1880. Reissue, 1969.
Nash, Margaret. "Rethinking Republican Motherhood: Benjamin Rush and the Young Ladies' Academy of Philadelphia." *Journal of the Early Republic* 17 (summer 1997): 171–191.

Nathans, Heather. *Early American Theatre from the Revolution to Thomas Jefferson*. Cambridge: Cambridge University Press, 2003.

Neufeld, Mary Diana. "The Adaptation of the Gothic Novel to the English Stage, 1765 to 1826." Ph.D. diss., Cornell, 1977.

Nichols, Nina da Vinci. "Place and Eros in Radcliffe, Lewis, and Bronte." In *The Female Gothic*. Montreal: Eden Press, 1983.

Nicoll, Allardyce. *A History of English Drama, 1660–1900*. 2nd ed. 6 vols. Cambridge: Cambridge University Press, 1963.

Odell, George C.D. *Annals of the New York Stage*. Vols. 1–3. New York: Columbia University Press, 1927.

Partin, Bruce Lynn. "The Horror Play: Its Transition from the Epic to the Dramatic Mode." Ph.D. diss., The Ohio State University, 1977.

Pinson, Ernest R. "The Black Sun: A Re-Evaluation of Gothic Drama and Its Influence." Ph.D. diss., The Ohio State University, 1970.

Pollock, Thomas. *The Philadelphia Theatre in the XVIII Century*. Philadelphia: University of Pennsylvania Press, 1933.

Pritner, Calvin. "William Warren's Management of the Chestnut Street Theatre Company." Ph.D. diss., University of Illinois, 1961.

Punter, David, ed. *A Companion to the Gothic*. Oxford: Blackwell, 2000.

Punter, David. *The Literature of Terror*. Vol. 1. Essex: Longman Group Limited, 1996.

Railo, Eino. *The Haunted Castle: A Study of the Elements of English Romanticism*. London: E.P. Dutton, 1927. Reprint, New York: Humanities Press, 1964.

Ranger, Paul. "Terror and Pity Reign in Every Breast." In *Gothic Drama in the London Patent Theatres, 1750–1820*. London: London Society for Theatre Research, 1991.

Reno, Robert. "James Boaden's *Fontainville Forest* and Matthew G. Lewis' *The Castle Spectre*. The Challenges of the Supernatural on the Late Eighteenth Century Stage." *Eighteenth Century Life*, October 1984, 95–103.

Richards, Jeffrey H. *Theater Enough*. Durham, NC: Duke University Press, 1991.

Ringe, Donald. *American Gothic*. Lexington: University Press of Kentucky, 1982.

Rollins, Richard. "Words as Social Control: Noah Webster and the Creation of the American Dictionary." *American Quarterly* 28 (Fall 1976).

Rosenfeld, Sybil. *Georgian Scene Painters and Scene Painting*. Cambridge: Cambridge University Press, 1981.

Savoy, Eric. "The Rise of American Gothic." In *The Cambridge Companion to Gothic Fiction*, 167–188. Cambridge: Cambridge University Press, 2002.

Sears, Donald A. "The Biographical Muddle of Mrs. Snelling Powell." *New England Quarterly* 33 (September 1960): 368–371.

Seilhamer, George. *History of the American Theatre*. Philadelphia: Globe Printing House, 1888–1891. Reprint, New York: Greenwood Press, 1968.

Shiffler, Harrold C. "Religious Opposition to the Eighteenth Century Philadelphia Stage." *Educational Theatre Journal* 14 (October 1962): 215–223.

Smith, Daniel Scott. "Family Limitation, Sexual Control and Domestic Feminism in Victorian America." In *A Heritage of Her Own*, ed. Nancy F. Cott and Elizabeth H. Pleck. New York: Simon and Schuster, 1979.

Stoddard, Richard. "Stock Scenery in 1798." *Theatre Survey* 13 (Nov. 1972): 102–103.

———. "The Haymarket Theatre, Boston." *Educational Theatre Journal* 27 (March 1975): 63–69.

Stevens, David. *The Gothic Tradition*. Cambridge: Cambridge University Press, 2000).

Summers, Montague. *The Gothic Quest: A History of the Gothic Novel*. London: Fortune Press, 1938. Reprint, New York: Russell and Russell, 1964.

Thorp, Willard. "Some Stage Adventures of Some Gothic Novels." *PMLA* 43 (1928): 476–486.

Tocqueville, Alexis de. *Democracy in America*. New York: Modern Library, 1981.

Trollope, Frances. *Domestic Manners of the Americans*. Edited by Donald Smalley. New York: Alfred A. Knopf, 1949.

Tropp, Martin. *Images of Fear*. Jefferson, NC: McFarland & Company, 1990.

Trusler, John. *Principles of Politeness and of Knowing the World; by the late Lord Chesterfield*. Philadelphia: Robert Bell, 1778.

Wemyss, Francis. *Twenty-Six Years of the Life of an Actor and Manager*. New York: 1847.

White, Shane. *Stories of Freedom in Black New York*. Cambridge, MA: Harvard University Press, 2002.

Winter, Kari J. *Subjects of Slavery, Agents of Change*. Athens The University of Georgia Press, 1992.

"Woman: Sketches of the History, Genius, Disposition, Accomplishments, Employments, Customs and Importance of the Fair Sex in All Parts of the World." London: G. Kearsley, 1790. Micropublished in *History of Women* New Haven, CT: Research Publications, Inc., 1975.

Wood, William Burke. *Personal Recollections of the Stage*. Philadelphia: H.C. Baird, 1855.

Zagarri, Roseemarie. "The Rights of Man and Woman in Post-Revolutionary America." *The William and Mary Quarterly* 55 (April 1998): 203–230.

Plays

Andrews, Miles. *The Mysteries of the Castle.* London: T.N. Longman, 1795. In *English and American Drama of the Nineteenth Century*, ed. Allardyce Nicoll and George Freedley. New Canaan, CT: Readex, 1963. Microfiche.

Arnold, Samuel. *The Woodman's Hut.* London: J. Miller, 1814. In *English and American Drama of the Nineteenth Century*, ed. Allardyce Nicoll and George Freedley. New Canaan, CT: Readex, 1963. Microfiche.

Baillie, Joanna. *De Monfort.* In *Seven Gothic Dramas*, 234–314, ed. Jeffrey N. Cox. Athens: Ohio University Press, 1992.

Barker, James Nelson. *Marmion.* New York: D. Longworth, 1816.

———. *Superstition.* Philadelphia: A.R. Poole, n.d.

Boaden, James. *Fountainville Forest.* In *The Plays of James Boaden*, ed. Steven Cohan. New York: Garland Publishing, Inc., 1980.

Colman, George. *Bluebeard.* London: W. Simpkin and R. Marshall, 1823. In *Plays by George Colman the Younger and Thomas Morton*. Cambridge: Cambridge University Press, 1983.

———. *The Iron Chest.* London: Hurst, Rees, and Orme, 1808. Reprint in *The British Theatre*, 21. New York: Georg Olms Verlag, 1970.

Cumberland, Richard. *The Carmelite.* In *The London Stage*, Vol. 3. London: Sherwood and Co., n.d.

Dunlap, William. *Bluebeard.* New York: D. Longworth, 1806. In *Three Centuries of Drama*. New Canaan, CT: Readex, 1963. Microfiche.

———. *Fontainville Abbey.* In *Adaptations of European Plays*. New York: Scholars' Facsimiles & Reprints, 1988.

———. *Ribbemont; or The Feudal Baron.* New York: D. Longworth, 1803. In *Three Centuries of Drama*. New Canaan, CT: Readex, 1963. Microfiche.

Hodgkinson, John. *The Man of Fortitude.* New York: David Longworth, 1807.

Holcroft, Thomas. *A Tale of Mystery.* In *The Hour of One*, ed. Stephen Wischhusen, London: Gordon Fraser, 1975.

Jephson, Robert. *The Count of Narbonne.* London: Longman, Hurst, Rees, and Ormer, n.d. In *The British Theatre*. Frankfurt: Minerva GMBH, 1969, 19.

Judah, Samuel. *The Mountain Torrent.* New York: T. Longworth, 1820. *Three Centuries of Drama*. New Canaan, CT: Readex, 1963. Microfiche.

———. *The Rose of Arragon, or The Vigil of St. Mark.* New York: S. King, 1822. *Three Centuries of Drama*. New Canaan, CT: Readex, 1963. Microfiche.

Lewis, Matthew G. *Adelmorn.* NewYork: D. Longworth, 1815. In *Early American Imprints*, Vol. 2, #35099.

———. *The Castle Spectre.* London: J. Bell, 1798. In *Seven Gothic Dramas*, ed. Jeffrey N. Cox. Athens: Ohio University Press, 1992, 149–224.

———. *One O'Clock!; or The Knight and the Wood Daemon.* London: Simpkin and R. Marshall, 1824.

———. *One O'Clock; or The Knight and the Wood Daemon.* London: Simpkin and R. Marshall, 1824. In *English and American Drama of the Nineteenth Century*, ed. Allardyce Nicoll and George Freedley. New Canaan, CT: Readex, 1963. Microfiche.

———. *Raymond and Agnes; or The Travelers Benighted.* New York: Samuel French, n.d. In *English and American Drama of the Nineteenth Century*, ed. Allardyce Nicoll and George Freedley. New Canaan, CT: Readex, 1963. Microfiche.

Maturin, Charles. *Bertram.* London: J. Murray, 1816. In *Seven Gothic Dramas*, 318–383, ed. Jeffrey N. Cox. Athens: Ohio State University Press, 1992.

Peake, R. B. *Presumption; or The Fate of Frankenstein.* In *Seven Gothic Dramas*, 385–426, ed. Jeffrey N. Cox. Athens: Ohio State University Press, 1992.

Planche, J.R. *The Vampire; or The Bride of the Isles.* In *The Hour of One*, ed. Stephen Wischhusen. London: Gordon Fraser, 1975.

Siddons, Henry. *The Sicilian Romance.* n.p., 1794. In *Three Centuries of Drama*. New Canaan, CT: Readex, 1963. Microfiche.

Stokes, John. *The Forest of Rosenwald.* New York: Dramatic Repository, 1821. In *Three Centuries of Drama*. New Canaan, CT: Readex, 1963. Microfiche.

192　Works Cited

Turnbull, J.D. *The Wood Daemon; or The Clock Has Struck.* Boston: B. True, 1808. In *Three Centuries of Drama.* New Canaan, CT: Readex, 1963. Microfiche.

Walker, C.E. *The Warlock of the Glen.* London: John Lowndes, 1820. In *English and American Drama of the Nineteenth Century,* ed. Allardyce Nicoll and George Freedley. New Canaan, CT: Readex, 1963. Microfiche.

West, Benjamin. *Melmoth the Wanderer.* London: J. Lowndes, n.d. In *English and American Drama of the Nineteenth Century,* ed. Allardyce Nicoll and George Freedley. New Canaan, CT: Readex, 1963. Microfiche.

White, John Blake. *Foscari.* Charleston: J. Hoff, 1806. In *Three Centuries of Drama.* New Canaan, CT: Readex, 1963. Microfiche.

———. *The Mysteries of the Castle.* Charleston, SC: John B. White, 1807.

Newspapers and Periodicals

American Monthly Magazine and Critical Review. April 1817, August 1817.
American Quarterly Review. June 1827.
Boston Daily Advertiser. 7 May, 1813.
Boston Gazette. 24 February 1794.
Boston Spectator. 7 January 1815; 10 November 1827.
Boston Spectator and Ladies' Album, 8 September, 1827.
Boston Weekly Magazine. 11 February 1804; 9 October, 12 October, 19 October, 9 November, 7 December 1816; 25 January 1817; 19 July 1817.
Charleston Courier. 2 May 1802; 9 February, 18 April, 6 May 1803; 2 October, 10, October, 1 November 1805; 1 February, 1806; 18 May, 14 November 1808; 15 November 1815.
City Gazette (Charleston). 6 June 1803; 29 October 1805.
Critic. 22 November 1828.
Cynick. 19 October 1811.

Dramatic Censor. 4 December 1805.
Emerald. (Boston) 10 July 1806; 10 January, 17 January, 19 September 1807.
Kaleidoscope, The. 12 December, 19 December 1818.
Massachusetts Mercury, The. 22 October, 1799.
Minerva. 20 April, 1822; 14 June 1823; 6 December 1823.
Mirror of Taste and Dramatic Censor. (Philadelphia). January, April, May, October, November 1810; January, April, May, October, November, 1811.
New York Mirror, and Ladies' Literary Gazette. 2 August, 13 December 1823; 24 January, 22 May, 29 May, 18 September, 13 November, 20 November 1824; 15 January, 12 February, 12 March, 23 April, 7 May, 28 May, 16 July, 30 July, 1825.
Philadelphia Gazette. 7 April 1795; 5 November, 1799; 12 April 1800.
Philadelphia Magazine. 28 February, 7 March, 16 May 1818.
Philadelphia Minerva, The. 13 February, 1796.
Philadelphia Repository. 31 October 1801.
Poulson's Daily Advertiser, 28 May 1812.
Polyanthos. 3 January 1801; 21 December 1805; March, April 1806; September, November 1813.
Port Folio. 17 January 1801; 23 January 1802; 14 September, 21 December 1805; 25 January 1806; 31 January, 23 May, 21 November 1807; October 1810; October 1818.
Rambler's Magazine. 1809; 1810.
Something. 18 November 1809.
Theatrical Censor. 4 December 1805; 2 June 1806.
The Times (London). 21 February 1852.
Thespian Mirror. 1 March 1806.

Collections

Jackson, Allan S., Vestal, NY.
The Historical Society of Pennsylvania, Philadelphia, PA, Chestnut Street Theatre File.
The Harvard Theatre Collection, Houghton Library, Harvard University, Cambridge, MA.

Index

actors: imported from Britain 21–22, 84; prejudice against 81–84; reputations 45, 84; salaries 81, 91
Adelmorn (Lewis) 31, 102
"American" traits: dependence on/resentment of British culture: 16, 19–22, 155–157; *see also* Nationalism
anti-theatrical laws (repeal) 16
audiences: changing demographics of audiences 25–26; prostitutes in "Third Tier" 18, 40–42, 63–64; "respectable" women 43–45; rude behavior 34–35, 40–44; seating in theatres 33–35

Bertram (Maturin): controversy 35; excerpt 33; synopsis 29; vehicle for stars 36, 146–147
Bluebeard (Colman): excerpt 118–119; synopsis 129
Bluebeard (Dunlap): differences between British and American versions 104, 127, 132; publicity for scenery 104; special effects 103–105; synopsis 28
Boaden, James (*Fontainville Forest*) 15, 56, 128
Booth, Junius Brutus, Sr. 145–146
Boston: Federal Street Theatre 28; gothic plays 31–32; Haymarket Theatre 28; population changes 16–17
Byron (George Gordon) Lord 10, 154

The Carmelite 67–68
The Castle of Otranto (Walpole) 6
The Castle Spectre (Lewis): criticism of 157; excerpt 5–6, 47, 54, 56, 66; publicity for 31, 80; synopsis 29
Charleston: audience behavior 34; gothic plays 31, 32; population increase 17, 28; theatre companies 27
The Chatham Garden Theatre (NY) 22, 27

Chesterfield, Lord (Philip Dormer Stanhope): *Letters of Advice to His Son* 48–50, 57–58
Chestnut Street Theatre: opening 25; scenery 97; ticket prices 25, 33–34
Colman, George: *Bluebeard* 28; *The Iron Chest* 30
Cooper, Thomas A. 21, 145, 146
The Count of Narbonne (Jephson) 66, 67, 68
Cox, Jeffrey 3
"The Cult of True Womanhood" (Welter) 62

Dark Shadows 1
DeLoutherbourg, Philippe Jacques 114
Duff, Mrs. Mary Ann 79
Dunlap, William: concerns about prostitutes 40–42; *Fontainville Abbey* 15–16, 127; negotiating with Mrs. Melmoth 87; negotiation with Mrs. Oldmixon 91–92; as playwright 20, 26, 102; reading Mary Wollstonecraft 70; *Ribbemont* 53; on status of actors 83

economic changes 17
Evans, Bertrand 3

Federal Street Theatre 28
Female Gothic: dangerous spaces 120–122; description 7–8, 63, 119
Fennell, James 25, 145
Fiedler, Leslie 10
Fleenor, Juliann (description of the Female Gothic) 7
Fontainville Abbey (Dunlap) 15, 26, 67, 95, 118; difference between British and American versions 15, 130–132, 137
Fordyce, James (*Sermons for Young Women*) 69, 70, 73, 74
The Forest of Rosenwald (Stokes) 102, 127, 128; difference between British and American versions 134–136; see also *Raymond and Agnes*

193

Forrest, Edwin 145, 146
Fountainville Forest (Boaden): excerpt 15, 56, 122; synopsis 128

gothic genre: changing definition 6; characteristics in fiction 6, 9; critical studies 6–8; objections to fiction 10
gothic heroes: fallen women 68–69, 77; older 53; qualities 50–52, 57, 61–62, 64–65; wives/mothers 67–68, 75–77; young 52–53, 65–67, 69–75
gothic plays: appeal 145–148; class differences in audience 149, 153, 154; contradictory nature of plays 77; criticism 31, 35, 142–143; description 11–12, 13; differences between British and American versions 130–138, 152; dispute over definition 12; instructive potential 75–77, 150, 155; popularity 9–10, 12, 141; relation to melodrama 11–12, 148, 153
gothic villains: qualities 59; types 54–57
Gregory, John (*A Father's Legacy to His Daughters*) 70, 71, 74, 75
Grimsted, David 3

Hodgkinson, John: in *The Castle Spectre* 145; performances in Charleston 27; request for scenic pieces 99
Holcroft, Thomas (*A Tale of Mystery*) 29

The Iron Chest 10, 146; excerpt 24, 54; synopsis 30; vehicle for stars 145–146, 147

Kean, Edmund 24, 36, 145, 146
Kotzebue 142

Lewis, Matthew Gregory ("Monk") 10, 31, 129

The Man of Fortitude (Hodgkinson) 51–52, 66
Marmion (Barker) 69, 108
Maywood, Robert 55, 145
McConachie, Bruce (*Melodramatic Formations*) 60
Melmoth, Mrs. (Charlotte) 79, 85–87
Melmoth the Wanderer 30, 111–112
melodrama: description 11, 107; gothic 12
Minerva Press 9
Moers, Ellen 7
Mortimer, Sir Edward (*The Iron Chest*) 24, 30, 54, 145–146, 147
The Mountain Torrent 30, 109–110
Murdoch, James 146
The Mysteries of the Castle (Andrews) 66
The Mysteries of the Castle (White): excerpt 61, 67, 68, 107; special effects 108; synopsis 107

Nationalism: dependence/resentment upon British culture 16, 19–22
New York: Chatham Garden Theatre 27; gothic plays 30–31; Park Theatre 26–27; population increases 16–17

Old American Company 28
Oldmixon, Mrs. (Georgina George) 25, 79, 90–93; contract negotiations with Dunlap 91–92; salary 91; singing in Charleston 92
Olympic Theatre 25
One O'Clock; or The Knight and the Wood Daemon (Lewis) 122, 129

Park Theatre 26–27
"Passionlessness" (Cott) 77, 139–140
Philadelphia: Chestnut Street Theatre 25; early theatre company 25; gothic plays 30–32; Olympic Theatre 25; population changes 17, 25; ticket prices 25, 33–34
Playwrights: prejudice against American 20–21, 127
Polidori, John (*The Vampyre*) 10
population: economic changes 17; increases 16–17, 28; social changes in deference 17–18
Powell, Charles Stuart 28
Powell, Mrs. Snelling (Elizabeth Harrison) 79, 89–90
Prescriptive literature: for men 48–50; popularity 10, 48–50; represented in gothic plays 57, 150, 155; warnings against loss of virginity 71–74; warnings against women's independence 69; warnings against women's learning 69–71; warnings against women's wit 71; *see also* Chesterfield, Lord; Fordyce, John; Gregory, John
Presumption; or The Fate of Frankenstein (Peake) 30, 110, 111
prostitutes: debates about presence 18, 63–64; public complaints 41–42
Punter, David: approaches to study of gothic genre 7

Radcliffe, Anne 10
Ranger, Paul 3
Raymond and Agnes; or The Bleeding Nun (Lewis) 8, 128
"Republican Motherhood" (Kerber) 139
Ribbemont; or The Feudal Baron (Dunlap) 26, 53
The Rose of Arragon (Judah) 30, 52

Second Great Awakening 18
Shelley, Mary (*Frankenstein*) 10
A Sicilian Romance 67, 68
social changes in U.S. 17–18, 57
Stokes, John (*The Forest of Rosenwald*) 127

A Tale of Mystery (Holcroft) 29, 107, 144
theatre: defense of theatre as morally instructive 37–39; lighting 100–101, 102, 109, 111, 114, 152, 154; popularity 37; potentially harmful effect on women 40; production 102, 103, 108, 109, 110–115, 154; scenic designers 97; ticket prices 22, 33–34; use of stock scenery 99–100, 102
theatrical criticism 37–39; criticism of gothic plays 142–143; description of critics 141; types of criticism 141–142
theatrical periodicals 37–38
"Theatricus" critiques 26, 88, 89
Tocqueville, Alexis de 138
Trollope, Mrs. Frances (*Domestic Manners of the Americans*) 63
Turnbull, John (*The Wood Daemon*) 127

The Vampire; or The Bride of the Isles (Planche) 109

Walnut Street Theatre 26
Walpole, Horace (*The Castle of Otranto*) 6

The Warlock of the Glen 67
Webster, Noah 19
West, Benjamin (adaptation of *Melmoth*) 10
West, (Thomas Wade) Company (Charleston) 27
White, John 107
Whitlock, Mrs. (Elizabeth Kemble) 79, 87–89
Wignell and Reinagle 25, 97; *see also* Chestnut Street Theatre
Wollstonecraft, Mary 70–71
women: in audience 62–64; restrictions in society 13
Wood, William: loss of scenery to fire 97; theatre manager records 5, 25, 35
The Wood Daemon (Lewis): excerpt 95; publicity 96, 106; special effects 102, 105–107; see also *One O'clock; or The Knight and the Wood Daemon*
The Wood Daemon (Turbull) 95, 127; differences between British and American versions 131, 133, 136, 137
The Woodman's Hut 108

www.ingramcontent.com/pod-product-compliance
Lightning Source LLC
Chambersburg PA
CBHW032101300426
44116CB00007B/835